ADMISSION TEST SERIES

THIS IS YOUR **PASSBOOK®** FOR ...

ARRT EXAMINATION IN RADIOGRAPHY

NATIONAL LEARNING CORPORATION®
passbooks.com

Copyright © 2020 by

National Learning Corporation

212 Michael Drive, Syosset, NY 11791
(516) 921-8888 • www.passbooks.com
E-mail: info@passbooks.com

PUBLISHED IN THE UNITED STATES OF AMERICA

PASSBOOK® SERIES

THE *PASSBOOK® SERIES* has been created to prepare applicants and candidates for the ultimate academic battlefield – the examination room.

At some time in our lives, each and every one of us may be required to take an examination – for validation, matriculation, admission, qualification, registration, certification, or licensure.

Based on the assumption that every applicant or candidate has met the basic formal educational standards, has taken the required number of courses, and read the necessary texts, the *PASSBOOK® SERIES* furnishes the one special preparation which may assure passing with confidence, instead of failing with insecurity. Examination questions – together with answers – are furnished as the basic vehicle for study so that the mysteries of the examination and its compounding difficulties may be eliminated or diminished by a sure method.

This book is meant to help you pass your examination provided that you qualify and are serious in your objective.

The entire field is reviewed through the huge store of content information which is succinctly presented through a provocative and challenging approach – the question-and-answer method.

A climate of success is established by furnishing the correct answers at the end of each test.

You soon learn to recognize types of questions, forms of questions, and patterns of questioning. You may even begin to anticipate expected outcomes.

You perceive that many questions are repeated or adapted so that you can gain acute insights, which may enable you to score many sure points.

You learn how to confront new questions, or types of questions, and to attack them confidently and work out the correct answers.

You note objectives and emphases, and recognize pitfalls and dangers, so that you may make positive educational adjustments.

Moreover, you are kept fully informed in relation to new concepts, methods, practices, and directions in the field.

You discover that you arre actually taking the examination all the time: you are preparing for the examination by "taking" an examination, not by reading extraneous and/or supererogatory textbooks.

In short, this PASSBOOK®, used directedly, should be an important factor in helping you to pass your test.

HOW TO TAKE A TEST

You have studied long, hard and conscientiously.

With your official admission card in hand, and your heart pounding, you have been admitted to the examination room.

You note that there are several hundred other applicants in the examination room waiting to take the same test.

They all appear to be equally well prepared.

You know that nothing but your best effort will suffice. The "moment of truth" is at hand: you now have to demonstrate objectively, in writing, your knowledge of content and your understanding of subject matter.

You are fighting the most important battle of your life—to pass and/or score high on an examination which will determine your career and provide the economic basis for your livelihood.

What extra, special things should you know and should you do in taking the examination?

I. YOU MUST PASS AN EXAMINATION

A. WHAT EVERY CANDIDATE SHOULD KNOW
Examination applicants often ask us for help in preparing for the written test. What can I study in advance? What kinds of questions will be asked? How will the test be given? How will the papers be graded?

B. HOW ARE EXAMS DEVELOPED?
Examinations are carefully written by trained technicians who are specialists in the field known as "psychological measurement," in consultation with recognized authorities in the field of work that the test will cover. These experts recommend the subject matter areas or skills to be tested; only those knowledges or skills important to your success on the job are included. The most reliable books and source materials available are used as references. Together, the experts and technicians judge the difficulty level of the questions.

Test technicians know how to phrase questions so that the problem is clearly stated. Their ethics do not permit "trick" or "catch" questions. Questions may have been tried out on sample groups, or subjected to statistical analysis, to determine their usefulness.

Written tests are often used in combination with performance tests, ratings of training and experience, and oral interviews. All of these measures combine to form the best-known means of finding the right person for the right job.

II. HOW TO PASS THE WRITTEN TEST

A. BASIC STEPS

1) Study the announcement

How, then, can you know what subjects to study? Our best answer is: "Learn as much as possible about the class of positions for which you've applied." The exam will test the knowledge, skills and abilities needed to do the work.

Your most valuable source of information about the position you want is the official exam announcement. This announcement lists the training and experience qualifications. Check these standards and apply only if you come reasonably close to meeting them. Many jurisdictions preview the written test in the exam announcement by including a section called "Knowledge and Abilities Required," "Scope of the Examination," or some similar heading. Here you will find out specifically what fields will be tested.

2) Choose appropriate study materials

If the position for which you are applying is technical or advanced, you will read more advanced, specialized material. If you are already familiar with the basic principles of your field, elementary textbooks would waste your time. Concentrate on advanced textbooks and technical periodicals. Think through the concepts and review difficult problems in your field.

These are all general sources. You can get more ideas on your own initiative, following these leads. For example, training manuals and publications of the government agency which employs workers in your field can be useful, particularly for technical and professional positions. A letter or visit to the government department involved may result in more specific study suggestions, and certainly will provide you with a more definite idea of the exact nature of the position you are seeking.

3) Study this book!

III. KINDS OF TESTS

Tests are used for purposes other than measuring knowledge and ability to perform specified duties. For some positions, it is equally important to test ability to make adjustments to new situations or to profit from training. In others, basic mental abilities not dependent on information are essential. Questions which test these things may not appear as pertinent to the duties of the position as those which test for knowledge and information. Yet they are often highly important parts of a fair examination. For very general questions, it is almost impossible to help you direct your study efforts. What we can do is to point out some of the more common of these general abilities needed in public service positions and describe some typical questions.

1) General information

Broad, general information has been found useful for predicting job success in some kinds of work. This is tested in a variety of ways, from vocabulary lists to questions about current events. Basic background in some field of work, such as sociology or economics, may be sampled in a group of questions. Often these are principles which have become familiar to most persons through exposure rather than through formal training. It is difficult to advise you how to study for these questions; being alert to the world around you is our best suggestion.

2) Verbal ability

An example of an ability needed in many positions is verbal or language ability. Verbal ability is, in brief, the ability to use and understand words. Vocabulary and grammar tests are typical measures of this ability. Reading comprehension or paragraph interpretation questions are common in many kinds of civil service tests. You are given a paragraph of written material and asked to find its central meaning.

IV. KINDS OF QUESTIONS

1. Multiple-choice Questions

Most popular of the short-answer questions is the "multiple choice" or "best answer" question. It can be used, for example, to test for factual knowledge, ability to solve problems or judgment in meeting situations found at work.

A multiple-choice question is normally one of three types:
- It can begin with an incomplete statement followed by several possible endings. You are to find the one ending which *best* completes the statement, although some of the others may not be entirely wrong.
- It can also be a complete statement in the form of a question which is answered by choosing one of the statements listed.
- It can be in the form of a problem – again you select the best answer.

Here is an example of a multiple-choice question with a discussion which should give you some clues as to the method for choosing the right answer:

When an employee has a complaint about his assignment, the action which will *best* help him overcome his difficulty is to
- A. discuss his difficulty with his coworkers
- B. take the problem to the head of the organization
- C. take the problem to the person who gave him the assignment
- D. say nothing to anyone about his complaint

In answering this question, you should study each of the choices to find which is best. Consider choice "A" – Certainly an employee may discuss his complaint with fellow employees, but no change or improvement can result, and the complaint remains unresolved. Choice "B" is a poor choice since the head of the organization probably does not know what assignment you have been given, and taking your problem to him is known as "going over the head" of the supervisor. The supervisor, or person who made the assignment, is the person who can clarify it or correct any injustice. Choice "C" is, therefore, correct. To say nothing, as in choice "D," is unwise. Supervisors have and interest in knowing the problems employees are facing, and the employee is seeking a solution to his problem.

2. True/False

3. Matching Questions
Matching an answer from a column of choices within another column.

V. RECORDING YOUR ANSWERS

Computer terminals are used more and more today for many different kinds of exams.

For an examination with very few applicants, you may be told to record your answers in the test booklet itself. Separate answer sheets are much more common. If this separate answer sheet is to be scored by machine – and this is often the case – it is highly important that you mark your answers correctly in order to get credit.

VI. BEFORE THE TEST

YOUR PHYSICAL CONDITION IS IMPORTANT
If you are not well, you can't do your best work on tests. If you are half asleep, you can't do your best either. Here are some tips:

1) Get about the same amount of sleep you usually get. Don't stay up all night before the test, either partying or worrying—DON'T DO IT!
2) If you wear glasses, be sure to wear them when you go to take the test. This goes for hearing aids, too.
3) If you have any physical problems that may keep you from doing your best, be sure to tell the person giving the test. If you are sick or in poor health, you relay cannot do your best on any test. You can always come back and take the test some other time.

Common sense will help you find procedures to follow to get ready for an examination. Too many of us, however, overlook these sensible measures. Indeed, nervousness and fatigue have been found to be the most serious reasons why applicants fail to do their best on civil service tests. Here is a list of reminders:

- Begin your preparation early – Don't wait until the last minute to go scurrying around for books and materials or to find out what the position is all about.
- Prepare continuously – An hour a night for a week is better than an all-night cram session. This has been definitely established. What is more, a night a week for a month will return better dividends than crowding your study into a shorter period of time.
- Locate the place of the exam – You have been sent a notice telling you when and where to report for the examination. If the location is in a different town or otherwise unfamiliar to you, it would be well to inquire the best route and learn something about the building.
- Relax the night before the test – Allow your mind to rest. Do not study at all that night. Plan some mild recreation or diversion; then go to bed early and get a good night's sleep.
- Get up early enough to make a leisurely trip to the place for the test – This way unforeseen events, traffic snarls, unfamiliar buildings, etc. will not upset you.

- Dress comfortably – A written test is not a fashion show. You will be known by number and not by name, so wear something comfortable.
- Leave excess paraphernalia at home – Shopping bags and odd bundles will get in your way. You need bring only the items mentioned in the official notice you received; usually everything you need is provided. Do not bring reference books to the exam. They will only confuse those last minutes and be taken away from you when in the test room.
- Arrive somewhat ahead of time – If because of transportation schedules you must get there very early, bring a newspaper or magazine to take your mind off yourself while waiting.
- Locate the examination room – When you have found the proper room, you will be directed to the seat or part of the room where you will sit. Sometimes you are given a sheet of instructions to read while you are waiting. Do not fill out any forms until you are told to do so; just read them and be prepared.
- Relax and prepare to listen to the instructions
- If you have any physical problem that may keep you from doing your best, be sure to tell the test administrator. If you are sick or in poor health, you really cannot do your best on the exam. You can come back and take the test some other time.

VII. AT THE TEST

The day of the test is here and you have the test booklet in your hand. The temptation to get going is very strong. Caution! There is more to success than knowing the right answers. You must know how to identify your papers and understand variations in the type of short-answer question used in this particular examination. Follow these suggestions for maximum results from your efforts:

1) Cooperate with the monitor
The test administrator has a duty to create a situation in which you can be as much at ease as possible. He will give instructions, tell you when to begin, check to see that you are marking your answer sheet correctly, and so on. He is not there to guard you, although he will see that your competitors do not take unfair advantage. He wants to help you do your best.

2) Listen to all instructions
Don't jump the gun! Wait until you understand all directions. In most civil service tests you get more time than you need to answer the questions. So don't be in a hurry. Read each word of instructions until you clearly understand the meaning. Study the examples, listen to all announcements and follow directions. Ask questions if you do not understand what to do.

3) Identify your papers
Civil service exams are usually identified by number only. You will be assigned a number; you must not put your name on your test papers. Be sure to copy your number correctly. Since more than one exam may be given, copy your exact examination title.

4) Plan your time
Unless you are told that a test is a "speed" or "rate of work" test, speed itself is usually not important. Time enough to answer all the questions will be provided, but this

does not mean that you have all day. An overall time limit has been set. Divide the total time (in minutes) by the number of questions to determine the approximate time you have for each question.

5) Do not linger over difficult questions

If you come across a difficult question, mark it with a paper clip (useful to have along) and come back to it when you have been through the booklet. One caution if you do this – be sure to skip a number on your answer sheet as well. Check often to be sure that you have not lost your place and that you are marking in the row numbered the same as the question you are answering.

6) Read the questions

Be sure you know what the question asks! Many capable people are unsuccessful because they failed to *read* the questions correctly.

7) Answer all questions

Unless you have been instructed that a penalty will be deducted for incorrect answers, it is better to guess than to omit a question.

8) Speed tests

It is often better NOT to guess on speed tests. It has been found that on timed tests people are tempted to spend the last few seconds before time is called in marking answers at random – without even reading them – in the hope of picking up a few extra points. To discourage this practice, the instructions may warn you that your score will be "corrected" for guessing. That is, a penalty will be applied. The incorrect answers will be deducted from the correct ones, or some other penalty formula will be used.

9) Review your answers

If you finish before time is called, go back to the questions you guessed or omitted to give them further thought. Review other answers if you have time.

10) Return your test materials

If you are ready to leave before others have finished or time is called, take ALL your materials to the monitor and leave quietly. Never take any test material with you. The monitor can discover whose papers are not complete, and taking a test booklet may be grounds for disqualification.

VIII. EXAMINATION TECHNIQUES

1) Read the general instructions carefully. These are usually printed on the first page of the exam booklet. As a rule, these instructions refer to the timing of the examination; the fact that you should not start work until the signal and must stop work at a signal, etc. If there are any *special* instructions, such as a choice of questions to be answered, make sure that you note this instruction carefully.

2) When you are ready to start work on the examination, that is as soon as the signal has been given, read the instructions to each question booklet, underline any key words or phrases, such as *least, best, outline, describe*

and the like. In this way you will tend to answer as requested rather than discover on reviewing your paper that you *listed without describing*, that you selected the *worst* choice rather than the *best* choice, etc.

3) If the examination is of the objective or multiple-choice type – that is, each question will also give a series of possible answers: A, B, C or D, and you are called upon to select the best answer and write the letter next to that answer on your answer paper – it is advisable to start answering each question in turn. There may be anywhere from 50 to 100 such questions in the three or four hours allotted and you can see how much time would be taken if you read through all the questions before beginning to answer any. Furthermore, if you come across a question or group of questions which you know would be difficult to answer, it would undoubtedly affect your handling of all the other questions.

4) If the examination is of the essay type and contains but a few questions, it is a moot point as to whether you should read all the questions before starting to answer any one. Of course, if you are given a choice – say five out of seven and the like – then it is essential to read all the questions so you can eliminate the two that are most difficult. If, however, you are asked to answer all the questions, there may be danger in trying to answer the easiest one first because you may find that you will spend too much time on it. The best technique is to answer the first question, then proceed to the second, etc.

5) Time your answers. Before the exam begins, write down the time it started, then add the time allowed for the examination and write down the time it must be completed, then divide the time available somewhat as follows:
    *   If 3-1/2 hours are allowed, that would be 210 minutes. If you have 80 objective-type questions, that would be an average of 2-1/2 minutes per question. Allow yourself no more than 2 minutes per question, or a total of 160 minutes, which will permit about 50 minutes to review.
    *   If for the time allotment of 210 minutes there are 7 essay questions to answer, that would average about 30 minutes a question. Give yourself only 25 minutes per question so that you have about 35 minutes to review.

6) The most important instruction is to *read each question* and make sure you know what is wanted. The second most important instruction is to *time yourself properly* so that you answer every question. The third most important instruction is to *answer every question*. Guess if you have to but include something for each question. Remember that you will receive no credit for a blank and will probably receive some credit if you write something in answer to an essay question. If you guess a letter – say "B" for a multiple-choice question – you may have guessed right. If you leave a blank as an answer to a multiple-choice question, the examiners may respect your feelings but it will not add a point to your score. Some exams may penalize you for wrong answers, so in such cases *only*, you may not want to guess unless you have some basis for your answer.

7) Suggestions
   a. Objective-type questions
      1. Examine the question booklet for proper sequence of pages and questions
      2. Read all instructions carefully
      3. Skip any question which seems too difficult; return to it after all other questions have been answered
      4. Apportion your time properly; do not spend too much time on any single question or group of questions
      5. Note and underline key words – *all, most, fewest, least, best, worst, same, opposite,* etc.
      6. Pay particular attention to negatives
      7. Note unusual option, e.g., unduly long, short, complex, different or similar in content to the body of the question
      8. Observe the use of "hedging" words – *probably, may, most likely,* etc.
      9. Make sure that your answer is put next to the same number as the question
      10. Do not second-guess unless you have good reason to believe the second answer is definitely more correct
      11. Cross out original answer if you decide another answer is more accurate; do not erase until you are ready to hand your paper in
      12. Answer all questions; guess unless instructed otherwise
      13. Leave time for review

   b. Essay questions
      1. Read each question carefully
      2. Determine exactly what is wanted. Underline key words or phrases.
      3. Decide on outline or paragraph answer
      4. Include many different points and elements unless asked to develop any one or two points or elements
      5. Show impartiality by giving pros and cons unless directed to select one side only
      6. Make and write down any assumptions you find necessary to answer the questions
      7. Watch your English, grammar, punctuation and choice of words
      8. Time your answers; don't crowd material

8) Answering the essay question

Most essay questions can be answered by framing the specific response around several key words or ideas. Here are a few such key words or ideas:

M's: manpower, materials, methods, money, management
P's: purpose, program, policy, plan, procedure, practice, problems, pitfalls, personnel, public relations
   a. Six basic steps in handling problems:
      1. Preliminary plan and background development
      2. Collect information, data and facts
      3. Analyze and interpret information, data and facts
      4. Analyze and develop solutions as well as make recommendations

5. Prepare report and sell recommendations
6. Install recommendations and follow up effectiveness

b. Pitfalls to avoid
1. *Taking things for granted* – A statement of the situation does not necessarily imply that each of the elements is necessarily true; for example, a complaint may be invalid and biased so that all that can be taken for granted is that a complaint has been registered
2. *Considering only one side of a situation* – Wherever possible, indicate several alternatives and then point out the reasons you selected the best one
3. *Failing to indicate follow up* – Whenever your answer indicates action on your part, make certain that you will take proper follow-up action to see how successful your recommendations, procedures or actions turn out to be
4. *Taking too long in answering any single question* – Remember to time your answers properly

EXAMINATION SECTION

EXAMINATION SECTION
TEST 1

DIRECTIONS: Each question or incomplete statement is followed by several suggested answers or completions. Select the one that BEST answers the question or completes the statement. *PRINT THE LETTER OF THE CORRECT ANSWER IN THE SPACE AT THE RIGHT.*

1. Gonadal shielding   1._____

    A.   can reduce exposure to a male by up to 95%
    B.   can reduce exposure to a female by up to 95%
    C.   cannot be provided during sterile procedures
    D.   all of the above

2. Positive Beam Limitation must be accurate to within   2._____

    A.   2% of collimation size   B.   5% of collimation size
    C.   2% of the SID   D.   5% of the SID

3. Film badges can measure exposures as low as _____ mrem.   3._____

    A. 1000   B.   100   C.   10   D.   1

4. A dose-response curve assuming that any dose of radiation is going to have some effect is BEST described as a _____ curve.   4._____

    A.   linear   B.   sigmoid
    C.   threshold   D.   non-threshold

5. Which of the following statements is TRUE regarding uncontrolled radiation areas?   5._____

    A.   They are areas such as waiting rooms and stairways
    B.   They need not be shielded
    C.   Exposure to individuals in these areas must be under 5 rem/year
    D.   All of the above

6. The most practical form of protection from radiation in most cases is   6._____

    A.   lead shielding   B.   concrete shielding
    C.   time   D.   distance

7. Categories for dose equivalent limits (maximum permissible dose) include: 7._____
       I.   Occupational
     II.   Non-occupational
    III.   Occasionally exposed
The CORRECT answer is:

    A. I *only*   B. II, III   C. I, III   D. I, II, III

8. A _____ shield is suspended in the light field of the beam-defining light.   8._____

    A.   flat contact   B.   shaped contact
    C.   shadow   D.   fluoroscopic

9. Which of the following is a somatic effect of radiation?
    I.   Leukemia
    II. Nausea
    III. Cataracts
The CORRECT answer is:

    A. I, II   B. II, III   C. I, III   D. I, II, III

9.____

10. X-ray tubes must be encased in a protective housing that reduces leakage radiation to less than 100 mR/hr at _____ from the housing.

    A. 1 foot   B. 1 meter   C. 10 feet   D. 10 meters

10.____

11. In vivo, the primary effect of radiation is by the _____ effect.

    A. direct   B. indirect   C. isolation   D. depth

11.____

12. In general, patient dose may be reduced (while maintaining density) through the use of _____ Kvp, _____ mAs techniques.

    A. high; low   B. high; high
    C. low; low   D. low; high

12.____

13. Hematologic depression can be caused by acute irradiation of the bone marrow. Which of the following cell types will be depressed most severely?

    A. Erythrocytes   B. Lymphocytes
    C. Granulocytes   D. Thrombocytes

13.____

14. What term describes the electron that is ejected from an atom during a photoelectric interaction?

    A. Photon   B. Recoil electron
    C. Photoelectron   D. Incident photon

14.____

15. Mental retardation and microcephaly will most likely occur with a dose of 250 rad between weeks _____ and _____.

    A. 1; 2   B. 2; 4   C. 4; 8   D. 11; 16

15.____

16. In which of the following groups has specific life-span shortening been observed?

    A. Radium dial painters
    B. A-bomb survivors
    C. Nurses who refuse to help lift
    D. None of the above

16.____

17. Hematologic system cells develop from what stem cell?

    A. Pluripotential   B. Pluridirectional
    C. Plurae   D. Platonic

17.____

18. The LD typically used in animal studies is

    A. 20/30   B. 50/30   C. 50/60   D. 100/30

18.____

19. The third stage of the radiation syndrome is   19.____

    A. NVD (nausea, vomiting, diarrhea)
    B. prodromal
    C. latent
    D. manifest

20. The malignancy with the shortest latent period is   20.____

    A. leukemia   B. thyroid   C. colon   D. breast

21. When a one-break effect does not reattach, it is called _____ deletion.   21.____

    A. applicable   B. terminal
    C. tolerance   D. radiation

22. The _____ of a cell survival curve represents _____.   22.____

    A. straight-line portion; repair   B. shoulder; repair
    C. shoulder; damage   D. none of the above

23. The main source of occupational exposure to the radiographer is   23.____

    A. the primary beam   B. off-focus radiation
    C. scatter radiation   D. none of the above

24. Which of the following provide radiation protection through a PA rather than AP projec- 24.____
    tion?

    A. Chest (protects the sternum)
    B. Skull (protects the lens of the eye)
    C. Lumbar spine (protects the gonads)
    D. All of the above

25. Which of the following dosimetric devices is particularly prone to misread when dropped? 25.____

    A. Film badge   B. Pocket dosimeter
    C. Thermoluminescent dosimeter   D. Fluorometric dosimeter

26. Which of the following are areas in which radiographers may receive higher-than-normal 26.____
    badge readings?

    A. Orthopedic radiography, fluoroscopy, and angiography
    B. Orthopedic radiography, portable radiography, and angiography
    C. Portable radiography, fluoroscopy, and angiography
    D. Portable radiography, angiography, and skull radiography

27. Fluoroscopic units with the x-ray tube over the patient and the image intensifier under the 27.____
    table

    A. no longer exist
    B. provide a higher occupational exposure to workers
    C. provide a lower occupational exposure to workers
    D. are currently under development

28. Although all of the following methods will reduce patient exposure for a PA chest, which of the following is the MOST effective, under the control of the radiographer, and will maintain or improve image quality?   28.____

    A. Use a portable lead apron
    B. Use a high ratio grid
    C. Collimate the beam to the size of the image receptor or smaller
    D. Increase the speed of the film/screen system

29. The control badge for the department reads 40 mrem. Your badge reads 60 mrem. What is your occupational exposure for that month?   29.____
    _____ mrem.

    A. 20   B. 40   C. 60   D. 80

30. An orthopedic surgeon continuously keeps his foot on the foot pedal of the C-arm. A chief technologist is asked to inform him of the advantages of intermittent fluoroscopy. These are: 30.____
    I.   Prolonged tube life, saving money
    II. Decreased patient dose
    III. Decreased occupational exposure to all workers in the surgical suite
The CORRECT answer is:

    A. I, II   B. I, III   C. II, III   D. I, II, III

KEY (CORRECT ANSWERS)

1.	A	16.	D
2.	C	17.	A
3.	C	18.	B
4.	D	19.	D
5.	A	20.	A
6.	D	21.	B
7.	D	22.	B
8.	C	23.	C
9.	D	24.	D
10.	B	25.	B
11.	B	26.	C
12.	A	27.	B
13.	B	28.	C
14.	C	29.	A
15.	D	30.	D

TEST 2

DIRECTIONS: Each question or incomplete statement is followed by several suggested answers or completions. Select the one that BEST answers the question or completes the statement. *PRINT THE LETTER OF THE CORRECT ANSWER IN THE SPACE AT THE RIGHT.*

1. The differences between x- and gamma rays can be stated as follows: 1.____

    A. X-rays are particulate and gamma rays are waves
    B. Gamma rays are particulate and x-rays are waves
    C. Gamma rays originate in the nucleus and x-rays originate through the deceleration of electrons
    D. X-rays originate in the nucleus and gamma rays originate through the deceleration of electrons

2. The measurement of radiation exposure to human beings is called   2.____

    A. densitometry   B. sensitometry
    C. dosimetry   D. goniometry

3. The active component of a thermoluminescent dosimeter is typically   3.____

    A. calcium tungstate   B. barium platinocyanide
    C. lithium fluoride   D. cesium iodide

4. The unit of radiation measurement for absorption in any medium is   4.____

    A. roentgen   B. rad   C. rem   D. curie

5. The quantity of electric charge produced in air would describe which of the following radi-   5.____
   ation units?

    A. Roentgen   B. Rad   C. Rem   D. Curie

6. Current standards calculate cumulative dose-equivalent limits by which of the following   6.____
   formulas?

    A. 50mSv x (age 18)   B. 5mSv x (age 18)
    C. 100mSv x age   D. 10mSv x age

7. Shielding equivalents are expressed in thicknesses of   7.____

    A. tungsten   B. rhenium   C. aluminum   D. lead

8. In general, the relationship between linear energy transfer (LET) and relative biologic   8.____
   effect (RBE) is a(n)

    A. direct proportion
    B. inverse proportion
    C. indirect proportion
    D. inverse proportion to the square of the LET

9. Which of the following are components of the target theory?   9.____
      I.   Radiation damage is random.
      II. *Hits* to the target may result in cell death.
      III. Simple cells are assumed to have multiple targets.
   The CORRECT answer is:

   A. I, II   B. I, III   C. II, III   D. I, II, III

10. A permanent sterility may be induced with a dose of   10.____

   A. 6 mGy (600 mrad)   B. 60 mGy (6 rad)
   C. 600 mGy (60 rad)   D. 6 Gy (600 rad)

11. A skin erythema would MOST likely be an example of a(n) _____ effect.   11.____

   A. early somatic   B. early genetic
   C. late somatic   D. late genetic

12. A fixed fluoroscopic unit must provide a minimum source-to-skin distance of _____ inches.   12.____

   A. 12   B. 15   C. 36   D. 40

13. Increasing _____ will tend to decrease entrance skin exposure (ESE).   13.____
      I. mAs
      II. kVp
      III. filtration
   The CORRECT answer is:

   A. I, II   B. I, III   C. II, III   D. I, II, III

14. Devices such as the Geiger-Mueller (G-M) counter and pocket ionization chamber operate on x-ray's ability to   14.____

   A. cause certain chemicals to fluoresce
   B. lyse water molecules
   C. darken a photographic emulsion
   D. ionize gases

15. If exposure is 1000 mrad per hour at 1 foot, and the radiographer stands at 2 feet from the source for 5 minutes, total exposure is approximately _____ mrad.   15.____

   A. 1000   B. 500   C. 200   D. 20

16. An increased incidence of breast cancer was noted in   16.____
      I. operators of shoe fluoroscopes
      II. women treated with radiation for postpartum mastitis
      III. survivors of the atomic bombs at Hiroshima and Nagasaki
   The CORRECT answer is:

   A. I, II   B. I, III   C. II, III   D. I, II, III

17. An effect that occurs randomly, and the probability of the effect is proportional to the dose received, BEST describes a _____ effect.   17.____

   A. somatic   B. genetic
   C. stochastic   D. nonstochastic

18. According to NCRP Report #91, the occupational exposure, annual effective absorbed dose equivalent limits for non-stochastic effects for all organs except the lens of the eye is _____ rem.

    A. 10   B. 15   C. 25   D. 50

18.____

19. According to NCRP Report #91, the level of negligible individual risk is _____ rem.

    A. 0.001   B. 0.01   C. 0.1   D. 1.0

19.____

20. Which of the following are examples of late somatic effects of radiation?
    I.   Hematopoietic syndrome
    II.   Carcinogenesis
    III.   Cataracogenesis
The CORRECT answer is:

    A. I, II   B. I, III   C. II, III   D. I, II, III

20.____

21. The MOST common response to low levels of ionizing radiation is

    A. no effect   B. free radical formation
    C. H_2O_2 formation   D. direct effect

21.____

22. Which of the following would be considered a radiosensitive organ?

    A. Brain   B. Muscle   C. Liver   D. Thyroid

22.____

23. Which of the following is considered to be the MOST radiosensitive blood cell?

    A. Erythrocyte   B. Lymphocyte
    C. Leukocyte   D. Thrombocytes

23.____

24. 100 rad of x- or gamma radiation is equivalent to _____ rem.

    A. 100   B. 200   C. 300   D. 1000

24.____

25. The dose-response relationship that states that there is a safe dose of radiation that results in responses that are not directly proportional to the dose received BEST describes the _____ relationship.

    A. linear, nonthreshold
    B. linear, threshold
    C. nonlinear, nonthreshold
    D. nonlinear, threshold

25.____

26. Which of the following are TRUE statements?
    I.   The DNA of a cell may be inactivated through direct or indirect interaction.
    II.   All photon-cell interactions occur by chance.
    III.   It can be determined by microscopic analysis whether a given cell death is due to direct or indirect interaction.
The CORRECT answer is:

    A. I, II   B. I, III   C. II, III   D. I, II, III

26.____

27. According to the law of Bergonie and Tribondeau, cells are the most radiosensitive if they   27.____
     I.   are mature
     II. are undifferentiated
     III. divide rapidly
    The CORRECT answer is:

    A. I, II   B. I, III   C. II, III   D. I, II, III

28. The Bucky slot shield must be covered with AT LEAST _____ mm lead equivalent.   28.____

    A. 0.15   B. 0.25   C. 0.5   D. 1.0

29. One of the determinants of barrier thickness for a radiographic room is workload, which   29.____
    is measured in mA

    A. min/week
    B. min/month
    C. x time x kVp
    D. x time x kVp x (multiplying factor)

30. The electron left over after the Compton effect is called a   30.____

    A. photoelectron   B. positron
    C. negatron   D. recoil electron

KEY (CORRECT ANSWERS)

1.	C	16.	C
2.	C	17.	C
3.	C	18.	D
4.	B	19.	A
5.	A	20.	B
6.	D	21.	A
7.	D	22.	D
8.	A	23.	B
9.	A	24.	A
10.	D	25.	D
11.	A	26.	A
12.	B	27.	C
13.	B	28.	B
14.	D	29.	A
15.	D	30.	D

EXAMINATION SECTION
TEST 1

DIRECTIONS: Each question or incomplete statement is followed by several suggested answers or completions. Select the one that BEST answers the question or completes the statement. *PRINT THE LETTER OF THE CORRECT ANSWER IN THE SPACE AT THE RIGHT.*

1. What term is used for the positively charged electrode of a modern diagnostic x-ray tube?

    A. Cathode   B. Anode   C. Stator   D. Rotor

1.____

2. Approximately _____ percent of the energy of the electrons accelerated to the anode is converted to heat.

    A. 99   B. 70   C. 50   D. 1

2.____

3. Which of the following components are normally located in the low voltage section of the x-ray circuit?
       I. Timer circuit
      II. Pre-reading Kvp meter
     III. Line voltage compensator
The CORRECT answer is:

    A. I, II   B. I, III   C. II, III   D. I, II, III

3.____

4. The unit of electrical potential is the

    A. volt   B. ohm   C. ampere   D. farad

4.____

5. Accuracy of milliamperage stations is tested by the _____ test.

    A. timer accuracy   B. half value layer
    C. milliamperage linearity   D. wire mesh

5.____

6. The unit of resistance is the

    A. ohm   B. volt   C. ampere   D. watt

6.____

7. The PRIMARY purpose of rectification is to _____ current.

    A. convert alternating to direct
    B. convert direct to alternating
    C. intensify alternating
    D. intensify direct

7.____

8. What term is used to describe the fastest time in which an automatic exposure control can terminate an exposure?

    A. Exposure time   B. Latensification
    C. Minimum reaction time   D. Backup time

8.____

9. A program that specifically addresses the safe and reliable operation of equipment is termed quality   9.____

    A. assurance   B. control
    C. improvement   D. assessment

10. The generator that will always use the shortest time possible to obtain a given mAs is the   10.____

    A. single phase, half-wave
    B. three-phase, six pulse
    C. three-phase, twelve pulse
    D. falling load

11. A three-phase, twelve pulse circuit will produce _____ pulses per second.   11.____

    A. 1   B. 12   C. 360   D. 720

12. A half value layer determination gave the following results: 12.____

X-ray output in mR	Thickness of Al in mm
200	0
150	1
100	2
70	3
50	4

Which one of the following is the half value layer?
_____ mm Al.

    A. 2.0   B. 2.5   C. 3.0   D. 4.0

13. Which type of generator should theoretically provide the LOWEST patient dose?   13.____

    A. Single-phase, half wave   B. Three-phase, six pulse
    C. Falling load   D. High frequency

14. The further an electron is from the nucleus, the weaker is its _____ energy.   14.____

    A. kinetic   B. electronic binding
    C. potential   D. free

15. In a transformer,   15.____

    A. both the input waveform and the output waveforms are AC
    B. the input waveform is AC and the output waveform is DC
    C. both the input waveform and the output waveform is DC
    D. the input waveform is DC and the output waveform is AC

16. Where might the anode heel have an effect?   16.____

    A. Finger x-ray
    B. Knee
    C. QC testing using the step wedge
    D. None of the above

17. A typical anode bevel would be _____ degree(s).   17.____

    A. 1   B. 17   C. 35   D. 45

18. Total filtration in an x-ray is the sum of _____ filtration.   18._____
        I.   inherent
        II. added
        III. lead
    The CORRECT answer is:

    A. I, II   B. I, III   C. II, III   D. I, II, III

19. Increasing filtration beyond about _____ mm Al eq. should begin to visibly affect radio- 19._____
graphic density.

    A. 1.0   B. 1.5   C. 2.5   D. 3.5

20. As a general rule, the optimum level of total filtration for equipment operating above 70 20._____
kVp is at least _____ mm Al eq.

    A. 1.5   B. 2.5   C. 3.5   D. 4.5

21. Off-focus radiation has similar effects to scatter.   21._____

    A. True   B. False

22. The two main types of portable equipment are   22._____

    A. three-phase and high frequency
    B. battery and capacitor-discharge
    C. wheeled and back-pack
    D. battery and high frequency

23. A department using a capacitor-discharge machine in ICU notes that films turn out light 23._____
every time the elevator is set in motion. Which device is probably not operating correctly
on this machine?

    A. Line-voltage meter   B. Line-voltage compensator
    C. mAs meter   D. mAs compensator

24. Mobile radiography tends to use   24._____

    A. wide latitude film   B. high ratio grids
    C. short latitude screens   D. all of the above

25. A machine has the *Dial-a-filter* seen on some units. For which class of patients will mis- 25._____
use of the filter (i.e., not changing the filter as needed) have the greatest effect?

    A. Pediatric patients
    B. Adolescents
    C. Adults
    D. Patients with fluid in their lungs

26. Tube currents for fluoroscopy typically range from   26._____

    A. 1 to 3 mA   B. 10 to 30 mA
    C. 100 to 300 mA   D. 100 to 300 mAs

27. The anode in an image intensifer

    A. is negatively charged
    B. has a hole in it to allow electrons to pass through
    C. is made of the same material as an x-ray tube anode
    D. all of the above

27.____

28. The gain in brightness that is calculated by the ratio of the input screen diameter to the output screen diameter is termed _____ gain.

    A. flux
    B. size
    C. minification
    D. voltage

28.____

29. The QC technologist at your hospital thinks the brightness of a fluoro system has degraded to unacceptable levels. How should she check this out?

    A. Measure the level of brightness with a photometer
    B. Ask the serviceman to come out and look at it
    C. Compare the old dose required for a standard image to the new dose required
    D. Use the wire mesh test

29.____

30. Which of the following are static imaging modalities?

    A. Cassettes
    B. Cine
    C. Video
    D. All of the above

30.____

KEY (CORRECT ANSWERS)

1.	B	16.	C
2.	A	17.	B
3.	D	18.	A
4.	A	19.	D
5.	C	20.	B
6.	A	21.	A
7.	A	22.	B
8.	C	23.	B
9.	B	24.	A
10.	B	25.	A
11.	D	26.	A
12.	A	27.	B
13.	D	28.	C
14.	B	29.	C
15.	A	30.	A

TEST 2

DIRECTIONS: Each question or incomplete statement is followed by several suggested answers or completions. Select the one that BEST answers the question or completes the statement. *PRINT THE LETTER OF THE CORRECT ANSWER IN THE SPACE AT THE RIGHT.*

1. The typical speed for a rotating anode is approximately _____ rpm.

    A. 30   B. 300   C. 3000   D. 30,000

1.____

2. A generator with a capacity of 1000 mA at 100 milliseconds and a maximum potential of 120 kVp has a power rating of _____ kW.

    A. 12   B. 120   C. 12,000   D. 120,000

2.____

3. If a transformer has a primary to secondary ratio of 1 to 20, and an input voltage of 120V, then the output voltage would be _____ V.

    A. 2.4   B. 24   C. 240   D. 2400

3.____

4. The pinhole camera, the slit camera, and the star resolution pattern are all used to evaluate

    A. kVp
    B. mAs reciprocity
    C. film speed and resolution
    D. focal spot size

4.____

5. Automatic brightness controls (ABCs) are found in

    A. phototimers   B. fluoroscopic units
    C. mammographic units   D. tomographic units

5.____

6. Using excessive *boost time* or preparation time for the rotor will MOST likely result in

    A. breakage of the filament
    B. shortened exposure times
    C. pitting of the anode
    D. cracking of the glass envelope

6.____

7. The accepted variance for exposure time, exposure reproducibility, and kilovoltage peak is _____ of the stated value.

    A. 2   B. 5   C. 10   D. 15

7.____

8. The tomographic motion MOST commonly used during intravenous urography is

    A. linear   B. circular
    C. hypocycloidal   D. star

8.____

9. The pinpoint from which x-rays emanate is the

    A. focal spot   B. cathode
    C. anode   D. electrode

9.____

10. If you want to make sure all mA stations give the same output, check for   10.____

    A. HVL   B. linearity
    C. reproducibility   D. timer accuracy

11. If you want to make sure that one mA station, or one combination of mA and time gives   11.____
constant results, check for

    A. HVL   B. linearity
    C. reproducibility   D. timer accuracy

12. To check the results of the _____ test, stand at 3 feet or more and look for dark areas   12.____
on the film.

    A. HVL
    B. timer accuracy
    C. phototimer reproducibility
    D. film-screen contact

13. For the _____ test, if you couldn't afford a phantom, you might simply radiograph a   13.____
bucket of water.

    A. HVL
    B. timer accuracy
    C. phototimer reproducibility
    D. film-screen contact

14. The chemical representation of cesium iodide is   14.____

    A. CI   B. CsI   C. CmI   D. cMi

15. A step-up transformer steps up _____ current.   15.____

    A. voltage and
    B. voltage and steps down
    C. resistance and
    D. resistance and steps down

16. A(n) _____ measures tube current.   16.____

    A. anode   B. cathode
    C. ionization chamber   D. mA meter

17. A(n) _____ is turned by a rotor.   17.____

    A. anode   B. cathode
    C. ionization chamber   D. mA meter

18. How many half-value layers make one tenth-value layer?   18.____

    A. 2.3   B. 3.3   C. 4.3   D. 5.3

19. If voltage is 220V, and amperage is 5A, then resistance is _____ ohm.   19.____

    A. 0.21   B. 44   C. 440   D. 1100

20. A rheostat is also known as a 20.____

    A. battery   B. diode
    C. transistor   D. variable resistor

21. Which of the following areas would probably have a grid-controlled x-ray tube? 21.____

    A. General radiography   B. Mammography
    C. Cineradiography   D. Computed tomography

22. Which of the following are common materials for the anode? 22.____
         I. Copper
        II. Molybdenum
       III. Graphite
The CORRECT answer is:

    A. I *only*   B. II *only*   C. I, II   D. I, II, III

23. The normal recommendation for large focal spot, due to heat capacity, is _____ mA or greater. 23.____

    A. 100   B. 200   C. 400   D. 600

24. Which of the following causes of tube failure would MOST likely lead to pitting and cracking of the anode? 24.____
         I. Failure to warm up the tube
        II. Single excessive exposure
       III. Filament vaporization
The CORRECT answer is:

    A. I, II   B. I, III   C. II, III   D. I, II, III

25. Heat units for a three-phase, twelve pulse unit, would be calculated through the formula kVp x 25.____

    A. mA   B. mA x s
    C. mA x s x 1.35   D. mA x s x 1.41

26. Which of the following causes of tube failure is similar to the burning out of a lightbulb? 26.____

    A. Failure to warm up the tube
    B. Single excessive exposure
    C. Excessive exposure times
    D. Filament vaporization

27. Except for those originating in the _____ shell, all characteristic x-rays produced by a tungsten target will have low energy. 27.____

    A. K   B. L   C. M   D. N

28. Increasing _____ will result in reduced x-ray intensity but increased effective energy. 28.____

    A. mAs
    B. kVp
    C. filtration
    D. atomic number of the target material

29. Which of the following materials will have the highest K-shell binding energy?   29.____

    A. Aluminum   B. Iodine   C. Barium   D. Lead

30. The generator with the greatest ripple would be   30.____

    A. single phase
    B. three phase, six pulse
    C. three phase, twelve pulse
    D. high frequency

KEY (CORRECT ANSWERS)

1.	C	16.	D
2.	B	17.	A
3.	D	18.	B
4.	D	19.	B
5.	B	20.	D
6.	A	21.	C
7.	B	22.	D
8.	A	23.	C
9.	A	24.	A
10.	B	25.	D
11.	C	26.	D
12.	D	27.	A
13.	C	28.	C
14.	B	29.	D
15.	B	30.	A

EXAMINATION SECTION
TEST 1

DIRECTIONS: Each question or incomplete statement is followed by several suggested answers or completions. Select the one that BEST answers the question or completes the statement. *PRINT THE LETTER OF THE CORRECT ANSWER IN THE SPACE AT THE RIGHT.*

1.   Which of the following conditions contribute to good recorded detail?   1._____
    I.   Short OID
    II. Short SID
    III. Large effective focal spot size

The CORRECT answer is:

  A. I *only*   B. I, II   C. II, III   D. I, II, III

2.   Which of the following combinations can produce a *decrease* in contrast without changing density?   2._____
    I.   Increasing kVp
    II. Decreasing kVp
    III. Increasing mAs
    IV. Decreasing mAs

The CORRECT answer is:

  A. I, III   B. II, III   C. I, IV   D. II, IV

3.   Which of the following are reducing agents used in automatic film processing developer solutions?   3._____
    I.   Hydroquinone
    II. Phenidone
    III. Potassium bromide

The CORRECT answer is:

  A. I, II   B. II, III   C. I, III   D. I, II, III

4.   Grid ratio is determined by dividing the _____ by the _____.   4._____

  A. lead strip height; interspace width
  B. lead strip thickness; interspace width
  C. lead strip thickness; lead strip height
  D. interspace width; lead strip thickness

5.   For an average abdomen, compression will have the LEAST effect on   5._____

  A. density   B. contrast
  C. part thickness   D. recorded detail

6. Magnification is calculated by dividing _____ by _____ .
      I.   SID
      II. OID
      III. SOD

6._____

The CORRECT answer is:

  A. I, II   B. II, III   C. I, III   D. II, I

7. Low resolution films typically have
      I.   high speed
      II. high contrast
      III. wide latitude

7._____

The CORRECT answer is:

  A. I, II   B. II, III   C. I, III   D. I, II, III

8. Sensitometric measurements on radiographic film processors of base-plus-fog, contrast index, and speed should be performed

8._____

  A. daily   B. weekly
  C. monthly   D. as needed

9. Orthochromatic film is sensitive to all wavelengths of light EXCEPT

9._____

  A. red   B. blue   C. yellow   D. green

10. Which of the following is a typical fixer replenishment rate for an automatic film processor?
_____ ml/in.

10._____

  A. 2 to 3   B. 6 to 8   C. 20 to 30   D. 50 to 80

11. The densities that make up a diagnostic image range from _____ to _____ OD.

11._____

  A. 0.1; 0.5   B. 1; 5   C. 0.25; 2.5   D. 1; 2.5

12. In automatic processing, the MOST common artifact linked to transport problems is

12._____

  A. scratches   B. dichroic stains
  C. excessive density   D. static

13. Quantum mottle would probably be most noticeable when _____ is used with _____ screens.

13._____

  A. low kVp; slow   B. low mAs; fast
  C. high kVp; slow   D. high mAs; slow

14. A radiograph is taken using 200 mAs and 0.15 seconds; however, it demonstrates motion. To reduce motion, 0.05 seconds is used.
What must the mA be to maintain density?

14._____

  A. 67   B. 100   C. 300   D. 600

15. A very large (weight of more than 350 lbs.) patient presents for an abdomen. With an automatic exposure control, which of the following is the BEST means of securing adequate density?

    A. Increasing kVp from 70 to 90
    B. Setting density on +1
    C. Setting density on +2
    D. Setting an adequate backup time

15.____

16. The anode heel effect is typically NOT important clinically as

    A. most equipment is designed so that it won't occur
    B. it is more important at short SIDs
    C. it is more important at very large field sizes
    D. all of the above

16.____

17. If a radiologist uses 10 mAs at 40" for an AP cervical spine, and the hospital starts doing obliques at 72", you would need to change the mAs to

    A. 3   B. 10   C. 32   D. 64

17.____

18. What does doubling your distance from the source do to the intensity of radiation?

    A. Halves it
    B. Doubles it
    C. Cuts it to 1/4 original value
    D. Increases it to 4x original value

18.____

19. Which of the following sets of technical factors would be more likely to see the anode heel effect?
_____" SID; _____ inch field length; _____ focal spot.

    A. 36; 5; small   B. 36; 14; large
    C. 72; 5; small   D. 72; 14; large

19.____

20. The fact that only those secondary photons which are emitted from the patient in a very forward direction of the primary beam are allowed to pass through the interspace describes grid

    A. efficiency   B. frequency
    C. selectivity   D. Bucky factor

20.____

21. Most modern grids have _____ lines per inch.

    A. 20-60   B. 40-90   C. 80-110   D. 100-140

21.____

22. If more light is produced by a screen, this is a potential increase in its _____ efficiency.

    A. conversion   B. absorption
    C. emission   D. all of the above

22.____

23. Intensifying screen speed is kVp-dependent.

    A. True   B. False

23.____

24. Modern x-ray film is _____ tinted.

    A. green   B. blue   C. gray   D. orange

24.____

25. The impurity used to make a sensitivity speck is   25._____

    A. silver bromide   B. silver sulfide
    C. gelatin   D. t-coat

KEY (CORRECT ANSWERS)

1.	A		11.	C
2.	C		12.	A
3.	A		13.	B
4.	A		14.	D
5.	D		15.	D
6.	C		16.	D
7.	C		17.	D
8.	A		18.	C
9.	A		19.	B
10.	B		20.	C

21.	C
22.	D
23.	A
24.	B
25.	B

TEST 2

DIRECTIONS: Each question or incomplete statement is followed by several suggested answers or completions. Select the one that BEST answers the question or completes the statement. *PRINT THE LETTER OF THE CORRECT ANSWER IN THE SPACE AT THE RIGHT.*

1. Thicker film emulsions will result in less sharpness of detail due to   1.____

    A. mottling   B. parallax
    C. halation   D. none of the above

2. High latitude films provide   2.____
        I.   a greater margin for error
        II. a longer gray scale
        III. increased contrast

    The CORRECT answer is:

    A. I, II   B. II, III   C. I, III   D. I, II, III

3. Which of the following film/screen speeds would most probably be used for chest radiog-   3.____
   raphy?

    A. 25   B. 50   C. 100   D. 400

4. Tissue differences are also called _____ contrast.   4.____

    A. subject   B. long scale
    C. short scale   D. reduced

5. When fogging occurs, gray scale is _____ and contrast is   5.____

    A. increased; increased   B. increased; reduced
    C. reduced; reduced   D. reduced; increased

6. The unit lp/mm is used for   6.____

    A. density   B. contrast
    C. magnification   D. resolution

7. The processing component connected to a microswitch to control replenishment is the   7.____
   _____ rack.

    A. detection   B. deep
    C. crossover   D. all of the above

8. Artifacts due to dried developer are more common in the _____ rack.   8.____

    A. detection   B. deep
    C. crossover   D. all of the above

9. Special end-loading cassettes are used for   9.____

    A. daylight processing   B. sensitometry
    C. duplicating film   D. none of the above

10. On an x-ray of the hand, the radiographer sees motion on the film. When she asks the patient if he moved, he says no.
What is a probable cause of this motion?

    A. Bucky tray movement
    B. Patient is lying
    C. Tube carriage was not locked in position
    D. The building shifted

10.____

11. Immobilizing the abdomen with a compression band
    I.   helps to eliminate motion
    II. increases scatter
    III. decreases scatter

The CORRECT answer is:

    A. I only   B. II only   C. I, II   D. I, III

11.____

12. Which of the following examinations could probably use a compensating filter?

    A. Foot   B. Hand   C. Wrist   D. Elbow

12.____

13. The optimum kVp for iodine is

    A. 80   B. 90   C. 100   D. 110

13.____

14. The optimum kVp for most barium studies is

    A. 80   B. 90   C. 100   D. 110

14.____

15. Scatter is increased with

    A. low kVp
    B. small field sizes
    C. large tissue thicknesses
    D. all of the above

15.____

16. Which of the following are equivalent?
    I.   200 mA; .1 sec
    II. 300 mA; .1 sec
    III. 400 mA; .05 sec

The CORRECT answer is:

    A. I, II   B. I, III   C. II, III   D. I, II, III

16.____

17. The general rule of thumb is that it takes a _____ % change in mAs to see a noticeable difference on a radiograph.

    A. 10   B. 20   C. 30   D. 50

17.____

18. The biggest problem with long exposure times is its ability to cause

    A. mottle   B. contrast changes
    C. motion   D. kVp variations

18.____

22

19. Which of the following would represent an optimum kVp for a hand?   19._____

    A. 55   B. 70   C. 90   D. 110

20. Exposure latitude can be seen as   20._____

    A. the maximum kVp allowed
    B. the minimum kVp allowed
    C. a margin for error
    D. a range within which optimal radiographs are produced

21. Which exam would tend to have the HIGHEST exposure latitude?   21._____

    A. Hand   B. Ribs
    C. Knee   D. Grid chest

22. How would you change technique if you were doing both an AP and lateral portable   22._____
chest on a premature infant?

    A. Use the same mAs for both
    B. Double mAs for the lateral
    C. Halve the mAs for the lateral
    D. None of the above

23. A radiographer takes a radiograph using an AEC. The first radiograph is light, and all   23._____
subsequent radiographs are also light.
Which of the following is the most likely cause?
_____ is set too _____.

    A. kVp; high   B. kVp; low   C. mA; high   D. mA; low

24. The minimum response time is a reason why _____ should not be phototimed.   24._____

    A. small anatomy   B. large anatomy
    C. ribs   D. sinuses

25. If the right and left photocell are chosen, and the right contains mostly bone and the left   25._____
air, the resultant radiograph will be

    A. just fine
    B. too dark
    C. too light
    D. too dark in one area and too light in another

KEY (CORRECT ANSWERS)

1.	B	11.	D
2.	A	12.	A
3.	D	13.	A
4.	A	14.	D
5.	C	15.	C
6.	D	16.	B
7.	A	17.	C
8.	C	18.	C
9.	A	19.	A
10.	C	20.	C

21.	D
22.	A
23.	B
24.	A
25.	D

———

EXAMINATION SECTION
TEST 1

DIRECTIONS: Each question or incomplete statement is followed by several suggested answers or completions. Select the one that BEST answers the question or completes the statement. *PRINT THE LETTER OF THE CORRECT ANSWER IN THE SPACE AT THE RIGHT.*

1. The same approximate image density will be provided with a technical factor selection of 20 mAs, 70 kVp or _____ mAs, _____ kVp.

   A. 10; 60   B. 10; 80   C. 20; 60   D. 20; 80

   1.____

2. The quality of the x-ray beam is influenced by
   - I.   kVp
   - II. filtration
   - III. mAs

   The CORRECT answer is:

   A. I, II   B. I, III   C. II, III   D. I, II, III

   2.____

3. Which one of the following changes will *increase* radiographic density without affecting contrast?

   A. Increasing kVp from 60 to 65
   B. Increasing mAs from 10 to 15
   C. Increasing SID from 40 to 50 inches
   D. Switching from the small to the large focal spot

   3.____

4. _____ is used for dissolution in both fixer and developer.

   A. Water   B. Potassium bromide
   C. Sodium carbonate   D. Acetic acid

   4.____

5. If _____ is not in the developer, the image might get too dark.

   A. water   B. potassium bromide
   C. sodium carbonate   D. acetic acid

   5.____

6. Collimation is always important; with an AEC _____ is even more important as this will cause the phototimer to shut off prematurely.

   A. patient size   B. backup time
   C. scatter radiation   D. primary radiation

   6.____

7. Since rare earth screen speed _____ with increasing kVp, it is best to use a _____ kVp technique chart.

   A. *decreases;* fixed   B. *increases;* fixed
   C. *decreases;* variable   D. *increases;* variable

   7.____

8. The factor of the image that is strictly geometric, and thus affects recorded detail or sharpness *only* is

   A. mAs   B. kVp
   C. filtration   D. focal spot size

   8.____

9. Increasing both kVp and mAs to influence the density of a radiograph will result in _____ density and _____.   9._____

    A. *increased;* contrast
    B. *increased;* decreased contrast
    C. *decreased;* contrast
    D. *decreased;* increased contrast

10. Image contrast can be predicted through the _____ ratio.   10._____

    A. photoelectric/Compton
    B. Compton/bresmsstrahlung
    C. photoelectric/bremsstrahlung
    D. Compton/characteristic

11. The PRIMARY property of barium and iodine that makes them effective at absorbing x-rays is their   11._____

    A. density
    B. high atomic number
    C. radioactivity
    D. unpaired outer shell electrons

12. The optimum kVp for the torso is   12._____

    A. 60   B. 70   C. 80   D. 90

13. Field size will have an effect on   13._____

    A. sharpness of recorded detail
    B. magnification
    C. distortion
    D. scatter production

14. The term _____ means *straight color* and refers to the narrow range of light emission from a screen.   14._____

    A. monochromatic   B. orthochromatic
    C. polychromatic   D. sigmochromatic

15. The _____ effect, resulting in a loss of recorded detail, is particularly acute with single emulsion film.   15._____

    A. reciprocity law failure   B. anode heel
    C. halation   D. crossover

16. If you are converting from 40 to 72 inches on a portable, what must you do to the mAs?   16._____

    A. Keep it the same
    B. Decrease it by a factor of 2
    C. Increase it by a factor of 2
    D. Increase it by a factor of 3

17. The PRIMARY advantage of tomography is improved image   17._____

    A. detail   B. contrast   C. density   D. clarity

18. Automated techniques (phototimers) should not be used for 18.____
      I.   small or narrow anatomy
      II. peripheral anatomy
      III. complex contrast anatomy
      IV. air-fluid levels
The CORRECT answer is:

  A. I, II   B. I, II, III
  C. II, III, IV   D. I, II, III, IV

19. Which of the following conditions contribute to a good recorded detail? 19.____
      I.   Long OID
      II. Long SID
      III. Large effective focal spot size
The CORRECT answer is:

  A. I *only*   B. II *only*   C. I, II   D. I, II, III

20. Which of the following would necessitate a repeat exposure? 20.____
      I.   No evidence of gonadal shielding
      II. An artifact that might represent pathology
      III. A positioning error that obscures anatomy
The CORRECT answer is:

  A. I, II   B. II, III   C. I, III   D. I, II, III

21. The area of highest exposure on an H&D curve is also known as the 21.____

  A. toe   B. gradient
  C. shoulder   D. straight-line portion

22. An increase in technique is often required for patients with 22.____

  A. emphysema   B. pulmonary edema
  C. osteoporosis   D. osteolytic disease

23. Which of the following sets of technical factors would produce an image with the greatest 23.____
radiographic density? _____ mA; _____ sec.; _____ kVp; _____ inches.

  A. 600; .1; 70; 40   B. 300; .2; 80; 72
  C. 300; .1; 80; 72   D. 400; .15; 80; 40

24. The basic tissue densities of an image that are the most difficult to differentiate when 24.____
they are adjacent to each other are

  A. air and bone   B. fat and bone
  C. air and muscle   D. fat and muscle

25. The most common cause of poor archival quality for films is _____ stain. 25.____

  A. acetate   B. boric acid
  C. silver sulfide   D. water

KEY (CORRECT ANSWERS)

1.	B		11.	B
2.	A		12.	C
3.	B		13.	D
4.	A		14.	B
5.	B		15.	C
6.	C		16.	D
7.	B		17.	B
8.	D		18.	D
9.	B		19.	B
10.	A		20.	B

21.	C
22.	B
23.	D
24.	D
25.	C

TEST 2

DIRECTIONS: Each question or incomplete statement is followed by several suggested answers or completions. Select the one that BEST answers the question or completes the statement. *PRINT THE LETTER OF THE CORRECT ANSWER IN THE SPACE AT THE RIGHT.*

1. The mechanical support for an intensifying screen is provided by the _____, which is usually made of _____.   1.____

    A. base; polyester
    B. base; gadolinium
    C. protective coating; polyester
    D. protective coating; gadolinium

2. What will the reflective layer of an intensifying screen -do?   2.____
    I. Control the spread of light
    II. Increase the x-ray to light conversion efficiency
    III. Increase image blur
The CORRECT answer is:

    A. I, II   B. II, III   C. I, III   D. I, II, III

3. The human eye is typically capable of resolving about _____ lp/mm.   3.____

    A. 6   B. 10   C. 25   D. 50

4. A radiographic technique that provides _____ contrast will allow for a _____ latitude in exposure factors.   4.____

    A. low; shorter   B. low; wider
    C. high; shorter   D. high; wider

5. For soft tissue imaging, it is BEST to   5.____

    A. *increase* kVp   B. *decrease* kVp
    C. *increase* mAs   D. *decrease* mAs

6. For imaging Paget's disease, it is BEST to   6.____

    A. *increase* kVp   B. *decrease* kVp
    C. *increase* mAs   D. *decrease* mAs

7. Radiographic density would decrease, but size distortion (magnification) would increase with an   7.____

    A. *increase* in SID   B. *decrease* in SID
    C. *increase* in mAs   D. *decrease* in mAs

8. Which of the following examinations makes the correct use of the heel effect?   8.____

    A. Abdomen: abdomen towards the cathode; pelvis towards the anode
    B. PA chest: neck towards the cathode; abdomen towards the anode
    C. Femur: knee towards the cathode; hip towards the anode
    D. Humerus: elbow towards the cathode; shoulder towards the anode

9. The smallest change in mAs that will result in a detectable difference in density by the human eye is

9.____

   A. 5-10%   B. 15-20%   C. 25-30%   D. 35-40%

10. Increasing focal spot size from 0.6 mm to 1.2 mm with no other changes in technical factors will result in

10.____

   A. *increased* image contrast
   B. *decreased* image contrast
   C. *increased* blur
   D. *decreased* blur

11. The production of scatter radiation in the patient would NOT be affected by

11.____

   A. field size   B. patient thickness
   C. using a grid   D. kVp

12. Increasing screen speed from 100 to 200 will require a change in mAs from an original value of 50 to

12.____

   A. 25   B. 75   C. 100   D. 200

13. Whereas the proper pH for the developer is _____, the proper pH for the fixer is _____.

13.____

   A. acidic; basic   B. basic; acidic
   C. acidic; neutral   D. basic; neutral

14. The usual means of handling patient motion is to *decrease*

14.____

   A. exposure time   B. mA
   C. kVp   D. focal spot size

15. True or shape distortion is sometimes called

15.____

   A. uneven magnification   B. absorption blur
   C. geometric blur   D. isometric blur

16. Which of the following screen speeds would probably provide the BEST recorded detail?

16.____

   A. 50   B. 100   C. 200   D. 400

17. _____ mAs, _____ speed system would provide the greates density.

17.____

   A. 100; 50   B. 50; 100   C. 25; 200   D. 12.5; 800

18. Minimum dryer temperature should be _____° F.

18.____

   A. 70   B. 90   C. 95   D. 120

19. Which one of the following would MOST likely use a high kVp of above 100?

19.____

   A. Adult grid chest   B. Pediatric chest
   C. Intravenous urogram   D. Extremity radiography

20. What is the MOST common cause of radiographic unsharpness?

20.____

   A. Large focal spot size   B. Short SIDs
   C. Long OIDs   D. Patient motion

21. The visible difference between adjacent radiographic densities best describes   21.____

    A. blur   B. contrast
    C. latitude   D. unsharpness

22. If a change in distance were to change the intensity of exit radiation from 10 mR to 2.5   22.____
mR, what change in mAs would be required to compensate?

    A. Double mAs
    B. Increase mAs 4x
    C. Halve mAs
    D. Decrease mAs to 1/4 original value

23. If 10 mAs were used without a grid, and a 12:1 grid was added to clean up scatter, which   23.____
one of the following is the amount of mAs needed with the grid?

    A. 2   B. 10   C. 20   D. 50

24. Which of the following would provide about the same magnification factor?   24.____
        I. SID, 40"; OID 3"
      II. SID, 108"; OID 8"
     III. SID, 120"; OID 10"
The CORRECT answer is:

    A. I, II   B. II, III   C. I, III   D. I, II, III

25. Reciprocity law failure is more likely to occur at _____ exposure times than _____   25.____
exposure times.

    A. long; short   B. short; long
    C. moderate; short   D. moderate; long

KEY (CORRECT ANSWERS)

1.	A		11.	C
2.	B		12.	A
3.	B		13.	B
4.	B		14.	A
5.	B		15.	A
6.	A		16.	A
7.	A		17.	D
8.	A		18.	D
9.	C		19.	A
10.	C		20.	D

21.	B
22.	B
23.	D
24.	D
25.	A

EXAMINATION SECTION
TEST 1

DIRECTIONS: Each question or incomplete statement is followed by several suggested answers or completions. Select the one that BEST answers the question or completes the statement. *PRINT THE LETTER OF THE CORRECT ANSWER IN THE SPACE AT THE RIGHT.*

1. The _____ vertical plane passes through the body parallel to the median plane or sagittal suture and divides the body into right and left portions.

    A. sagittal   B. coronal
    C. transpyloric   D. transverse

    1.____

2. The movement by which the two elements of any jointed part are drawn away from each other is termed

    A. abduction   B. adduction   C. extension   D. flexion

    2.____

3. If the patient is semiprone or standing with the left side closest to the film, this is a _____ oblique.

    A. right anterior (RAO)   B. left anterior (LAO)
    C. right posterior (RPO)   D. left posterior (LPO)

    3.____

4. A projection in which the central ray *skims* (passes between or by) body parts and projects anatomic structures in profile and free of superimposition is a(n)

    A. axial   B. tangential
    C. lateral   D. oblique

    4.____

5. The landmark of the mastoid tips corresponds to what internal structure?

    A. Body of C1
    B. Body of C2
    C. Intervertebral space of C2-C3
    D. Body of C4

    5.____

6. Broad and deep thorax, ribs almost horizontal, shallow thoracic cavity; short lungs, narrowed above and broad at bases; and high diaphragm describes which body habitus?

    A. Hypersthenic   B. Sthenic
    C. Hyposthenic   D. Asthenic

    6.____

7. The bone which serves as a base of the trunk and provides the connection between the vertebral column and the lower limbs is the

    A. femur   B. tibia   C. pelvis   D. coccyx

    7.____

8. The articulation of the head of the femur with the pelvis occurs at the

    A. acetabulum   B. bicipital groove
    C. ischial depression D. glenoid fossa

    8.____

9. When the pelvis is correctly positioned for an A. P. projection, the _____ will not be visible (or will be barely visible) on the resultant radiograph.

    A. lesser trochanter   B. greater trochanter
    C. femoral heads   D. symphysis pubis

9.____

10. In the bilateral *frog-leg* position of the pelvis, the central ray is directed to the center of the film at a point

    A. one inch cephalad to the symphysis pubis
    B. two inches distal to the obturator foramen
    C. corresponding to the level of the ASIS
    D. corresponding to the level of the iliac crests

10.____

11. The central ray for the AP axial projection of the sacroiliac joints enters a point midway between the

    A. obturator foramen and the head of the femur
    B. greater trochanters
    C. level of the ASIS and the symphysis pubis
    D. level of the ASIS and iliac crests

11.____

12. To demonstrate the inferior or distal portion of the SI joint more clearly, the central ray may be directed

    A. 5-10 degrees caudally   B. 15-20 degrees cephalad
    C. 15-20 degrees caudally   D. 5-10 degrees cephalad

12.____

13. Which of the following structures is NOT shown in the crosstable lateral projection of the hip?

    A. Femoral neck   B. Acetabulum
    C. Ischial tuberosity   D. Ischial spine

13.____

14. Which of the following positions of the knee will BEST demonstrate narrowing of the knee joint due to arthritis?

    A. AP/supine
    B. Lateral/recumbent
    C. AP/weight-bearing
    D. Axial/with knee flexed 40 degrees

14.____

15. The upper portion of the sternum is the

    A. manubrium   B. suprasternal notch
    C. manubrial notch   D. jugular notch

15.____

16. The only bony connection between the upper extremities and the bony thorax is the

    A. manubrium   B. suprasternal notch
    C. manubrial notch   D. sternoclavicular joint

16.____

17. Which of the following is usually not well-visualized on the chest radiograph?

    A. Clavicles   B. Scapulae   C. Ribs   D. Sternum

17.____

18. Right ribs in the oblique position are best shown using   18.____

    A. LPO   B. RAO
    C. RPO   D. any oblique

19. On a PA chest, if the Valsalva maneuver is used to increase the size of a small pneu-   19.____
mothorax, kVp is _____ by _____.

    A. decreased; 5   B. decreased; 10
    C. increased; 5   D. increased; 10

20. The AP lordotic projection, Lindblom method,   20.____
         I.   is an AP axial
        II. demonstrates the apices
      III. demonstrates conditions such as interlobar effusions
The CORRECT answer is:

    A. I, II   B. I, III   C. II, III   D. I, II, III

21. Any frontal position of the chest will superimpose which of the following structures?   21.____
         I.   Sternum
        II. Esophagus
      III. Heart
The CORRECT answer is:

    A. I, II   B. I, III   C. II, III   D. I, II, III

22. When abdominal structures are located behind the lining of the abdominopelvic cavity,   22.____
they are said to be _____ in location.

    A. retrosternal   B. retroperitoneal
    C. retroperiosteum   D. post-peristaltic

23. All of the following will be well-demonstrated on the AP recumbent abdomen EXCEPT   23.____

    A. the diaphragm
    B. tumor masses
    C. the gallbladder
    D. the outline of the psoas muscles

24. Abnormal lateral curvature of the spine is known as   24.____

    A. kyphosis   B. lordosis
    C. diverticulosis   D. scoliosis

25. The two processes extending laterally from each vertebra are called _____ processes.   25.____

    A. transverse   B. spinous
    C. superior articular   D. inferior articular

26. For the AP projection of the cervical spine, the head (chin) is extended to   26.____

    A. place the chin and mastoid tips in the same transverse plane
    B. make the patient more comfortable
    C. place the occlusal plane and odontoid process in the same transverse plane
    D. place the occlusal plane and mastoid tips in the same transverse plane

27. For the AP odontoid position of the cervical spine, the patient should open the mouth as wide as possible. Then the head should be adjusted so that a line from the _____ to the _____ is perpendicular to the cassette.

    27.____

   A. lower edge of the upper incisor; the tip of the mastoid process
   B. upper edge of the lower incisors; the tip of the mastoid process
   C. middle of the open mouth; the tip of the mastoid process
   D. mastoid; jaw

28. If the shoulder farthest from the film cannot be sufficiently depressed for the Twining method of the cervicothoracic region, the central ray should be directed

    28.____

   A. 20 degrees cephalic   B. 15 degrees caudad
   C. 10 degrees cephalic   D. 5 degrees caudad

29. Recent evidence suggests that the PA projection of the lumbar spine accomplishes all of the following EXCEPT

    29.____

   A. it may be more comfortable for the patient
   B. it places the intervertebral disk spaces at an angle more parallel with the divergence of the beam
   C. it places the spinous processes at an angle more conducive to visualization
   D. it provides superior radiation protection to the patient

30. The evaluation criteria for PA projections of the skull includes which of the following?

    30.____

   I. The distance from the lateral border of the skull to the lateral border of the orbit should be equal on both sides
   II. Petrous ridges should fill the orbits
   III. Frontal bone should be penetrated

The CORRECT answer is:

   A. I, II   B. I, III   C. II, III   D. I, II, III

KEY (CORRECT ANSWERS)

1. A	11. C	21. A
2. C	12. B	22. B
3. B	13. D	23. C
4. B	14. C	24. D
5. A	15. A	25. A
6. A	16. D	26. D
7. C	17. D	27. A
8. A	18. C	28. D
9. A	19. C	29. C
10. A	20. D	30. D

TEST 2

DIRECTIONS: Each question or incomplete statement is followed by several suggested answers or completions. Select the one that BEST answers the question or completes the statement. *PRINT THE LETTER OF THE CORRECT ANSWER IN THE SPACE AT THE RIGHT.*

1. To localize the sella turcica on the lateral aspect of the cranium, one must measure 3/4 inch   1.____

    A. inferior and 3/4 inch posterior to the EAM
    B. lateral to the EAM
    C. anterior and 3/4 inch superior to the OML
    D. superior and anterior to the EAM

2. The small intestine is approximately _____ ft. in length.   2.____

    A. 3   B. 10   C. 21   D. 30

3. The islets of Langerhans are composed of _____ and _____ cells.   3.____

    A. alpha; omega   B. red; white
    C. platelets; muscle   D. alpha; beta

4. The primary indications for radiographic evaluation of the esophagus include   4.____

    A. esophageal reflux
    B. esophageal varices
    C. presence of foreign bodies
    D. all of the above

5. The radiographic examination of choice for demonstration of the distal esophagus, stomach, and proximal small bowel is the   5.____

    A. barium swallow
    B. minimal hiatal hernia - Wolf's method
    C. UGI series
    D. laryngogram

6. Structures demonstrated on the AP radiograph of the stomach include the entire opacified stomach and the   6.____

    A. esophagus   B. terminal ileum
    C. cecum   D. duodenum

7. For the PA oblique position of the stomach, the degree of obliquity is approximately _____ degrees for the average patient.   7.____

    A. 30   B. 35   C. 40   D. 45

8. In hypotonic duodenography, the object of the exam is to   8.____

    A. eliminate peristalsis of the pylorus
    B. eliminate peristalsis of the duodenum

C. distend the head of the pancreas by two times to visualize pathology there
D. distend the duodenum by two to three times its normal diameter to visualize pathology of the pancreatic head or duodenum

9. In excretory urography, the greatest concentration of contrast appears at _____ minutes.   9._____

    A. 2 to 5   B. 5 to 10   C. 10 to 15   D. 15 to 20

10. Which of the following is the introduction of a drainage catheter into the collecting system   10._____
of the kidney?

    A. Excretory urography
    B. Retrograde cystography
    C. Percutaneous nephrostomy
    D. Voiding cystourethrography

11. In knee arthrography, the medial meniscus is visualized through a(n) _____ projection.   11._____

    A. ap   B. oblique
    C. mediolateral   D. tangential

12. Which of the following are part of the appendicular skeleton?   12._____
    I. Humerus
    II. Clavicle
    III. Scapula
The CORRECT answer is:

    A. I, II   B. I, III   C. II, III   D. I, II, III

13. Which of the following body parts are normally radiographed with and without weights?   13._____

    A. Humerus
    B. Shoulder
    C. Acromioclavicular joints
    D. Clavicle

14. For an AP projection of the 2nd finger, direct the central ray perpendicular to the _____   14._____
joint.

    A. proximal interphalangeal
    B. distal interphalangeal
    C. first carpometacarpophalangeal
    D. second carpometacarpophalangeal

15. Soft tissue radiography of the upper extremity is used for all of the following EXCEPT   15._____

    A. bursitis of the shoulder
    B. arthritis of the shoulder
    C. calcification in tendons
    D. foreign body localization

16. The radiograph of the AP or PA positions of the hand should include anatomy from the distal ends of the fingers to the

    A. proximal end of the metacarpal
    B. distal end of the metacarpal
    C. mid-carpal area
    D. radial and ulnar styloid processes

16._____

17. Which body type has a barrel-like torso?

    A. Hypersthenic   B. Sthenic
    C. Asthenic   D. Hyposthenic

17._____

18. Which body type tends to be thin, but with muscle/fat tissue ratios similar to sthenic patients?

    A. Hypersthenic   B. Sthenic
    C. Asthenic   D. Hyposthenic

18._____

19. Which group(s) tend(s) to have a greater collection of body fat?

    A. Children   B. Women
    C. Older people   D. All of the above

19._____

20. Which group(s) tend(s) to have less mineral content in their bones?

    A. Children   B. Women
    C. Older people   D. All of the above

20._____

21. For a PA axial projection of the clavicle, angle the central ray

    A. 10 to 15 degrees cephalad
    B. 10 to 15 degrees caudad
    C. 25 to 30 degrees cephalad
    D. 25 to 30 degrees caudad

21._____

22. For a lateral projection of the knee, _____ the knee _____ degrees.

    A. flex; 5 to 10   B. extend; 5 to 10
    C. flex; 20 to 30   D. extend; 20 to 30

22._____

23. Breathing instructions for a PA chest are to hold the breath at the end of

    A. one full expiration   B. one full inspiration
    C. two full expirations   D. two full inspirations

23._____

24. For a tangential projection of the patella, with the patient prone, angle the central ray _____ degrees _____ .

    A. 25; cephalad   B. 25; caudad
    C. 45; cephalad   D. 45; caudad

24._____

25. To image the frontal bone with a PA skull projection,
      I. place the OML perpendicular to the cassette
     II. direct the central ray perpendicular to the cassette
     III. direct the central ray to exit at the glabella
The CORRECT answer is:

25._____

A. I, II   B. I, III   C. II, III   D. I, II, III

26. For the parieto-orbital projection of the optic foramen, place the MSP _____ degrees   26.____
from perpendicular.

     A. 5   B. 7   C. 25   D. 37

27. Demonstration of the sigmoid colon with minimal super-imposition of bowel loops would   27.____
be provided by a _____ with a 30 degree _____ angle.

     A. PA; cephalad   B. PA; caudal
     C. LPO; caudal   D. LPO; cephalad

28. Which of the following would be used to demonstrate a transverse fracture of the patella?   28.____
     I. Tangential (Settegast)
     II. PA
     III. Lateral
The CORRECT answer is:

     A. I, II   B. I, III   C. II, III   D. I, II, III

29. To show the entire fibula without bony superimposition, perform a(n)   29.____

     A. PA   B. AP
     C. AP medial oblique   D. AP lateral oblique

30. The bone lying mostly below the floor of the cranium is the   30.____

     A. ethmoid   B. frontal   C. parietal   D. sphenoid

KEY (CORRECT ANSWERS)

1. D	11. D	21. D
2. C	12. C	22. C
3. D	13. C	23. D
4. D	14. A	24. C
5. C	15. B	25. A
6. D	16. D	26. D
7. D	17. A	27. D
8. D	18. D	28. C
9. D	19. D	29. C
10. C	20. D	30. A

EXAMINATION SECTION
TEST 1

DIRECTIONS: Each question or incomplete statement is followed by several suggested answers or completions. Select the one that BEST answers the question or completes the statement. *PRINT THE LETTER OF THE CORRECT ANSWER IN THE SPACE AT THE RIGHT.*

1. On a lateral projection of the ankle, the talus is _____ to the calcaneus.   1._____

    A. superior   B. inferior   C. lateral   D. medial

2. If the patient cannot be rotated from the supine position, an oblique projection of the cervical spine can still be accomplished by angling the central ray _____ degrees with the coronal plane.   2._____

    A. 10   B. 15   C. 25   D. 45

3. Demonstration of a diaphragmatic hernia during an upper GI is best accomplished with the _____ position.   3._____

    A. Trendelenburg   B. right anterior oblique
    C. prone   D. supine

4. Performing chest radiography in the upright position is preferred as   4._____
    I. the shape of the heart will not be distorted
    II. the size of the heart will not be distorted
    III. deeper inspiration is usually possible
The CORRECT answer is:

    A. I, II   B. I, III   C. II, III   D. I, II, III

5. Blood is pumped from the left ventricle into the   5._____

    A. aorta   B. pulmonary arteries
    C. pulmonary veins   D. vena cava

6. The formation of the elbow joint is through the articulation of the trochlea and the   6._____

    A. olecranon process   B. coracoid process
    C. clavicle   D. semilunar notch

7. The sigmoid and rectosigmoid areas are best demonstrated by which of the following projections during a lower GI examination?   7._____

    A. AP; central ray angled 40 degrees caudally
    B. PA; central ray angled 40 degrees cephalad
    C. Left lateral decubitus
    D. Right lateral decubitus

8. Skull sutures are _____ joints.   8._____

    A. amphiarthroidal   B. biarthroidal
    C. diarthroidal   D. synarthroidal

9. The junction of the lateral and medial borders of the scapula is the _____ angle.   9.____

   A. anterior   B. inferior   C. medial   D. lateral

10. More individuals fall into the category of _____ body habitus than any other.   10.____

   A. asthenic   B. hyposthenic
   C. hypersthenic   D. sthenic

11. For the parietoacanthial (Waters) projection for sinuses, the central ray exits at the   11.____

   A. acanthion   B. glabella   C. gonion   D. nasion

12. The right sacroiliac joint would best be demonstrated through a _____ degree _____   12.____
   posterior oblique position.

   A. 25; left   B. 25; right   C. 45; left   D. 45; right

13. The brachycephalic skull will have an angulation of _____ degrees between the petrous   13.____
   ridges and the median sagittal plane.

   A. 15   B. 37   C. 45   D. 55

14. The usual recommendation to demonstrate the knee joint in the anteroposterior position   14.____
   is to direct the central ray

   A. 5 to 7 degrees cephalad
   B. 5 to 7 degrees caudad
   C. 10 to 12 degrees cephalad
   D. 10 to 12 degrees caudad

15. The proper demonstration of the mortise joint in a medial oblique position of the ankle   15.____
   requires a _____ degree internal rotation of the leg.

   A. 5   B. 15   C. 35   D. 45

16. All of these are considered to be parts of a typical vertebra EXCEPT the   16.____

   A. body
   B. spinous process
   C. superior articular facet
   D. transverse foramen

17. The only one of the following facial bones that is UNPAIRED is the   17.____

   A. inferior nasal concha   B. mandible
   C. maxilla   D. palatine

18. To demonstrate the floor of the orbits, modify the PA projection of the cranium by direct-   18.____
   ing the central ray _____ degrees caudally.

   A. 10   B. 20   C. 30   D. 45

19. For an IVU, the AP oblique projection is generally taken with a body rotation of _____   19.____
   degrees.

   A. 10   B. 30   C. 45   D. 60

20. Nephroptosis would best be demonstrated by placing the patient in the AP _____ posi-   20.____
    tion.

    A. supine   B. prone
    C. upright   D. Trendelenburg

21. The sphenoid and ethmoid sinuses are best demonstrated through the _____ projec-   21.____
    tion.

    A. PA axial   B. parietoacanthial
    C. lateral   D. submentovertex

22. A variation of urography that takes several radiographs immediately following a bolus   22.____
    injection of contrast media to look for indications of a narrowed renal artery is _____
    urography.

    A. retrograde   B. voiding
    C. hypertensive intravenous   D. percutaneous antegrade

23. Prolapse of the bladder is best demonstrated through a(n)   23.____

    A. AP supine   B. AP upright
    C. AP postvoid   D. RPO postvoid

24. A patient with suspected regional enteritis (Crohn's disease) would most likely present   24.____
    for a(n)

    A. esophagram   B. lower GI
    C. small bowel series   D. upper GI

25. A patient with suspected diverticulosis would most likely present for a(n)   25.____

    A. esophagram   B. lower GI
    C. small bowel series   D. upper GI

26. The classic *apple-core pattern* of annular carcinoma would probably be visualized on a   26.____
    radiographic examination of the

    A. colon   B. esophagus
    C. small bowel   D. stomach

27. For a lateral nasal bone examination, the   27.____
        I. MSP is adjusted parallel to the cassette
        II. IOML is parallel to the transverse axis of the cassette
        III. central ray enters 3/4 inch above the nasion
    The CORRECT answer is:

    A. I, II   B. I, III   C. II, III   D. I, II, III

28. For a PA projection of the sternoclavicular joints, the central ray is directed perpendicular   28.____
    to

    A. T1   B. T3   C. T5   D. T7

29. To visualize ribs above the diaphragm, have the patient suspend respiration on   29.____

    A. full inspiration   B. full expiration
    C. partial inspiration   D. partial expiration

30. The most inferior structure visualized on a chest radiograph would be the
    30.____

    A. costophrenic angle   B. esophagus
    C. heart shadow   D. hilar region

KEY (CORRECT ANSWERS)

1.	A		16.	D
2.	D		17.	B
3.	A		18.	C
4.	B		19.	B
5.	A		20.	C
6.	D		21.	D
7.	B		22.	C
8.	D		23.	B
9.	B		24.	C
10.	D		25.	B
11.	A		26.	A
12.	A		27.	A
13.	D		28.	B
14.	A		29.	A
15.	B		30.	A

TEST 2

DIRECTIONS: Each question or incomplete statement is followed by several suggested answers or completions. Select the one that BEST answers the question or completes the statement. *PRINT THE LETTER OF THE CORRECT ANSWER IN THE SPACE AT THE RIGHT.*

1. In the radiographic examination of the coccyx, the

     I.   MSP is centered to the table
     II. central ray is directed 10 degrees cephalad
     III. central ray enters 2 inches superior to the symphysis pubis

    The CORRECT answer is:

    A. I, II   B. I, III   C. II, III   D. I, II, III

1.____

2. For a lateral cervicothoracic region radiograph (Twining method), the central ray enters at the level of

    A. C6   B. T2   C. T4   D. T6

2.____

3. During which radiograph of the cervical spine is the patient often instructed to phonate an *ah* during the exposure?

    A. AP   B. Obliques
    C. Open mouth   D. Lateral

3.____

4. For which of the following projections of the foot is the central ray directed perpendicular?

     I.   AP
     II. Medial oblique
     III. Lateral

    The CORRECT answer is:

    A. I, II   B. I, III   C. II, III   D. I, II, III

4.____

5. The central ray is directed approximately 2 inches inferior to the coracoid process for a radiograph of the AP

    A. elbow
    B. scapula
    C. acromioclavicular articulations
    D. clavicle

5.____

6. In a shoulder radiography,

     I.   for an AP position of the humerus, adjust the hand in external rotation
     II. for a lateral position of the humerus, adjust the hand in internal rotation
     III. direct the central ray perpendicular to the coracoid process

    The CORRECT answer is:

    A. I, II   B. I, III   C. II, III   D. I, II, III

6.____

7. For a medial oblique of the elbow, it is NOT true that the

    A. patient's hand is supinated
    B. arm is rotated medially
    C. anterior surface of the epicondyles are adjusted to an angle of 40 to 45 degrees
    D. central ray is directed perpendicular to the elbow joint

7.____

8. For a radiographic demonstration of the scaphoid (navicular), it is NOT true that 8.____

    A. the elbow is flexed 90 degrees
    B. the wrist is placed in extreme radial flexion
    C. the central ray is usually directed perpendicular to the scaphoid
    D. delineation of fractures may require an angulation of 10 to 15 degrees proximally

9. Which of the following projections of the hand direct the central ray perpendicular to the 9.____
third metacarpophalangeal joint?
    I. PA
    II. Oblique
    III. Lateral
The CORRECT answer is:

    A. I, II   B. I, III   C. II, III   D. I, II, III

10. The male urethra is typically _____ cm. long. 10.____

    A. 4   B. 10   C. 20   D. 30

11. The gland that has both endocrine and exocrine functions is the 11.____

    A. adrenal gland   B. pancreas
    C. pineal gland   D. pituitary gland

12. A stomach that sits high in the abdomen, almost in the chest cavity, is considered 12.____

    A. atonic   B. hypertonic
    C. hypotonic   D. orthotonic

13. There are two phalanges in the _____ toe. 13.____

    A. 1st (great)   B. 2nd
    C. 3r   D. 4th

14. The longest and strongest bone in the body is the 14.____

    A. femur   B. hip   C. mandible   D. skull

15. An exaggerated convexity in the thoracic region is termed 15.____

    A. kyphosis   B. lordosis
    C. sarcoidosis   D. scoliosis

16. The right and left lower quadrants together contain which of the following abdominal 16.____
regions?
    I. Right hypochondrium
    II. Hypogastrium
    III. Right iliac
The CORRECT answer is:

    A. I, II   B. I, III   C. II, III   D. I, II, III

17. A longitudinal angulation of the central ray with the long axis of the body part refers to 17.____
a(n) _____ projection

    A. axial   B. decubitus
    C. oblique   D. tangential

18. The surgical neck of the humerus is located   18.____

    A.   above the greater and lesser tubercules
    B.   between the greater and lesser tubercules
    C.   below the greater and lesser tubercules
    D.   obliquely on the posterior surface of the humerus

19. Stensen's duct is also called the _____ duct.   19.____

    A.   lesser sublingual   B.   greater sublingual
    C.   parotid   D.   submandibular

20. Which of the following are NOT secreted by the stomach?   20.____

    A.   Gastric lipase   B.   Insulin
    C.   Pepsin   D.   Renin

21. For the thumb, the central ray is directed in all projections perpendicular to the   21.____

    A.   base of the thumb
    B.   body of the thumb
    C.   metacarpophalangeal joint
    D.   proximal interphalangeal joint

22. The patient is erect or prone, in an oblique position, with the midcoronal plane forming a   22.____
60 degree angle with the cassette. The anterior surface of the cassette is centered to the
cassette. The central ray is directed perpendicular to the shoulder joint at the level of the
scapulohumeral joint.
This BEST describes the

    A.   AP shoulder
    B.   PA axial clavicle
    C.   PA oblique shoulder (scapular Y)
    D.   transthoracic lateral shoulder

23. The patient is initially prone with the foot resting on the table. The affected knee is flexed   23.____
so that the tibia and fibula form a 50 to 60 degree angle with the film. The central ray is
directed cephalad through the patellofemoral joint.
This BEST describes which of the following?

    A.   Axial knee
    B.   Intercondylar fossa (tunnel view)
    C.   Lateral knee
    D.   Tangential patella (Settegast method)

24. The patient is turned from supine to the affected side in a posterior oblique body position.   24.____
The affected knee is flexed, and the affected hip is centered to the midline of the table.
The central ray is directed perpendicular to a point midway between the ASIS and the
symphysis pubis.
This BEST describes which of the following?

    A.   Lateral knee   B.   Oblique knee
    C.   Lateral hip   D.   Oblique hip

25. For which cervical spine projection is 72 inch SID often recommended?

    A. AP   B. Obliques
    C. Open mouth   D. Lateral

25.____

26. For a scoliosis series, the first radiograph has the MSP centered to the film and the film is adjusted to include _____ of the iliac crests.

    A. 1 inch   B. 2 inches
    C. 3 inches   D. the entire length

26.____

27. A lateral soft tissue neck to show subepiglottic narrowing is often taken for

    A. asthma
    B. atelectasis
    C. croup
    D. chronic obstructive pulmonary disease

27.____

28. The Caldwell method (PA axial) is adapted from the PA skull by directing the central ray

    A. perpendicular to the film
    B. at a 5 degree caudal angle to the OML
    C. at a 15 degree cephalic angle to the OML
    D. at a 15 degree caudal angle to the OML

28.____

29. On a lateral skull, when the sella turcica is of primary interest, the central ray is directed _____ to the EAM.

    A. 1 inch superior
    B. 2 inches superior
    C. 3/4 inch superior and 3/4 inch anterior
    D. 3/4 inch inferior and 3/4 inch posterior

29.____

30. For an RAO (PA oblique) of the esophagus, the patient's _____ and the central ray is directed perpendicular to the cassette at the level of _____.

    A. left side is obliqued 10 to 15 degrees; T2 or T3
    B. left side is obliqued 35 to 40 degrees; T5 or T6
    C. right side is obliqued 10 to 15 degrees; T2 or T3
    D. right side is obliqued 35 to 40 degrees; T5 or T6

30.____

KEY (CORRECT ANSWERS)

1.	B		16.	C
2.	B		17.	A
3.	C		18.	C
4.	C		19.	C
5.	B		20.	B
6.	D		21.	C
7.	A		22.	C
8.	B		23.	D
9.	A		24.	C
10.	C		25.	D
11.	B		26.	A
12.	B		27.	C
13.	A		28.	C
14.	A		29.	C
15.	A		30.	B

EXAMINATION SECTION
TEST 1

DIRECTIONS: Each question or incomplete statement is followed by several suggested answers or completions. Select the one that BEST answers the question or completes the statement. *PRINT THE LETTER OF THE CORRECT ANSWER IN THE SPACE AT THE RIGHT.*

1. The median _____ vein is the usual preferred site for injection of contrast in excretory urography.

    A. basilic
    C. femoral
    B. antecubital
    D. carotid

1.____

2. What is the average amount of contrast injected in the average adult patient for excretory urography?
_____ ml.

    A. 10 to 25
    C. 120 to 250
    B. 30 to 100
    D. 300 to 1000

2.____

3. Percutaneous renal puncture and antegrade pyelography are sometimes combined with which diagnostic method?

    A. CT
    C. Ultrasound
    B. MRI
    D. Nuclear medicine

3.____

4. Which of the following are possible complications of retrograde cystography?
    I. Urinary sepsis
    II. Elevated pulse/respiration rate
    III. Chills and fever
The CORRECT answer is:

    A. I, II   B. I, III   C. II, III   D. I, II, III

4.____

5. What are the most common puncture sites for myelography?
_____ interspace.
    I. L2-L3
    II. L3-L4
    III. L4-L5
The CORRECT answer is:

    A. I, II   B. I, III   C. II, III   D. I, II, III

5.____

6. With what procedure is myelography often combined?

    A. CT
    C. Ultrasound
    B. MRI
    D. Nuclear medicine

6.____

7. The patient positions for introduction of contrast and removal of spinal fluid (spinal puncture) include which of the following?
    I. Prone
    II. Sitting, hunched over
    III. On side, in fetal position
The CORRECT answer is:

7.____

A. I, II   B. I, III   C. II, III   D. I, II, III

8. What is the most common approach used for the Seldinger Technique?   8._____

     A. Brachial   B. Axillary
     C. Femoral   D. Translumbar

9. What term describes a solution with an ionic concentration higher than normal body   9._____
fluid?

     A. Isotonic   B. Hyperstatic
     C. Hyperosmolar   D. Osmotic

10. What drug should be readily available if a patient develops hives several minutes follow-   10._____
ing injection of an iodinated contrast medium?

     A. Atropine   B. Benadryl
     C. Vasopressin   D. Tolazoline

11. When dressing for a sterile operating room procedure, which of the following should be   11._____
put on last?

     A. Gloves   B. Gown
     C. Shoe covers   D. Face mask

12. The normal range of adult systolic blood pressure is _____ mm Hg.   12._____

     A. 10 to 60   B. 70 to 100
     C. 110 to 140   D. 140 to 170

13. A surgical creation of an opening between the colon and the surface of the body is a(n)   13._____

     A. ileostomy   B. colostomy
     C. ostomy   D. colileostomy

14. Levin and Cantor are examples of _____ tubes.   14._____

     A. urinary   B. gastric
     C. cranial   D. endotracheal

15. Which of the following procedures must be performed with sterile techniques?   15._____

     A. Knee arthrogram   B. Lumbar myelogram
     C. Renal arteriography   D. All of the above

16. A common drug given to a patient who is having a reaction to contrast during an intrave-   16._____
nous urogram is

     A. furosemide   B. potassium
     C. heparin   D. diphenhydramine

17. To preserve sterile integrity when a person's path is crossed, contact should be made   17._____

     A. face to face   B. side to side
     C. back to back   D. none of the above

18. A sterile tray has been opened and the procedure has been delayed for an hour. When you look back at the tray, it is damp.
What should you do?

    A. Discard it
    B. Use it anyway
    C. Wipe all devices with alcohol
    D. Wipe all devices with diluted bleach

18.____

19. The term pneumothorax means

    A. inflammation of the lung
    B. fluid in the lungs
    C. air in thoracic cavity
    D. normal aeration of lungs

19.____

20. The feeling of light-headedness that many patients suffer caused by a long period of rest is

    A. orthostatie hypertension
    B. orthostatie hypotension
    C. fatigue
    D. inner ear infections

20.____

21. Compared to a cleansing enema, a barium enema typically uses
    I. a larger amount of liquid
    II. a larger rectal catheter
    III. colder water
The CORRECT answer is:

    A. I, II   B. II, III   C. I, III   D. I, II, III

21.____

22. Which of the following is TRUE regarding rectal and oral temperatures?
Rectal temperatures are

    A. 0.5 to 1.0° higher than oral temperatures
    B. 0.5 to 1.0° lower than oral temperatures
    C. the same as oral temperatures
    D. considered to be inaccurate

22.____

23. In cases of bowel perforation, what type of contrast medium is preferred?

    A. Air   B. Iodine   C. Barium   D. Oil-based

23.____

24. The resistance of a contrast medium to free flow is termed

    A. viscosity   B. impaction
    C. impedance   D. compression

24.____

25. One of the most important instructions to give patients, especially older patients, following a barium enema is to

    A. drink plenty of fluids
    B. see if their doctor wants them to eat

25.____

C. take a strong laxative
D. rest for 2 to 3 days

26. Which of the following can lead to legal difficulties?   26.____
      I.   Not checking the patient's name by wristband or oral affirmation
      II. Not asking the patient if it is agreeable for you to
      III. perform the examination
      IV. Mismarking the radiograph
The CORRECT answer is:

   A. I, II   B. I, III   C. II, III   D. I, II, III

27. A patient's chart indicates he has bradycardia. This means that he has a(n)   27.____

   A. slow heart rate   B. fast heart rate
   C. enlarged heart   D. small heart

28. A former patient presents herself at your department and demands her radiographs. In   28.____
most states and facilities, the proper response is that

   A. she may take them at any time
   B. she may take them if she pays a fee
   C. the facility owns the radiographs, but she may be provided with copies
   D. the facility owns the radiographs and she has no right to them

29. Proper body mechanics include: 29.____
      I.   Keeping the knees locked
      II. Keeping the back straight
      III. Using the legs rather than the back to lift
The CORRECT answer is:

   A. I, II   B. I, III   C. II, III   D. I, II, III

30. A reaction to contrast caused by patient anxiety would be classified as   30.____

   A. overdose   B. anaphylactic
   C. cardiovascular   D. psychogenic

KEY (CORRECT ANSWERS)

1.	B		16.	D
2.	B		17.	C
3.	C		18.	A
4.	D		19.	C
5.	A		20.	B
6.	A		21.	A
7.	D		22.	A
8.	C		23.	B
9.	C		24.	A
10.	B		25.	A
11.	A		26.	D
12.	C		27.	A
13.	B		28.	C
14.	B		29.	C
15.	D		30.	D

TEST 2

DIRECTIONS: Each question or incomplete statement is followed by several suggested answers or completions. Select the one that BEST answers the question or completes the statement. *PRINT THE LETTER OF THE CORRECT ANSWER IN THE SPACE AT THE RIGHT.*

1. All of these patients arrive at 8 A.M. for their examination. In which order should they be performed?   1.____
     I.   35 year old outpatient for a chest x-ray
     II. 50 year old diabetic for an intravenous urogram
     III. 7 year old for an upper GI
     IV. 35 year old for an upper GI
   The CORRECT answer is:

   A. I, II, III, IV   B. II, III, IV, I
   C. III, IV, I, II   D. IV, I, II, III

2. Which of the following are strategies used to alleviate patient cramping during a barium enema?   2.____
     I.   Remove the enema tip
     II. Have the patient take slow, deep breaths
     III. Stop the flow of barium
   The CORRECT answer is:

   A. I, II   B. I, III   C. II, III   D. I, II, III

3. A patient who exhibits hives as a result of contrast media injection would MOST likely be provided with which of the following drugs?   3.____

   A. Analgesic   B. Anesthetic
   C. Anticoagulant   D. Antihistamine

4. Documented means of HIV transmission include: 4.____
     I.   Air
     II. Blood and body fluids
     III. Fomites such as countertops
   The CORRECT answer is:

   A. I *only*   B. II *only*   C. I, II   D. II, III

5. All of the following are effective means of preventing disease transmission in certain circumstances. Which of them is a simple, effective method often ignored by healthcare professionals?   5.____

   A. Wearing masks   B. Wearing gloves
   C. Wearing gowns   D. Handwashing

6. How many workers are required to correctly perform a radiographic examination on a patient in strict isolation?   6.____

   A. 1   B. 2   C. 3   D. 4

7. Blunt trauma to the skull is MOST likely to result in a _____ fracture.   7._____

    A. comminuted   B. depressed
    C. linear   D. spiral

8. Informed consent for an invasive radiographic procedure for most adults is provided by   8._____
the

    A. patient   B. patient's family member
    C. referring physician   D. witness

9. BUN and creatinine levels provide indications of _____ function.   9._____

    A. cardiac   B. liver   C. pulmonary   D. renal

10. Another name for a diarthroidal joint is _____ joint.   10._____

    A. fibrous   B. gliding
    C. synarthroidal   D. synovial

11. Ionizing radiation would NOT be employed for which of the following examinations?   11._____
        I.   Single photon emission computed tomography (SPECT)
        II. Magnetic resonance imaging
        III. Ultrasound
The CORRECT answer is:

    A. I, II   B. I, III   C. II, III   D. I, II, III

12. Imaging of joints such as knee and shoulder, once performed exclusively by arthrogra-   12._____
phy, is now being slowly replaced by

    A. angiography
    B. computed tomography (CT)
    C. magnetic resonance imaging (MRI)
    D. ultrasound

13. Barium sulfate and water-soluble iodine are contrast agents routinely used in plain film   13._____
radiography as well as

    A. angiography
    B. computed tomography (CT)
    C. magnetic resonance imaging (MRI)
    D. ultrasound

14. The highest incidence of contrast medium reactions occur with which of the following   14._____
media?

    A. Air
    B. Barium sulfate
    C. Ionic iodinated contrast media
    D. Non-ionic iodinated contrast media

15. The BEST place for a urinary catheter is   15._____

    A. on the patient's abdomen
    B. on the x-ray table

C. held up high by one of the transporters
D. below the level of the urinary bladder

16. An intestinal obstruction caused by immobility of the bowel is a(n) _____ ileus.   16._____

    A. adynamic   B. bifocal
    C. mechanical   D. segmented

17. The ethical principle that BEST correlates with *first do no harm* is   17._____

    A. autonomy   B. beneficence
    C. fidelity   D. nonmaleficence

18. Which of the following are consistent with the ASRT and the ARRT Code of Ethics?   18._____
        I.   The physician is responsible for all actions of the technologist.
        II.   Radiographers may not diagnose.
        III.   Radiographers may reveal confidential information only as required by law.
The CORRECT answer is:

    A. I, II   B. I, III   C. II, III   D. I, II, III

19. A radiographer who reveals information that subjects the patient to ridicule, scorn or con-   19._____
tempt may be guilty of

    A. assault   B. battery
    C. defamation   D. negligence

20. A term that is often used interchangeably with infiltra-tion is   20._____

    A. coagulation   B. extravasation
    C. intravenous   D. topical

21. An unusual response to a drug that is peculiar to an individual would be called   21._____

    A. contraindication   B. idiopathic
    C. idiosyncratic   D. psychogenic

22. Which of the following positioning/immobilization devices are typically radiopaque?   22._____
        I.   Head clamps
        II.   Positioning sponges
        III.   Sandbags
The CORRECT answer is:

    A. I, II   B. I, III   C. II, III   D. I, II, III

23. Which of the following age groups cannot usually take the view of another and have a   23._____
view of time that only includes the here and now?

    A. Toddlers (1 to 3 years)
    B. Preschoolers (3 to 5 years)
    C. Schoolchildren (6 to 10 years)
    D. Adolescents (10 to 20 years)

24. What percentage of individuals above the age of 65 exhibit memory loss?   24._____

    A. 10   B. 20   C. 30   D. 50

25. Which of the following positions is often useful for the male using a urinal?   25._____

    A. Fowler's   B. Sim's
    C. Trendelenburg   D. Lithotomy

26. An infection that results from a physician's intervention is called   26._____

    A. iatrogenic   B. idiopathic
    C. idiosyncratic   D. nosocomial

27. Which of the following terms BEST describes an individual serving as a reservoir for an   27._____
infection?

    A. Carrier   B. Fomite   C. Host   D. Vector

28. Self-gloving   28._____
    I. requires the removal of all jewelry first
    II. is performed before gowning
    III. may be performed through 2 methods: open or closed
The CORRECT answer is:

    A. I, II   B. I, III   C. II, III   D. I, II, III

29. Patients with symptomatic bradycardia are typically candidates for   29._____

    A. angioplasty   B. open heart surgery
    C. pacemaker insertion   D. ventriculography

30. Which of the following would be the MOST likely cause of hypovolemic shock?   30._____

    A. Damage to the spinal cord
    B. Loss of blood or tissue fluid
    C. Myocardial infarction
    D. Sepsis, deep anesthesia, or anaphylaxis

KEY (CORRECT ANSWERS)

1.	B	16.	A
2.	C	17.	D
3.	D	18.	C
4.	B	19.	C
5.	D	20.	B
6.	B	21.	C
7.	B	22.	B
8.	A	23.	A
9.	D	24.	A
10.	D	25.	A
11.	C	26.	A
12.	C	27.	A
13.	B	28.	B
14.	C	29.	C
15.	D	30.	B

———

EXAMINATION SECTION
TEST 1

DIRECTIONS: Each question or incomplete statement is followed by several suggested answers or completions. Select the one that BEST answers the question or completes the statement. *PRINT THE LETTER OF THE CORRECT ANSWER IN THE SPACE AT THE RIGHT.*

1.   The Law position is used to obtain x-rays of the   1.____

    A.   jugular foramina   B.   mandible
    C.   mastoid process   D.   petrous portions

2.   Assume that the roentgenologist has requested a ventral decubitus view of the lungs.   2.____
The technician adjusts the patient's body to a true anteroposterior position with the arms above the head. He places the cassette vertically against the affected side. The exposure is then made at the end of a full inhalation.
In reviewing the procedure described above, it would be CORRECT to say that the

    A.   body should have been in a true posteroanterior position
    B.   patient should have been in an erect position
    C.   exposure should have been made on expiration
    D.   technician followed the correct procedure

3.   If a fracture of the lateral malleolus is suspected, the films which should be taken are   3.____

    A.   AP and lateral views of the knee
    B.   AP, lateral, and oblique views of the ankle
    C.   AP, lateral, and oblique views of the elbow
    D.   skull, submentovertex view

4.   For an infusion nephropyelography, it is necessary to use a table that is equipped with   4.____

    A.   a cystoscopy unit   B.   cine radiography
    C.   enema apparatus   D.   tomographic apparatus

5.   In pneumoencephalography, the area which is studied is the   5.____

    A.   heart
    B.   lungs
    C.   spinal cord
    D.   ventricular system of the brain

6.   In order to determine fluid level in the chest, the position which should be used, in addi-   6.____
tion to routine views, is

    A.   AP decubitus   B.   LAO and RAO
    C.   lateral decubitus   D.   PA decubitus

7.   The position for the cervical spine which should be used to obtain views of the atlas and   7.____
axis is

    A.   AP, open mouth   B.   LAO
    C.   lateral   D.   RAO

8. The palpation points for a lateral position of the sternum are the   8.____

    A. acromion process and the xyphoid process
    B. apex of the scapula and the manubrium
    C. manubrium and the xyphoid process
    D. sterno-clavicular articulation and the shaft of the clavicle

9. The one of the following procedures which does NOT require the use of a contrast   9.____
medium is

    A. cerebral angiography   B. cholangiography
    C. myelography   D. xeroradiography

10. In order to secure a radiograph of the pars petrosapro-jected at right angles to its long   10.____
axis, one should use

    A. Fuch's position
    B. Hickey's position
    C. Stenver's position
    D. the anterior tangential view

11. In an I.V.P. examination of the average adult patient, the compensation for the kidney   11.____
drop when the patient is moved from the supine to the erect position is approximately
_____ inches.

    A. twelve   B. six   C. two   D. zero

12. The Chassard-Lapine position is used to demonstrate the   12.____

    A. cervical spine   B. hip joint
    C. pelvis   D. sigmoid

13. The lordotic projection of the chest is used MAINLY to demonstrate the   13.____

    A. apices   B. diaphragm
    C. great vessels   D. size of the heart

14. In the Granger position for an x-ray of the sella turcica, the central ray is directed   14.____

    A. $10°$ caudad   B. $10°$ cephalad
    C. $30°$ cephalad   D. perpendicularly

15. In a radiograph of the kidneys, the left kidney when compared with the right kidney is   15.____
USUALLY

    A. much larger   B. on the same level
    C. slightly higher   D. slightly lower

16. Of the following, the one which is a measurement of x-ray quantity is   16.____

    A. a milliampere   B. a roentgen
    C. an angstrom   D. the half-value layer

17. The quality of an x-ray beam is MAINLY dependent on the   17.____

    A. heat of the filament   B. KvP impressed on the tube
    C. size of the focal spot   D. size of the target

18. The *half-value layer* is the measure which has been adopted internationally to indicate   18.____

    A.   radiation quality
    B.   radiation quantity
    C.   the amount of filtration to be added in x-ray therapy
    D.   the inherent filtration in an x-ray tube

19. An increase in the kilovoltage across the x-ray tube results in   19.____

    A.   no alteration in wave length
    B.   radiation of longer wave length
    C.   radiation of shorter wave length
    D.   twice as many impulses per second

20. The CHIEF purpose of a filter of aluminum placed beneath the aperture of a radiographic   20.____
tube is to

    A.   control the latitude of the radiographic image
    B.   eliminate the light given off by the filament
    C.   absorb some of the longer wave lengths
    D.   filter out undesirable stem radiation

21. The autotransformer is used to   21.____

    A.   dissipate the heat in the x-ray tube
    B.   measure the time of exposure
    C.   select the milliamperes to be used
    D.   select the voltage to the high tension transformer

22. The ratio of a transformer expresses the relationship of   22.____

    A.   the number of turns in the primary winding to the number of turns in the secondary
        winding
    B.   the weight of the primary to the weight of the secondary
    C.   the size of the wire in the primary to the size of the wire in the secondary
    D.   watts output to watts input

23. The milliamperage through the x-ray tube for any given exposure is CHIEFLY dependent   23.____
upon the

    A.   heat of the anode
    B.   heat of the filament
    C.   size of the target
    D.   voltage applied to the tube

24. A rheostat changes the voltage by   24.____

    A.   cutting out part of the transformer
    B.   increasing the number of windings in the primary of the transformer
    C.   shortening the filament transformer
    D.   varying the amount of resistance

25. If an x-ray tube is gassy, it will USUALLY be noted that   25.____

    A. no reading will be obtained on the primary voltmeter
    B. the milliammeter is not registering
    C. there are irregular fluctuations in the milliamperage
    D. the tube filament does not light up

26. The ADVANTAGE of a rotating anode x-ray tube over stationary anode tube is that the   26.____
rotating anode tube

    A. is low in cost
    B. permits lower energies to be used
    C. is small and easily manipulated
    D. permits high energies with a small focal spot

27. During a 100 Ma exposure with full-wave rectified equipment, a milliammeter which is   27.____
known to be accurate indicates only 50 Ma.
Of the following, the MOST probable reason for this is that

    A. a valve tube is not functioning properly
    B. one of the fuses is burned out
    C. the high tension transformer has developed a short circuit
    D. the timer is not properly set

28. A double focus x-ray tube is one which has   28.____

    A. two cathodes
    B. two electrodes
    C. two focal spots
    D. rotating and stationary anodes

29. A spinning top is used to check the timer of a full-wave rectified x-ray machine.   29.____
If an exposure is made at 1/10 of a second, and the timer is accurate, the number of
black dots which will show on the processed film is

    A. 6   B. 8   C. 10   D. 12

30. In a full-wave rectified x-ray unit, if one of the valve-tubes is nonfunctioning, the milliam-   30.____
meter will register

    A. double the selected Ma
    B. slightly more than one-half of the selected Ma
    C. the same as the selected Ma
    D. zero

31. High speed screens are NOT ordinarily useful in   31.____

    A. intravenous urography
    B. magnification radiography
    C. pediatric radiography
    D. radiography of the hand

32. Of the following, the MOST important reason for keeping records in an x-ray department   32.____
is to provide

A. a basis for evaluating the performance of the individual employees in the department
B. an easy way to predict the next year's work load
C. better health care to the patients and families in the community
D. statistical information for reporting on the activities of the x-ray department

33. The one of the following which it is LEAST necessary for the technician to record on every x-ray film is the 33.____

    A. date of examination   B. name of the doctor
    C. name of the patient   D. side (R or L)

34. The MOST important reason for paying attention to a complaint from a patient who has come for an examination is that 34.____

    A. people appreciate the attention given to their complaints
    B. employees should always be considerate to patients
    C. there is no harm in listening, even if the complaint is not justified
    D. there may be good reason for the patient's complaint

35. To gain the confidence of the patient, it would be MOST advisable for the technician to 35.____

    A. discuss the patient's symptoms with the patient
    B. let the patient know he is friendly with the physicians
    C. present an efficient and careful manner of work
    D. tell the patient about his training and experience as a technician

36. Assume that one of the two x-ray rooms is unavailable for use on a day when a large number of patients have been scheduled for examination.
Of the following, it would be BEST to 36.____

    A. proceed with the examination of all patients, taking them in order as scheduled
    B. reschedule all of the afternoon patients since it will be impossible to reach them before closing time
    C. see if any of the patients can come on another date and arrange for appointments at the next suitable date for these patients
    D. take only half of the patients called for each hour, and tell the others to come back on another date

37. An elderly woman who is scheduled for a series of radio-grans tells the technician half-way through the session that she feels nauseous and does not want to continue.
Of the following, it would be BEST for the technician to 37.____

    A. ask her if she can come back the next day since it is important that the series be completed
    B. ask her if she would like to rest outside while he takes another patient, and say that he will continue her examination when she feels better
    C. tell her he has not completed the series but that, if she chooses to stop, it is her responsibility
    D. tell her that she will have to continue until the full series is completed

38. For a technician to discuss the x-ray findings with the patient's family would be

    A. *wise,* because the family would be favorably impressed with the technician's knowledge and ability
    B. *unwise,* because the family should be told by the radiologist or doctor in charge of the case of the diagnosis and treatment required
    C. *wise,* because he would be able to assure them that the patient's condition is not serious since he has seen the films
    D. *unwise,* because the technician is too busy to be able to enter into discussion of the patient's condition with the family

38.____

39. The radiologist who is in charge of the section frequently, and without prior announcement, gives the technicians assignments in the department which conflict with those of their immediate supervisor.
In order to resolve the conflict, it would be BEST for the

    A. supervisor to discuss the matter with the radiologist at some convenient time
    B. technicians to discuss the matter with the radiologist while the supervisor is present
    C. supervisor to tell the technicians to follow the radiologist's orders
    D. supervisor to tell the technicians to ignore the radiologist and do the work he has assigned

39.____

40. One of the technicians is trying hard to do a good job but seems to lack the needed skills for good work.
In this situation, it would be BEST for the supervisor to

    A. arrange to give this technician additional training
    B. assign less difficult work to this technician
    C. let the technician learn by doing
    D. set lower performance standards for this technician

40.____

KEY (CORRECT ANSWERS)

1. C	11. C	21. D	31. D
2. A	12. D	22. A	32. C
3. B	13. A	23. B	33. B
4. D	14. B	24. D	34. D
5. D	15. C	25. C	35. C
6. C	16. B	26. D	36. C
7. A	17. B	27. A	37. B
8. C	18. A	28. C	38. B
9. D	19. C	29. D	39. A
10. C	20. C	30. B	40. A

TEST 2

DIRECTIONS: Each question or incomplete statement is followed by several suggested answers or completions. Select the one that BEST answers the question or completes the statement. *PRINT THE LETTER OF THE CORRECT ANSWER IN THE SPACE AT THE RIGHT.*

1. The primary purpose of filters in a film badge used for x-ray detection is to   1.____

    A. absorb scattered radiation
    B. increase the gamma of the H and D curve
    C. permit dose measurements over a wide range of energies
    D. prevent fogging

2. Of the following, the statement about grids which is NOT correct is: 2.____

    A. Focused grids should be used only within fixed target-film distance ranges
    B. Grids reduce the scattered radiation that reaches the film
    C. Simple grids limit the size of the radiograph
    D. To prevent grid shadows, the grid and tube are moved separately

3. Of the following, the statement about screens which is NOT correct is: 3.____

    A. Generally, faster screens give poorer resolution
    B. Screens give better resolution
    C. Screens reduce the x-ray exposure of the film
    D. Screens should be used only with screen film

4. A Potter-Bucky diaphragm is used CHIEFLY to   4.____

    A. eliminate a large percentage of secondary radiation
    B. increase the diameter of the primary beam
    C. limit the diameter of the primary beam
    D. produce radiographs free from distortion

5. A crosshatched grid is NOT useful   5.____

    A. at a 20° angle into the grid
    B. at 60 inch anode-film distance
    C. in pediatric radiology
    D. with off-center perpendicular beam techniques

6. Sharpness of detail on a diagnostic radiograph is NOT ordinarily affected by   6.____

    A. grid ratio   B. movement of the patient
    C. screen speed   D. target size

7. In fluoroscopy, reducing the size of the field results in an improved image because of less   7.____
scatter from the

    A. collimator shutters   B. table top
    C. patient   D. room

8. A film is taken with a target-film distance of 40 inches and an object-film distance of 10 inches.
   The magnification factor is   8.____

   A. .45   B. .60   C. 1.20   D. 1.33

9. In half-wave rectified x-ray machines operating with a 60 cycle current, the number of impulses per second passing through the tube is   9.____

   A. 20   B. 40   C. 50   D. 60

10. An x-ray tube with a heat-storage capacity of 100,000 heat units has a cooling rate of 10,000 heat units per minute. Starting with a cold tube, a certain procedure calls for 5 exposures of 100 Kv, 500 Ma and 1/5 second each. After 3 minutes, a second series of 10 films is to be taken.   10.____
    Which of the following techniques would NOT damage this tube?
    _____ Kv, _____ Ma, _____ second(s).

   A. 80; 100; 2   B. 80; 500; 1/5
   C. 100; 500; 1/5   D. 120; 300; 1/3

11. All other factors being equal, which of the following exposures would produce the greatest radiographic density?   11.____
    _____ second and _____ milliamperes.

   A. 1/10; 100   B. 1/20; 200   C. 1/40; 500   D. 1; 10

12. Fine focus (0.3 mm.) anode tubes   12.____

   A. allow direct magnification radiography
   B. are not desirable for vascular radiology
   C. cannot be used with rotating anodes
   D. require three phase input

13. In an image-amplifier fluoroscopic system with automatic brightness control, moving to a thicker part of the patient AUTOMATICALLY   13.____

   A. decreases the Kv to give more contrast
   B. increases the brightness setting on the TV monitor
   C. increases the gain of the image-amplifier tube
   D. increases the Kv or Ma of the x-ray tube

14. Three phase x-ray units   14.____

   A. allow shorter exposure times
   B. are not useful in serial rapid film techniques
   C. increase contrast at the same Kv settings as in single phase units
   D. require higher Kv settings

15. The thickness of cut in linear tomography depends on the   15.____

   A. anatomy of the patient   B. Kv used
   C. length of sweep   D. Ma used

16. The one of the following which is NOT a function of a radiographic cone is to   16.____

    A. decrease contrast
    B. decrease secondary scatter
    C. improve detail visibility
    D. limit the field of exposure

17. If all other factors are kept constant, the change from a two mm to a one mm focal spot   17.____
    will produce a radiograph with

    A. increased distortion   B. magnification
    C. poorer definition   D. sharper image

18. If all other factors are kept constant, the change from non-grid to grid technique will pro-   18.____
    duce a radiograph with

    A. decreased contrast
    B. increased contrast
    C. increased density
    D. no change in contrast or density

19. The optimum distance between the x-ray tube and the grid is determined by the   19.____

    A. distance between lead strips
    B. grid ratio
    C. height of lead strips
    D. number of lead strips

20. Suppose that a film has been taken with Kv of 60. A second film, taken at Kv of 70, with   20.____
    all other factors unchanged, would show ALMOST_____ the exposure.

    A. one-seventh   B. one-sixth
    C. one-half   D. twice

21. Assume that for a particular radiograph which is normally taken at 72 inch distance and   21.____
    10 MaS, it is necessary to reduce the distance to 36 inches.
    The new MaS should be

    A. 2.5   B. 5   C. 10   D. 20

22. To reduce patient exposure to radiation, the x-ray beam should be filtered by the equiva-   22.____
    lent of

    A. 3 cm of aluminum   B. 3 mm of aluminum
    C. 3 mm of copper   D. 3 mm of tungsten

23. The maximum permissible milliamperage during fluoroscopy is   23.____

    A. 1   B. 3   C. 5   D. 7

24. The maximum permissible dose in rads to the whole body for a radiation worker who is   24.____
    30 years old is

    A. 30   B. 60   C. 90   D. 120

25. The radiation dose to a technician should not exceed 25._____

    A. 3 rem in 13 weeks   B. 3 rem in 1 year
    C. 15 rem in 1 year   D. 30 rem in 1 month

26. Reversal of the radiographic image is produced by 26._____

    A. chemical fog
    B. exposure of film to white light
    C. film touching the sides of the tank
    D. overexposure of film to radiation

27. The yellowing of processed radiographs after they have been stored for a period of time is the result of 27._____

    A. inadequate developing
    B. inadequate rinsing after developing
    C. inadequate washing
    D. weak developer

28. The suspended crystals embedded in the gelatin of the x-ray film are 28._____

    A. calcium tungstate   B. silver bromide
    C. silver nitrate   D. zinc sulfide

29. Film artifacts appearing as branching, twig-like lines are caused by 29._____

    A. fingernail scratches
    B. improper processing
    C. improper safelight exposure
    D. static

30. Elon and hydroquinone in the developer acts as 30._____

    A. acidifiers   B. developing agents
    C. preservatives   D. restrainers

31. If a patient must be held during radiography, the person who holds the patient should be 31._____

    A. a technician who is most familiar with the position used
    B. anyone who is available at the time
    C. one who is not regularly exposed to radiation
    D. the technician who has had the lowest radiation exposure in the past six months

32. Compared to a 14 x 17 PA chest film exposure, a miniature chest photofluorogram will 32._____

    A. be equally satisfactory for diagnostic purposes
    B. give better definition for diagnostic purposes
    C. result in a higher radiation dose to the patient
    D. result in a lower radiation dose to the patient

33. A patient presents the technician with a note signed by his doctor, requesting that he be allowed to borrow films of his gall bladder series in order for a comparison to be made with an earlier series.
Of the following, it would be BEST for the technician to 33._____

A. give him the films but keep the doctor's note
B. give him the films since they are his
C. obtain the permission of the radiologist to give him the films
D. inform him that the films cannot be borrowed

34. You have instructed an aide who is responsible for the supply room to use those supplies which have been on hand longest before using newer stock.
Of the following, the MOST practical way to do this is to

    A. keep a file for each item in supply, with records of dates when supplies are received and used
    B. place new supplies behind those of different items which are already in stock
    C. put newly-received supplies in the supply closet only after all supplies of the same item are used up
    D. put supplies that are needed most often in the front of the supply closet

34.____

35. Assume that, because of alterations in the building, the x-ray department in the health center is being redesigned and you have been asked to make suggestions.
Before planning the new layout, it would be MOST important to know

    A. how many employees will be assigned to the x-ray department
    B. how much money will be available for the alterations in the x-ray department
    C. the probable location of the x-ray department in the building
    D. what types and numbers of x-ray examinations will be required of this department

35.____

36. Suppose a meeting of the technicians has been called to discuss ways of improving certain procedures and practices in the x-ray departments at the various locations.
Of the following, the LEAST desirable result of the meeting would be

    A. the adjustment of differences in point of view within the group
    B. the demonstration of the supervisor's ability to lead rather than control the group by command
    C. the motivation of the members of the group to work in harmony
    D. to show the group that the supervisor's ideas are always correct

36.____

37. Suppose the services of part-time aides have been made available. These aides will be assigned, as needed, to work in the x-ray departments of the various health centers. One of the technicians objects to working with these aides.
Of the following, the action which would be MOST appropriate for the supervisor to take to change this technician's attitude would be to

    A. agree with him that part-time aides will not be very useful, but explain to him that he cannot refuse to use them
    B. discuss with him some of the ways that aides might be useful in the x-ray department
    C. explain to him that these part-time aides need and are entitled to work experience
    D. tell him that use of part-time aides may result in large raises for the technicians because of increased work output

37.____

38. Assume that you are attending a training session for a group of x-ray technicians.
Of the following, the LEAST important reason for asking questions during the session is to

38.____

A. check on the effectiveness of the teaching
B. find out who is the best technician in the group
C. focus attention on an important point in the lesson
D. motivate the group to pay attention to the lecture

39. In the orientation training of a newly-appointed technician, it would be LEAST helpful to

39.____

    A. discuss the importance of careful positioning of patients in x-ray examination
    B. point out the charts used in determining exposure factors for the available equipment
    C. review the anatomical terms commonly used in radiography
    D. stress the clinical importance of accurate radiography in the treatment of patients

40. Assume that you are teaching a less experienced technician the correct way to take one of the more complicated radiographs.
Of the following, the BEST procedure to follow is to

40.____

    A. explain what is to be done; then demonstrate how it is done; then observe him as he does it himself, making corrections if needed; then follow up
    B. prepare a detailed, step-by-step explanation in writing for the technician to follow, and tell him to speak to you if he has any questions
    C. show him how to do the easier steps first; then, after he has had some experience, show him the more difficult steps
    D. tell him to watch another, more experienced technician as he performs this task, and to consult with this employee if he has any problems when he has to do it himself

_____

KEY (CORRECT ANSWERS)

1. C	11. C	21. A	31. C
2. C	12. A	22. D	32. C
3. B	13. D	23. C	33. C
4. A	14. A	24. B	34. A
5. A	15. C	25. A	35. D
6. A	16. A	26. B	36. D
7. C	17. D	27. C	37. B
8. D	18. B	28. B	38. B
9. D	19. B	29. D	39. C
10. B	20. D	30. B	40. A

_____

TEST 3

DIRECTIONS: Each question or incomplete statement is followed by several suggested answers or completions. Select the one that BEST answers the question or completes the statement. *PRINT THE LETTER OF ThE CORRECT ANSWER IN THE SPACE AT THE RIGHT.*

1. Vessels which convey blood away from the heart are called   1.____

    A.   arteries   B.   lymphatics
    C.   veins   D.   ventricles

2. The cardiac orifice is the opening between the   2.____

    A.   bronchus and trachea
    B.   esophagus and stomach
    C.   left ventricle and aorta
    D.   superior vena cava and left atrium

3. The double-walled serous membrane enclosing each lung is called the   3.____

    A.   pericardium   B.   pleura
    C.   meninges   D.   omentum

4. The muscle of the heart is called the   4.____

    A.   endocardium   B.   mesocardium
    C.   myocardium   D.   pericardium

5. After urine is formed in the kidney, the structures through which it passes until it is voided are, *in order,* the   5.____

    A.   bladder, ureter, urethra
    B.   ureter, bladder, uvula
    C.   ureter, bladder, urethra
    D.   urethra, bladder, ureter

6. A sac-like bulging or ballooning of the wall of a blood vessel is known as   6.____

    A.   a diverticulum   B.   an aneurysm
    C.   a thrombus   D.   phlebitis

7. The collapse of the lung or any portion of it is called   7.____

    A.   atelectasis   B.   emphysema
    C.   infarct   D.   pneumonitis

8. The angle formed by the lungs and the diaphragm at the lateral chest wall is called the _____ angle.   8.____

    A.   costal   B.   costophrenic
    C.   intercostal   D.   phrenic

9. The condition in which there is air in the pleural cavity is   9.____

    A.   atelectasis   B.   bronchiectasis
    C.   empyema   D.   pneumothorax

10. The Islets of Langerhans are ductless glands located in the   10.____

     A. kidneys   B. pancreas
     C. small intestine   D. spleen

11. The appendix is attached to the   11.____

     A. cecum   B. descending colon
     C. ileum   D. transverse colon

12. The common bile duct empties into the   12.____

     A. duodenum   B. gall bladder
     C. liver   D. stomach

13. The ribs that articulate with the sternum are   13.____

     A. costochondrals   B. false ribs
     C. floating ribs   D. true ribs

14. The organ which lies posterior to the stomach and whose head fits into the duodenal loop is the   14.____

     A. gall bladder   B. kidney
     C. pancreas   D. pylorus

15. The space between the lungs is called the   15.____

     A. ilium   B. mediastinum
     C. thoracic cavity   D. thoracic inlet

16. The S-shaped portion of the descending colon is called the   16.____

     A. anal canal   B. ileo-cecal valve
     C. rectum   D. sigmoid

17. The outer portion of the kidney is the   17.____

     A. cortex   B. hilum
     C. medulla   D. renal pelvis

18. The head of the femur articulates with the innominate bone to form the hip joint. The cavity in the innominate bone into which the femur fits is the   18.____

     A. acetabulum   B. femoral neck
     C. glenoid fossa   D. sacro-iliac joint

19. The large opening at the base of the skull through which the spinal cord passes is the   19.____

     A. external auditory meatus
     B. foramen magnum
     C. olfactory foramen
     D. optic foramen

20. The three MAJOR divisions of the small intestine, beginning at its upper *end*, are the   20.____

     A. duodenum, jejunum, and ileum
     B. duodenum, jejunum, and ischium
     C. ileum, duodenum, and jejunum
     D. jejunum, duodenum, and ileum

21. Striated muscles would be found in the   21.____

    A. intima or muscle walls of blood vessels
    B. pituitary gland
    C. biceps
    D. stomach

22. The receptors that are stimulated when the head is rested on the table in front of the   22.____
chair are in the

    A. temporal lobe   B. semicircular canals
    C. utricle   D. middle ear

23. The neuron that transmits the impulse from the receptor to the spinal cord is the   23.____

    A. associative neuron   B. afferent neuron
    C. efferent neuron   D. synaptic connection

24. Those organs or mechanisms that register the movements and position of the body are   24.____
called

    A. proprioceptors   B. interoceptors
    C. exteroceptors   D. glands

25. The one of the following that does not belong with the others is   25.____

    A. axon   B. dendrite   C. end brush   D. pons

26. The MAIN path of communication from higher to lower coordination centers is the   26.____

    A. spinal lemniscus   B. pyramidal tracts
    C. pons Varoli   D. medial lemniscus

27. The LARGEST interlobular fissure of the brain is the   27.____

    A. fissure of Rolando
    B. parietal-occipital fissure
    C. fissure of Sylvius
    D. longitudinal fissure

28. The pathway the nerve impulse will take through the nervous system is determined by   28.____

    A. the length of the central axis from where the impulse enters
    B. the thalamus
    C. synaptic resistance
    D. the cerebellum

29. The four language centers (speaking, writing, hearing, reading) are found in   29.____

    A. the cerebellum
    B. both hemispheres of the cerebrum
    C. the spinal cord
    D. the frontal lobe

30. The *motor area* is located in the   30.____

    A. cuneas
    B. ascending parietal convolution
    C. superior temporal convolution
    D. precentral gyrus

31. The white matter of the nervous system is due to the   31.____

    A. function of conduction   B. synapses present
    C. medullary sheaths   D. structure of nerve cell

32. The one of the following that is NOT related to the other three is   32.____

    A. iris   B. pupil   C. retina   D. cochlea

33. The region in the retina in which the vision is clearest is called the   33.____

    A. vitreous humor   B. fovea
    C. rod   D. lens

34. The semicircular canals are concerned with   34.____

    A. balance   B. muscle sense
    C. hearing   D. pain sensitivity

35. The part of the brain which acts as a relay station for all afferent tracts (except the olfac-   35.____
tory and vestibular) and passes these sensory impulses on to the cerebrum is the

    A. medulla   B. precentral gyrus
    C. thalamus   D. cuneas

36. The middle ear consists of the   36.____

    A. ossicular chain, the tensor tympani, and the stapedius
    B. tympanic membrance, the malleus, the incus, and the stapes
    C. oval window, the malleus, the incus, and the stapes
    D. Eustachian tube, the malleus, the incus, and the stapes

37. Of the following parts of the larynx, the one which is NOT a cartilage is the   37.____

    A. cricoid   B. thyroid
    C. glottis   D. epiglottis

38. Of the following nerves, the one which is NOT concerned with breathing is_____ nerve.   38.____

    A. a branch of the 12th thoracic
    B. the phrenic
    C. the vagus
    D. a branch of the 2nd cervical

39. Of the following activities of the body, the one which is NOT under the control of the cen-   39.____
tral nervous system is

    A. digestion   B. breathing
    C. movements of the jaw   D. movements of the tongue

40. Of the following, the one which does NOT involve the use of the cerebrum is   40.____

    A. the sensation of light
    B. the reflex blinking of the eye
    C. the sensation of color awareness
    D. speaking

_____

KEY (CORRECT ANSWERS)

1. A	11. A	21. C	31. C
2. B	12. A	22. C	32. D
3. B	13. D	23. B	33. B
4. C	14. C	24. A	34. A
5. C	15. B	25. D	35. C
6. B	16. D	26. B	36. A
7. A	17. A	27. C	37. C
8. B	18. A	28. C	38. C
9. D	19. B	29. B	39. A
10. B	20. A	30. D	40. B

_____

EXAMINATION SECTION
TEST 1

DIRECTIONS: Each question or incomplete statement is followed by several suggested answers or completions. Select the one that BEST answers the question or completes the statement. *PRINT THE LETTER OF THE CORRECT ANSWER IN THE SPACE AT THE RIGHT.*

1. X-rays were discovered by

   A. Coolidge   B. Edison   C. Marconi   D. Roentgen

   1._____

2. The *most desirable* end-result of x-ray examination is

   A. proper use of equipment   B. sufficient number of films
   C. adequate diagnosis   D. a complete hospital record

   2._____

3. *Generally,* an x-ray technician should gain the patient's confidence by

   A. an analysis of the patient's case
   B. indicating the type and length of his service in other hospitals
   C. an efficient and thorough manner
   D. friendship with many physicians

   3._____

4. If a patient asks the x-ray technician a technical diagnostic question dealing with the patient's case, the x-ray technician *should*

   A. answer the question to the best of his ability
   B. refer him to the physician or surgeon
   C. tell the patient to ask again after the films are developed
   D. mention the title of the proper medical textbook dealing with the case

   4._____

5. An x-ray technician knows that a program to protect himself against the harmful effects of radiation would employ each of the following EXCEPT

   A. sunlight   B. frequent x-ray examinations
   C. available protective devices   D. frequent blood counts

   5._____

6. An ambulatory patient is one who

   A. comes in an ambulance
   B. can walk
   C. is confined to bed
   D. cannot walk, but may come to x-ray in a chair

   6._____

7. An artefact is a(n)

   A. bone specialist
   B. experienced technician
   C. film defect
   D. film taken at a kilovoltage of over 200 KVP

   7._____

8. A cervical spine is 8.____

    A. part of the neck
    B. part of the pelvis
    C. a projection on the top of an autotransformer
    D. any bony prominence

9. In roentgenology, a filter is used to 9.____

    A. lower kilovoltage
    B. lower milliamperage
    C. reduce soft radiation
    D. reduce the emulsion

10. A cathode is a part of the 10.____

    A. voltmeter   B. cable
    C. condenser   D. x-ray tube

11. An x-ray tube has 11.____

    A. air at atmospheric pressure
    B. an almost complete vacuum
    C. neon
    D. freon

12. A sphere gap can be used to measure 12.____

    A. kilovoltage   B. amperage
    C. resistance   D. impedance

13. A solenoid is a form of 13.____

    A. high-tension rectifier   B. timer
    C. voltmeter   D. coil magnet

14. A thermostat is a device 14.____

    A. attached to a tilt table
    B. employed in radium treatments
    C. used in controlling temperature
    D. for calibrating an x-ray machine

15. A photo-electric cell may be a component part of a(n) 15.____

    A. interval timer   B. rectifying tube circuit
    C. photoroentgen apparatus   D. kenetron

16. A photoroentgen unit 16.____

    A. employs a camera
    B. does tomography
    C. does planigraphy
    D. produces standard density radiographs

17. Tube targets are made of   17.____

    A. iron   B. uranium
    C. tungsten   D. beryllium

18. For protective reasons, some x-ray tubes are housed in a bath of   18.____

    A. mercury   B. oil
    C. graphite   D. tellurium

19. The *usual* contrast material used in a gastro-intestinal series is   19.____

    A. bismuth   B. barium
    C. bromine   D. borax

20. A substance *commonly* used in bronchography is   20.____

    A. pantopaque   B. priodax
    C. lipiodol   D. skiodan

21. A chemical *commonly* used in intensifying screens is   21.____

    A. calcium oxalate   B. calcium thiocyanate
    C. calcium tungstate   D. calcium bicarbonate

22. Filters are used in the x-ray beam to   22.____

    A. increase contrast
    B. reduce film density
    C. remove low energy x-ray photon
    D. reduce exposure time

23. X-ray tables should be grounded to **prevent**   23.____

    A. motion   B. shocks
    C. secondary radiation   D. fire hazard

24. A milliampere represents one _____ of an ampere.   24.____

    A. *millionth*   B. *thousandth*
    C. *hundredth*   D. *tenth*

25. The resistance of a conductor to the flow of an electric current is measured by   25.____

    A. amperes   B. ohms
    C. volts   D. watts

26. A rotating anode tube is of value because   26.____

    A. a smaller effective focal spot can be used than on ordinary tubes
    B. the rotation of the filament keeps it centered
    C. the rotating anode makes it unnecessary to have a vacuum x-ray tube
    D. a rotating anode makes rectification of current unnecessary

27. On a rotating anode tube, the *average* effective size of the smallest focal spot is *about*   27.____
    _____ sq. mm.

    A. 1 to 2   B. 4 to 8
    C. 16 to 32   D. 50 to 100

28. If the exposure factors are correct for a certain film at 36 inches tube to film distance, and you keep all other factors constant, a film at 6 feet distance will require _____ the time.

    A. one-quarter   B. one-half
    C. twice   D. four times

28.____

29. Compared with intensifying screens, cardboard holders require *about* _____ times as much exposure time.

    A. two   B. eight
    C. sixteen   D. thirty-two

29.____

30. Intensifying screens are used *primarily to*

    A. obtain better detail
    B. obtain better contrast
    C. reduce x-ray energy
    D. shorten target-skin distance

30.____

31. Fluoroscopes are *usually* set at about _____ milliamperes.

    A. 5   B. 10   C. 20   D. 40

31.____

32. Shock-proof equipment indicates *primarily*

    A. protection from secondary radiation
    B. resistance to rough handling
    C. protection from high tension current
    D. resistance to the pulsation effect in current

32.____

33. Technique charts should be used for each of the following reasons EXCEPT to

    A. shorten exposure time   B. prevent tube overload
    C. reduce film wastage   D. reduce technical error

33.____

34. Chest films are *customarily* taken at 6 feet to

    A. protect patient   B. reduce motion effect
    C. decrease distortion   D. remove artefacts

34.____

35. The *minimum* distance of acceptable safety between patient and fluoroscopy tube is _____ inches.

    A. 5   B. 10   C. 20   D. 25

35.____

36. Films of the chest for lung detail are *usually* taken on

    A. inspiration   B. expiration
    C. phonation   D. deglutition

36.____

37. When a patient is directly facing the cassette, the position is

    A. A.P   B. P.A
    C. supine   D. lateral

37.____

38. The *opposite* to pronation is

    A. flexion   B. extension
    C. lordosis   D. supination

38.____

39. To demonstrate fluid levels in the chest or abdomen, the x-ray beam **should be**   39.____

    A. converging   B. of low kilovoltage
    C. vertical   D. horizontal

40. Planigraphy is   40.____

    A. soft tissue technique
    B. stereoscopic study
    C. sectional radiography
    D. myelography

41. By "prone" is meant   41.____

    A. face down   B. flat on back
    C. lying on side   D. semi-recumbent

42. A tangential view means, most nearly, one that is   42.____

    A. ordered by radiologist
    B. ordered by head technician
    C. far oblique
    D. taken across a visible mass

43. A bronchogram consists of   43.____

    A. stereoscopic chest studies
    B. P.A. and lateral chest
    C. films showing visualization of bronchi with lipiodol
    D. planigraphy

44. An examination of the ilium for fracture involves the   44.____

    A. skull   B. leg
    C. pelvis   D. foot

45. The knee cap is known technically as the   45.____

    A. fabella   B. patella
    C. os calcis   D. calvarium

46. The exit of the stomach is called the   46.____

    A. cardia   B. antrum
    C. lesser ourvature   D. pylorus

47. The urethra is the   47.____

    A. inlet to the bladder
    B. outlet of the bladder
    C. upper part of the kidney
    D. lower part of the kidney

48. The *longest* bone in the body is called the   48.____

    A. femur   B. humerus
    C. radius   D. tibia

49. The pancreatic and bile ducts enter into the

    A. esophagus   B. stomach
    C. duodenum   D. colon

49.____

50. The opening in the base of the skull where the spinal cord enters is called foramen

    A. of Morgagni   B. magnum
    C. rotundum   D. ovale

50.____

KEY (CORRECT ANSWERS)

1. D	11. B	21. C	31. A	41. A
2. C	12. A	22. C	32. C	42. D
3. C	13. D	23. B	33. A	43. C
4. B	14. C	24. B	34. C	44. C
5. B	15. C	25. B	35. B	45. B
6. B	16. A	26. A	36. A	46. D
7. C	17. C	27. A	37. B	47. B
8. A	18. B	28. D	38. D	48. A
9. C	19. B	29. B	39. D	49. C
10. D	20. C	30. C	40. C	50. B

EXAMINATION SECTION

TEST 1

DIRECTIONS: Each question or incomplete statement is followed by several suggested answers or completions. Select the one that BEST answers the question or completes the statement. *PRINT THE LETTER OF THE CORRECT ANSWER IN THE SPACE AT THE RIGHT.*

1. The symphysis pubis is part of the
    A. pelvis   B. jaw   C. thorax   D. foot
    1.____

2. The sella turcia is in the
    A. center of the base of the skull   B. vertex of the skull
    C. occipital region   D. frontal region
    2.____

3. Stenver's position is used in examination of the
    A. innominate bone   B. os calcis
    C. navicular   D. temporal bone or petrous pyramid
    3.____

4. A tarsal bone is a small bone in the
    A. skull   B. wrist   C. foot   D. pelvis
    4.____

5. In the parotid region, one might look for a _____ calculus.
    A. biliary   B. urinary   C. prostatic   D. salivary
    5.____

6. It is important to have media numbered MAINLY to
    A. prevent loss
    B. replace missing media
    C. locate defective screens and artifacts
    D. keep a good property inventory
    6.____

7. It is important to identify films, but this will NOT lead to
    A. the radiologist knowing left and right
    B. keeping accurate records
    C. hastening film taking
    D. avoiding mixups
    7.____

8. You have obtained a film of proper density of a spine on a 14 x 17 film. You are asked to get a film of one vertebra using a small cone. The exposure factors will be _____ for a 14 x 17 cone.
    A. half as much as   B. slightly less than
    C. slightly greater than   D. twice as much as
    8.____

9. Static marks on films are MOST likely to occur in _____ weather.
    A. hot dry   B. cold dry   C. hot wet   D. cold wet
    9.____

10. The ingredient that forms the bulk of the emulsion coating an x-ray film is   10.____
    A. silver bromide   B. iodine   C. gelatin   D. zinc sulphate

11. When a short stop bath is used, the PRINCIPAL ingredient is   11.____
    A. nitric acid   B. sodium hydroxide
    C. elbon   D. acetic acid

12. Normal temperature of a developing solution is _____ degrees F.   12.____
    A. 58 to 60   B. 68 to 70   C. 78 to 80   D. 88 to 90

13. A stop bath is used to   13.____
    A. prevent further developing
    B. retard fixing
    C. give greater detail
    D. prepare emulsion for warmer hypo and wash water

14. Which one of the following is NOT found in developer?   14.____
    A. Metol   B. Hydroxyquinone
    C. Hydroquinone   D. Sodium carbonate

15. A common preservative in developers to prolong life is sodium   15.____
    A. thiosulphite   B. alpha sulphite
    C. sulphate   D. sulphite

16. Sodium carbonate is used as a component of developer to   16.____
    A. soften black tones   B. harden black tones
    C. retard hydroquinone   D. soften emulsion

17. Which one of the following is NOT found in fixor?   17.____
    A. Sodium hyposulphite   B. Sodium monosulphite
    C. Alum   D. Sodium sulphite

18. The MOST economical way to cool developer is to   18.____
    A. add ice or cold water to solution
    B. add ice or cold water to surrounding bath
    C. blow a fan over surface of tank
    D. add powdered developer to solution

19. The life of developer depends in part on all of the following EXCEPT   19.____
    A. temperature   B. dark room ventilation
    C. age   D. number of films processed

20. Film fog is NOT produced by   20.____
    A. hot developer
    B. exposure of leaded cassette to stray radiation
    C. a safe light that is too strong
    D. failure to use a short stop bath

21. Use of a warm developer will NOT result in   21.____
    - A. reduced contrast
    - B. softened emulsion
    - C. under-exposure
    - D. lengthened fixing period

22. Replenishers will keep the tank level up but will NOT   22.____
    - A. shorten developing time
    - B. renew and prolong developer life
    - C. prevent oxidation
    - D. give contrast

23. Alum is used in fixer to   23.____
    - A. hasten fixing time
    - B. give better contrast
    - C. preserve and harden emulsion
    - D. shorten washing time

24. Solutions, when not in use, should be covered to prevent each of the 24.____
    following EXCEPT
    - A. evaporation
    - B. contamination
    - C. oxidation
    - D. expansion

25. PRIMARILY, colored paper is left on films used in cardboard to prevent 25.____
    - A. static marks
    - B. "nail defects"
    - C. fogging if cardboard is not light-tight
    - D. scratching

26. Developer is added to developer to   26.____
    - A. speed up developer
    - B. maintain tank level
    - C. prevent oxidation
    - D. delay reduction

27. Hypo is NOT used to   27.____
    - A. speed processing
    - B. remove all silver salts
    - C. preserve emulsion
    - D. chemically neutralize film prior to washing

28. With new developer, the time of development is controlled DIRECTLY by 28.____
    - A. number of films
    - B. film exposure
    - C. temperature of bath
    - D. film area

29. Developers become weak through each of the following EXCEPT 29.____
    - A. hydration   B. saturation   C. oxidation   D. induction

30. A good way to make a rough estimate of hypo deterioration is based on a 30.____
    rule of thumb which provides that hypo is expended when, compared with new
    solution, the old solution takes _____ time as long to clear a film.
    - A. 3   B. 6   C. 9   D. 12

Questions 31-50.

DIRECTIONS: Questions 31 through 50 consist of statements. You are to decide whether each statement is true or false. If the statement is true or correct, print the letter T; if the statement is false or incorrect, print the letter F.

31.   A roentgen ray is the same as an x-ray.   31._____

32.   A Coolidge tube is *primarily* a form of rectifying tube.   32._____

33.   An x-ray machine is *more likely* to spark in cold, dry weather.   33._____

34.   A stationary grid is used to cut down secondary radiation effect on a film.   34._____

35.   A rheostat is a form of darkroom timer.   35._____

36.   A Lysholm grid is a device for partially eliminating secondary radiation effect from a film.   36._____

37.   The number of watts in a circuit is *equal* to the volts multiplied by the amperes.   37._____

38.   Chest films should *never* be taken in the antero-posterior projection.   38._____

39.   The closer a structure is to a cassette, the greater is the degree of distortion of its image, all other factors remaining constant.   39._____

40.   In tomography, the cassette moves during the exposure.   40._____

41.   A small intestinal study is obtained in every barium clysma.   41._____

42.   A prone pressure device is *frequently* employed in urinary tract work.   42._____

43.   The aorta is a large artery.   43._____

44.   The right lung *normally* has fewer lobes than the left lung.   44._____

45.   The dorsal spine is the same as thoracic spine.   45._____

46.   Darkroom tunnels or light traps should be painted white so the technician can see better.   46._____

47.   On film processing, the exposed film is first put in hypo and then in the developer.   47._____

48.   The chemical name for hypo is hydroquinone.   48._____

49.   After fixing, x-ray films should be washed for from 15 to 30 minutes.   49._____

50.   Films which are sensitive to x-rays are *not* sensitive to ordinary light.   50._____

KEY (CORRECT ANSWERS)

1.	A	11.	D	21.	C	31.	T	41.	F
2.	A	12.	B	22.	C	32.	F	42.	F
3.	D	13.	A	23.	C	33.	F	43.	T
4.	C	14.	B	24.	D	34.	T	44.	F
5.	D	15.	D	25.	C	35.	F	45.	T
6.	C	16.	D	26.	B	36.	T	46.	F
7.	C	17.	B	27.	A	37.	T	47.	F
8.	C	18.	B	28.	C	38.	F	48.	F
9.	B	19.	B	29.	D	39.	F	49.	T
10.	C	20.	D	30.	A	40.	T	50.	F

EXAMINATION SECTION
TEST 1

DIRECTIONS: Each question or incomplete statement is followed by several suggested answers or completions. Select the one that BEST answers the question or completes the statement. *PRINT THE LETTER OF THE CORRECT ANSWER IN THE SPACE AT THE RIGHT.*

1. Which of the following is the APPROXIMATE skin dose, in rads, for 10 minutes of fluoroscopy performed at 1.5 mA?

    A. 10   B. 15   C. 20   D. 30

1.____

2. Which of the following would MOST likely cause a decrease in patient exposure?

    A. Increasing kVp 15% and cutting mAs in half
    B. Two tomographic cuts instead of two plain films
    C. Changing from a non-grid technique to an 8:1 grid
    D. Changing from a 400 film/screen combination to a 200 film/screen combination

2.____

3. Undifferentiated cells are

    A. highly radiosensitive
    B. immature
    C. without a specific function
    D. all of the above

3.____

4. Which of the following is LEAST radiosensitive?

    A. Blood forming cells   B. Nerves
    C. Lens   D. Gonads

4.____

5. The effects of radiation exposure are dependent upon the

    A. amount of radiation
    B. size of the irradiated area
    C. length of exposure
    D. all of the above

5.____

6. The occupational MPD is valid for all of the following rays EXCEPT

    A. alpha   B. beta   C. gamma   D. x-rays

6.____

7. A greater Linear Energy Transfer (LET) is delivered by particles with a velocity and _____ charge.

    A. faster; greater   B. slower; greater
    C. faster; lesser   D. slower; lesser

7.____

8. As the amount of Linear Energy Transfer increases (from interaction occurring between radiation and biologic material), the amount of biologic effect or damage will

    A. remain the same   B. decrease
    C. increase   D. not be calculable

8.____

9. Follow-up studies have been done on individuals receiving accidental exposure to radiation. Pioneer radiation workers have been shown to have a GREATER incidence of _____ compared with the normal population.

    A. leukemia and other cancers
    B. cataract formation
    C. shortened life span
    D. all of the above

9.____

10. _____ is the single BEST method of protecting a patient from excessive radiation.

    A. Shielding   B. Pulsing
    C. Beam restriction   D. All of the above

10.____

11. The radiation exposure of a patient receiving an entrance dose of 400 mR at 1 meter is _____ mR.

    A. 0.4   B. 4.0   C. 40   D. 400

11.____

12. If an infant cannot be held by mechanical restraints, all of the following may be used to assist EXCEPT a

    A. friend of the family   B. relative
    C. radiology employee   D. nurse

12.____

13. All of the following positions can demonstrate the air-fluid level in an infant EXCEPT

    A. recumbent AP   B. erect
    C. decubitus   D. none of the above

13.____

14. The formation of electrons within the x-ray tube is accomplished by

    A. induction   B. thermionic emission
    C. conduction   D. all of the above

14.____

15. With three-phase equipment, the voltage never drops to zero, and x-ray intensity is significantly

    A. less   B. unchanged   C. greater   D. lost

15.____

16. Proper care of leaded apparel includes

    A. not folding lead aprons or gloves after use
    B. hanging lead aprons on an appropriate rack after use
    C. annual fluoroscopy of aprons and gloves to check for cracks
    D. all of the above

16.____

17. All of the following statements are true regarding tracheostomy patients EXCEPT:

    A. The tracheostomy patient will have difficulty speaking
    B. A gurgling or rattling sound coming from the trachea indicates the need for suctioning
    C. Any movement of the tracheostomy tube will not cause obstruction of the airway
    D. Rotation of the tracheostomy tube may cause the tube to become dislodged

17.____

18. When multiple films are taken on a patient, each radiograph must include all of the follow-   18.____
ing information EXCEPT the

    A. right or left side marker
    B. patient's name or ID number
    C. time and date of the examination
    D. patient's birthdate

19. The MOST common adverse reaction of a patient receiving iodinated contrast medium is   19.____

    A. severe headache   B. fever
    C. hives   D. abdominal pain

20. Fractures of the humerus and shoulder girdle are quite painful due to difficulties in immo-   20.____
bilizing the upper extremities.
All of the following are true statements regarding the radiographic examination of such
patients EXCEPT:

    A. They should be performed as quickly as possible
    B. They should be performed with the fewest number of changes in body position
    C. The best position is upright
    D. PA and left lateral decubitus must be taken

21. A complete patient history is required prior to injection of an iodinated contrast medium.   21.____
The patient should be questioned regarding

    A. allergy history
    B. asthma and hay fever history
    C. previous reactions to contrast media
    D. all of the above

22. Areas of the body that are susceptible to bed sores or decubitus ulcers include all of the   22.____
following EXCEPT the

    A. scapulae   B. trochanters
    C. toes   D. sacrum

23. A patient undergoing radiographic examination starts to experience a seizure.   23.____
You should

    A. continue taking the x-rays
    B. stop the radiography and give a sedative
    C. stop the radiography and protect the patient from hitting any hard surfaces or falling
       off the examination table
    D. stop the radiography and wait for the seizure to end

24. The intraspinal method of contrast medium administration is used in myelography and   24.____
may be performed in the _____ position.

    A. seated   B. lateral
    C. prone   D. all of the above

25. Aseptic techniques used for the administration of contrast media are given via   25.____

    A. oral route   B. rectal route
    C. nasogastric tube   D. all of the above

KEY (CORRECT ANSWERS)

1.	D	11.	A
2.	A	12.	C
3.	D	13.	A
4.	B	14.	B
5.	D	15.	C
6.	A	16.	D
7.	B	17.	C
8.	C	18.	D
9.	D	19.	C
10.	C	20.	D

21.	D
22.	C
23.	C
24.	D
25.	D

TEST 2

DIRECTIONS: Each question or incomplete statement is followed by several suggested answers or completions. Select the one that BEST answers the question or completes the statement. *PRINT THE LETTER OF THE CORRECT ANSWER IN THE SPACE AT THE RIGHT.*

1. When the antecubital vein is inaccessible, the _____ vein is used to administer contrast media.   1._____

   A. basilic   B. cephalic   C. femoral   D. ulnar

2. The movement of a synovial joint that decreases the angle between articulating surfaces is called   2._____

   A. protraction   B. adduction
   C. flexion   D. extension

3. After a barium enema examination, the patient should be instructed to   3._____

   A. increase intake of fluid and fiber
   B. monitor bowel movements and have at least one in the next 24 hours
   C. expect white colored stool until all barium is expelled
   D. all of the above

4. Cyanosis resulting from oxygen deficiency is characterized by a bluish discoloration of the   4._____

   A. gums   B. lips
   C. nail beds   D. all of the above

5. All of the following are iodinated contrast media EXCEPT   5._____

   A. metrizamide   B. barium sulfate
   C. ethiodized oil   D. meglumine diatrizoate

6. Barium sulfate may be used for GI radiography in all of the following clinical conditions EXCEPT   6._____

   A. perforation of the gastrointestinal tract
   B. GI polyps
   C. colorectal cancer
   D. pancreatitis

7. Shock occurs when blood pressure is unable to provide sufficient oxygenated blood to body tissues.   7._____
   Common symptoms of shock include

   A. a drop in blood pressure
   B. increased pulse rate
   C. restlessness and apprehension
   D. all of the above

8. The protrusion of a portion of an organ through a wall that normally contains it is called a(n)

   8.____

   A. extravasation
   B. herniation
   C. diverticulosis
   D. excretion

9. It is the radiographer's responsibility to provide the radiologist with all of the following EXCEPT

   9.____

   A. films of diagnostic quality
   B. pertinent patient history
   C. diagnosis and prognosis
   D. none of the above

10. Substances or chemicals that retard the growth of pathogenic bacteriae, but do not necessarily kill them, are termed

    10.____

    A. germicides
    B. disinfectants
    C. antiseptics
    D. toxins

11. All of the following parts of the gastrointestinal tract can be shown through oral administration of barium sulfate EXCEPT the

    11.____

    A. esophagus
    B. stomach
    C. sigmoid colon
    D. small bowel

12. The consent given by a patient upon admission to the hospital is sufficient for all of the following radio-graphic examinations EXCEPT

    12.____

    A. chest x-ray
    B. renal arteriogram
    C. abdominal x-rays
    D. sialography

13. All of the following are advantages of low-osmolality and non-ionic water soluble contrast media over ionic contrast media EXCEPT:

    13.____

    A. They are less costly
    B. Allergic reactions are less likely
    C. They can be used for intrathecal and intravascular injections
    D. Side effects are less severe

14. The *recumbent* position means lying

    14.____

    A. on the back
    B. face downward
    C. down in any position
    D. down with a horizontal x-ray beam

15. The position in which the body is rotated with the left anterior portion closest to the film is called the _____ oblique.

    15.____

    A. right anterior
    B. left anterior
    C. right posterior
    D. left posterior

16. Which of the following should be done prior to bringing the patient into the x-ray examination room?   16.____

    A. Clean the x-ray table
    B. Prepare the room for the examination to be performed
    C. Make sure that the x-ray room is clean and orderly
    D. All of the above

17. A fracture caused by a fall onto an outstretched hand in order to *brake* a fall is called a _____ fracture.   17.____

    A. greenstick   B. Colles'
    C. Salter   D. none of the above

18. The thorax is composed of the   18.____

    A. 12 pairs of ribs   B. sternum
    C. thoracic vertebrae   D. all of the above

19. The lateral elbow and lateral forearm must be flexed 90° in order to superimpose all of the following EXCEPT the   19.____

    A. distal radius   B. distal ulna
    C. humeral epicondyles   D. medial ulna

20. The sacroiliac joints angle posteriorly and medially 25° to the mid sagittal plane. In order to show them with the patient in the AP position, the affected side must be elevated   20.____

    A. 20°   B. 25°   C. 50°   D. 75°

21. In which of the following projections would the greater tubercle be seen in profile?   21.____

    A. AP humerus   B. Lateral humerus
    C. AP elbow   D. Lateral elbow

22. Small amounts of fluid are BEST demonstrated in the   22.____

    A. lateral decubitus position, affected side up
    B. lateral decubitus position, affected side down
    C. lateral recumbent position
    D. prone position

23. Small amounts of air are BEST demonstrated in the _____ if the erect position cannot be obtained.   23.____

    A. lateral decubitus position, affected side up
    B. lateral recumbent position, affected side down
    C. AP Trendelenberg position
    D. lateral recumbent position

24. Full or forced expiration is used to elevate the diaphragm and demonstrate the   24.____

    A. ribs above the diaphragm
    B. ribs above the diaphragm, while obliterating pulmonary vascular markings
    C. ribs below the diaphragm to best advantage
    D. heart

25. Shallow breathing technique is occasionally used to visualize   25.____

    A. above the diaphragm ribs
    B. below the diaphragm ribs
    C. pulmonary vascular marking
    D. cardiac vessels

———

KEY (CORRECT ANSWERS)

1.	A		11.	C
2.	C		12.	B
3.	D		13.	A
4.	D		14.	C
5.	B		15.	B
6.	A		16.	D
7.	D		17.	B
8.	B		18.	D
9.	C		19.	D
10.	C		20.	B

21.	A
22.	B
23.	A
24.	C
25.	A

———

EXAMINATION SECTION
TEST 1

DIRECTIONS: Each question or incomplete statement is followed by several suggested answers or completions. Select the one that BEST answers the question or completes the statement. *PRINT THE LETTER OF THE CORRECT ANSWER IN THE SPACE AT THE RIGHT.*

1. For an intravenous cholangiogram, the area of the abdomen which you should radiograph is the _____ quadrant.   1.____
   A. left upper   B. left lower
   C. right upper   D. right lower

2. The ilium is part of the   2.____
   A. pelvis   B. small intestine
   C. colon   D. pancreas

3. The olecranon is a part of the   3.____
   A. shoulder   B. knee   C. hip   D. elbow

4. The outlet of the bladder is known as the   4.____
   A. urethra   B. ureter   C. kidney   D. anus

5. The coracoid process is part of the   5.____
   A. pelvis   B. scapula
   C. forearm   D. cervical spine

6. The manubrium is part of the   6.____
   A. ankle   B. hip   C. shoulder   D. sternum

7. The one of the following glands which is located in the abdominal cavity is the   7.____
   A. thymus   B. pineal   C. adrenal   D. pituitary

8. The greater trochanter will be seen on films of the   8.____
   A. knee   B. shoulder   C. leg   D. hip

9. The external canthus of the eye should be used as a landmark when taking a(n) _____ view of the _____ .   9.____

   A. lateral; skull
   B. lateral; sella turcica
   C. lateral; paranasal sinuses
   D. AP; malar bone

10. The one of the following landmarks which should be used when radiographing a patient's abdomen for kidneys, ureters, and bladder (KUB) is the   10.____
    A. xiphoid process of the sternum   B. ischial tuberosities
    C. crest of the ilium   D. umbilicus

11. To take a PA of the skull, the landmark which should be used is the

    A. cantho-meatal line
    B. external auditory meatus
    C. internal canthus of the eye
    D. petrous pyramid

11.____

12. In order to determine the anatomical landmarks for a lateral film of the fifth lumbar vertebra, one should locate the

    A. plane connecting the anterior-superior iliac spines
    B. area just below the top of the iliac crests
    C. pubic symphysis
    D. plane connecting the hips

12.____

13. Reid's base line is a landmark used in taking radiographs of the

    A. bony pelvis   B. skull
    C. small intestines   D. thoracic inlet

13.____

14. To take a PA of the chest for the heart, the landmark which should be used is the

    A. coracoid process   B. crest of the ilium
    C. 2nd dorsal vertebra   D. 9th dorsal vertebra

14.____

15. To take an AP of the shoulder, the landmark which should be used is the

    A. coracoid process   B. 5th dorsal vertebra
    C. 9th dorsal vertebra   D. 7th cervical vertebra

15.____

16. In radiography, the term *distal* means MOST NEARLY

    A. farthest from the center of the body
    B. toward the back
    C. toward the head
    D. closest to the center of the body

16.____

17. In radiography, the term *cephalad* means MOST NEARLY toward the

    A. front   B. head   C. center   D. feet

17.____

18. A tunnel view of the knee should be made with the knee

    A. rotated medially   B. moderately flexed
    C. completely extended   D. turned into the lateral

18.____

19. The hand should be placed in pronation when taking a(n)

    A. PA of the wrist
    B. AP of the wrist
    C. lateral of the thumb
    D. oblique of the third finger

19.____

20. In radiography, the term *caudad* means MOST NEARLY

    A. lying on the stomach   B. inverted
    C. toward the head   D. toward the feet

20.____

21. In order to visualize the extent of the duodenal loop MOST advantageously, the projection should be made   21._____

    A. RPO   B. AP   C. LAO   D. RAO

22. In order to visualize the external malleolus of the ankle MOST advantageously, it should be positioned   22._____

    A. in the true AP position
    B. in the true lateral position
    C. with the ankle flexed and the leg rotated internally
    D. with the foot extended and the leg rotated externally

23. In order to remove the scapulae from the lung fields when taking a PA radiograph of the chest, the x-ray technician should   23._____

    A. angle the tube 15 toward the feet
    B. use a 72-inch target-film distance
    C. roll the patient's shoulders forward
    D. have the patient take a deep breath

24. When doing an intravenous pyelogram, the BEST projection to show both kidneys on a single film is   24._____

    A. AP   B. PA   C. RL   D. LAO

25. When all other factors remain unchanged, the density or blackness of the film will vary in _____ proportion to the _____.   25._____

    A. *inverse*; time
    B. *inverse*; Kv
    C. *direct*; square of the distance
    D. *inverse*; square of the distance

———

KEY (CORRECT ANSWERS)

1.	C	11.	A
2.	A	12.	B
3.	D	13.	B
4.	A	14.	D
5.	B	15.	A
6.	D	16.	A
7.	C	17.	B
8.	D	18.	B
9.	C	19.	A
10.	C	20.	D

21.	D
22.	C
23.	C
24.	A
25.	D

———

TEST 2

DIRECTIONS: Each question or incomplete statement is followed by several suggested answers or completions. Select the one that BEST answers the question or completes the statement. *PRINT THE LETTER OF THE CORRECT ANSWER IN THE SPACE AT THE RIGHT.*

1. Of the following, it is usually BEST to increase bone contrast in the film by   1._____

    A. increasing Kv   B. decreasing time
    C. increasing MaS   D. decreasing MaS

2. In a transformer, the Kv may be increased or decreased depending on the ratio of the   2._____
    number of turns of wire in the primary coil to the secondary coil.
    If there are 100 turns in the primary coil and the secondary has 100,000 turns, then
    the voltage imparted in the secondary is _____ times _____ than in the primary.

    A. 1000; greater   B. 100; greater
    C. 1000; less   D. 100,000 greater

3. Assume that, when taking a radiograph, the Kv is increased but the average density   3._____
    remains the same. The contrast will

    A. remain the same
    B. be increased
    C. be decreased
    D. change in proportion to the change in MaS

4. Of the following, the way to reduce magnification is by the use of   4._____

    A. increased object-film distance
    B. longer target-film distance
    C. shorter target-film distance
    D. a small focal spot

5. If all other factors remain unchanged, the one of the following combinations of time and 5._____
    milliamperes which gives the GREATEST density is _____ second and _____ milliam-
    peres.

    A. 1/10; 100   B. 1/5; 50
    C. 1/5; 200   D. 1/10; 500

6. Assume that you are checking the accuracy of a timer on a four valve (full-wave) x-ray   6._____
    machine, using a spinning top.
    If the timer is accurate, the number of dots you should see in a 1/10 second exposure
    is

    A. 6   B. 12   C. 18   D. 24

7. Assume that the technician, when making a radiograph of the chest, used the usual milli-   7._____
    amperage and time settings, but noticed that the MaS recorded on the meter during
    exposure was only one-half of the setting. The film, when developed, was light.
    The MOST likely source of the difficulty is the

    A. autotransformer
    B. valve tubes in the rectifier circuit

    C.   line voltage compensator
    D.   x-ray tube

8.   When using portable x-ray machines, an external ground wire is *essential* PRIMARILY   8.____
    because the

    A.   machine will operate more efficiently
    B.   electrical circuits will be stabilized
    C.   hazard of electrical shock will be reduced
    D.   machine will not operate without a ground wire

9.   In radiography, a collimator is useful to   9.____

    A.   increase the output of the x-ray machine
    B.   increase the life of the tube
    C.   reduce the amount of unnecessary radiation reaching the patient
    D.   reduce the exposure time

10.   The function of an autotransformer in an x-ray machine is to control   10.____

    A.   kilovoltage
    B.   milliamperage
    C.   time of exposure
    D.   rectifying valve tube current

11.   A rapid film changer would be used in   11.____

    A.   scanography   B.   laminography
    C.   small intestinal series   D.   angiocardiography

12.   To get BEST detail when using screen film, the x-ray technician should use the _____   12.____
    screen.

    A.   slow   B.   medium
    C.   fast   D.   extra fast

13.   As compared to the Ma used in equipment for diagnostic radiology, the Ma used in ther-   13.____
    apy equipment is GENERALLY

    A.   higher   B.   lower   C.   the same   D.   varied

14.   Generally, a patient is asked to hold his breath when being x-rayed.   14.____
    Of the following, the one which permits quiet shallow breathing, while using a long
    exposure time and low Ma, is a

    A.   cholecystogram
    B.   10 minute film of intravenous pyelogram
    C.   PA of the chest
    D.   lateral of the dorsal spine

15.   Assume that you are to radiograph a patient's hips utilizing 70 Kv,   15.____
    Of the following, the grid ratio which you should select to insure a SATISFACTORY
    radiograph is

    A. 8:1   B. 10:1   C. 12:1   D. 16:1

16. Cardboard technique in radiographic work is ESPECIALLY useful for an examination of the   16._____

     A.   chest   B.   skull   C.   heart   D.   wrist

17. With the patient lying on his side, the x-ray beam should be horizontal when taking a radiograph of the   17._____

     A.   abdomen to demonstrate fluid level
     B.   skull to demonstrate hairline fracture
     C.   colon to determine diverticulitis
     D.   spine to demonstrate "whiplash" fracture

18. A patient with a clinically diagnosed pneumonia in the right middle lobe is referred to the radiology department for PA and lateral films of the chest.   18._____
The BEST position in which to take the lateral film is

     A.   left lateral erect
     B.   right lateral
     C.   right lateral decubitus with the horizontal beam
     D.   right semilateral with the patient rotated 30

19. A thick pasty mixture of barium sulphate and water is USUALLY employed when doing a radiographic examination of the   19._____

     A.   colon   B.   stomach
     C.   esophagus   D.   small intestine

20. Assume that several patients are scheduled for radiographs of the abdominal region.   20._____
If the abdomens are of the same thickness and the same Kv is used, the one of the following patients who will usually require the MOST MaS for a good film is a(n)

     A.   old woman   B.   young woman
     C.   cancer patient   D.   young man

21. The single view for BEST demonstrating the maxillary sinuses is the   21._____

     A.   Caldwell   B.   Waters
     C.   submentovertical   D.   Towne

22. In the Stenvers projection (posterior profile view) of the mastoids, the patient faces the film and the head is rotated 45°.   22._____
The tube should be angled toward the vertex of the skull

     A.   5°   B.   12°   C.   25°   D.   45°

23. In the Caldwell (posterior-anterior) projection of the frontal and ethmoid sinuses, the patient faces the film and the orbitomeatal line is perpendicular to the film. The tube should be angled APPROXIMATELY   23._____

     A.   15-20° toward the head
     B.   15-20° laterally
     C.   15-20° toward the feet
     D.   parallel to the orbitomeatal line

24. The technician is asked to take a film of the left hip of a pregnant woman.   24._____
It is MOST important to

    A. take a film of the right hip as well for comparison
    B. shield the abdomen
    C. take multiple projections
    D. warn the patient of the possible hazards of radiation

25. In the Law projection (lateral) of the mastoids, the patient is prone and the head is posi-   25._____
tioned in the true lateral position.
The central ray enters two inches above and two inches posterior to the external auditory meatus, and the tube is angled _____ toward the _____.

    A. 25°; feet
    B. 10°; feet and 35° toward the face
    C. 25°; face
    D. 15°; feet and 15° toward the face

KEY (CORRECT ANSWERS)

1.	C		11.	D
2.	A		12.	A
3.	C		13.	B
4.	B		14.	D
5.	D		15.	A
6.	B		16.	D
7.	B		17.	A
8.	C		18.	B
9.	C		19.	C
10.	A		20.	D

21.	B
22.	B
23.	C
24.	B
25.	D

EXAMINATION SECTION
TEST 1

DIRECTIONS: Each question or incomplete statement is followed by several suggested answers or completions. Select the one that BEST answers the question or completes the statement. *PRINT THE LETTER OF THE CORRECT ANSWER IN THE SPACE AT THE RIGHT.*

1. The Ma and Kv which are used in conventional fluoroscopy, without image intensification, in the adult is _____ Ma and _____ Kv.   1.____

    A. 3 to 4; 40 to 50   B. 3 to 5; 80 to 90
    C. 1; 85 to 90   D. 15; 80 to 90

2. Of the following, erect films of the abdomen are USUALLY used   2.____

    A. to demonstrate free air in the peritoneal cavity
    B. routinely for fracture of the lumbar spine
    C. for fracture of the rib below the diaphragm
    D. to demonstrate the position of the colon

3. Assume that the conventional PA film of the chest is not adequate and that another projection is required for better demonstration of the highest portion of the upper lobes. The MOST suitable projection to use for this purpose is the   3.____

    A. apical lordotic
    B. decubitus with the horizontal beam
    C. lateral
    D. photofluorogram

4. Examination of the skull after injection of air into the spine is known as   4.____

    A. salpingography   B. ventriculography
    C. pneumoencephalography   D. arteriography

5. The contrast agents used in urography, cholecystography, and cholangiography are opaque to x-ray because of the presence of   5.____

    A. tungsten   B. methylglucamine
    C. barium   D. iodine

6. Myelography is the study of the   6.____

    A. spinal canal   B. uterus and tubes
    C. birth canal   D. gall bladder

7. Cholangiography is the study of the   7.____

    A. thyroid   B. kidney
    C. chest   D. biliary ducts

8. Sialography is the study of the   8.____

    A. heart chambers   B. salivary ducts
    C. spinal canal   D. biliary ducts

9. Arthrography is the study of the

   A. joints　　　B. arteries　　　C. aorta　　　D. heart

9.____

10. In oral cholecystography, the time that should elapse after the patient takes the pre-scribed contrast agent before the film is taken is MOST NEARLY

   A. 10 minutes　　　　B. 2 hours
   C. 12 hours　　　　　D. 3 days

10.____

11. For soft tissue radiography, the x-ray technician should

   A. increase both the Kv and MaS
   B. lower both the Kv and MaS
   C. increase the Kv and lower the MaS
   D. lower the Kv and increase the MaS

11.____

12. Assume that a film of normal density is obtained with an exposure time of 1/4 second. If the distance is doubled, but the Kv and Ma remain the same, then the exposure time should be _____ second(s).

   A. 1/8　　　B. 1/2　　　C. 1　　　D. 2

12.____

13. When taking an AP view of the right thumb, the x-ray technician turned the palm down, with the thumb turned outward. He used cardboard technique at a 40 inch distance, with a setting of 80 Kv, 100 Ma, 1/10 second. The BEST appraisal of the x-ray technician's work is that he

   A. took the radiograph properly
   B. should have turned the palm up
   C. should have used screen film
   D. should have used lower Kv

13.____

14. The MOST probable cause of a fuzzy area in the image of a film which is otherwise clear and sharp is

   A. a defective grid
   B. poor screen contact
   C. a defect in the film before exposure
   D. poor processing technique

14.____

15. A minimum target-film distance of 72 inches is USUALLY employed when doing chest radiography because

   A. the lungs are usually very easy to penetrate
   B. it tends to reduce magnified distortion, especially of the heart
   C. the patient will receive less radiation
   D. it tends to reduce secondary radiation

15.____

16. Assume that a satisfactory film of a chest is obtained at a 72 inch target-film distance using 100 Ma and 1/10 second exposure. If 200 Ma were used and all other factors were unchanged, the exposure time should be

   A. the same　　　　　B. 1/40 second
   C. 1/20 second　　　　D. 2/10 second

16.____

17. When taking radiographs of extremities measuring 10 cm or less, maximum detail can   17.____
USUALLY be obtained by using

    A.   a large focal spot
    B.   non-screen film
    C.   fast intensifying screens
    D.   a Potter-Bucky diaphragm

18. Of the following examinations to be made of a pregnant woman, the one which gives the   18.____
MOST significant radiation exposure is

    A.   AP of the pelvis
    B.   lateral of the skull
    C.   laminograms of the left foot
    D.   PA of the chest

19. In angiocardiography, the exposure to the patient is higher than in a conventional radio-   19.____
graph of the chest CHIEFLY because

    A.   the Kv is much greater for each radiograph
    B.   the MaS is much greater for each radiograph
    C.   many films of the same part of the body must be taken
    D.   the x-rays are concentrated upon a thin layer of tissue

20. In a photofluorogram of the chest, as compared to a conventional 14 x 17 PA film, the   20.____
quantity of radiation to which the patient is exposed

    A.   is the same   B.   is greater
    C.   is less   D.   varies

21. The MOST dangerous time for a mother to receive excessive radiation as far as the baby   21.____
is concerned is

    A.   the second month of pregnancy
    B.   the sixth month of pregnancy
    C.   the ninth month of pregnancy
    D.   immediately after delivery

22. A seriously injured patient with possible hip fracture can be BEST examined by use of   22.____

    A.   flexion-extension films   B.   the knee-chest position
    C.   lateral decubitus films   D.   stereoscopic AP films

23. A patient is brought from the emergency room with an immobilized right lower extremity.   23.____
A request is made for frontal and lateral projection of the right knee. It is BEST to

    A.   remove the immobilizing material from the right leg before taking the radiograph
    B.   remove the immobilizing material only from the right knee before taking the radio-
        graph
    C.   take the radiograph without removing the immobilizing material
    D.   return the patient to the emergency room with the notation that films cannot be
        taken

24. In linear body section radiography, the x-ray tube and the Bucky tray move simultaneously

    A. in the same direction
    B. in opposite directions
    C. in the same and opposite directions alternately
    D. perpendicularly to each other

24.____

25. In making a stereoscopic pair of films, the patient remains in the same position for the two exposures while the tube is shifted. The total tube shift depends PRIMARILY on

    A. focal-film distance
    C. position of the patient
    B. thickness of the part
    D. part of the body examined

25.____

KEY (CORRECT ANSWERS)

1.	B		11.	D
2.	A		12.	C
3.	A		13.	B
4.	C		14.	B
5.	D		15.	B
6.	A		16.	C
7.	D		17.	B
8.	B		18.	A
9.	A		19.	C
10.	C		20.	B

21.	A
22.	D
23.	C
24.	B
25.	A

TEST 2

DIRECTIONS: Each question or incomplete statement is followed by several suggested answers or completions. Select the one that BEST answers the question or completes the statement. *PRINT THE LETTER OF THE CORRECT ANSWER IN THE SPACE AT THE RIGHT.*

1. Scanograms are used for   1.____

   A. determination of bone length
   B. examination of the duodenal bulb
   C. cerebral arteriograms
   D. examination of the orbits

2. Laminography is LEAST likely to be used to radiograph the   2.____

   A. skull   B. chest   C. liver   D. finger

3. When choosing a darkroom safe light, to be used at a 40 inch distance from the loading   3.____
   bench, it is BEST to obtain a _____ bulb and a _____ filter.

   A. 25 Watt; 2 mm aluminum   B. 2 1/2 Watt; red acetate
   C. 10 Watt; Wratten 6-B   D. red glass; clear white

4. In order to obtain maximum radiographic quality when processing non-screen x-ray film   4.____
   rather than regular x-ray film, the developing and fixing time should be APPROXIMATELY

   A. the same   B. doubled
   C. increased 10%   D. decreased 60%

5. In processing solutions, sodium thiosulphite acts as a(n)   5.____

   A. hardener   B. reducer
   C. acidifier   D. silver bromide solvent

6. In developing solutions, elon and hydroquinone act as   6.____

   A. silver bromide solvents   B. reducers
   C. preservatives   D. hardeners

7. Incomplete washing of films, following completion of fixing, results in   7.____

   A. fogging of the film
   B. breaks in the emulsion
   C. eventual fading and staining of the film
   D. almost immediate development of artifacts

8. Assume that you are in a hospital whose x-ray department is open from 8 A.M. to 12   8.____
   Noon and from 1 P.M. to 6 P.M. You have assigned one of your technicians to schedule
   all the x-ray appointments for the clinic cases. Your instructions to him are not to make
   more than 12 appointments per half hour in the morning session and not more than 15
   per hour for the afternoon session.
   The GREATEST number of patients he can schedule in the entire day will be

   A. 75   B. 96   C. 123   D. 171

Questions 9-13.

DIRECTIONS: Questions 9 through 13 are based on the following annual report which was submitted by Hospital A.

HOSPITAL A
CASES HANDLED IN THE X-RAY DEPARTMENT FOR THE YEAR

Type of Case	1st Quarter	2nd Quarter	3rd Quarter	4th Quarter
Fractures:				
Simple	1254	3885	4067	4390
Compound	835	2331	2032	1463
Angiograms	427	1793	1656	934
G.I. Studies	142	1076	1104	810
Myelograms	72	359	553	437
Pulmograms	1068	2510	2208	2805

9. On the basis of the above chart, the GREATEST number of cases handled in the year was in the _____ quarter.

    A. first   B. second   C. third   D. fourth

10. The SHARPEST decrease in the number of cases from one quarter to the next involved

    A. angiograms
    C. compound fractures
    B. G.I. Studies
    D. pulmograms

11. If all fracture cases were combined for the year, these cases would represent APPROXIMATELY _____ of all cases.

    A. 21%   B. 35%   C. 53%   D. 68%

12. The decrease in the number of cases during the third quarter was PRIMARILY due to the decreased numbers of cases involving

    A. simple and compound fractures
    B. compound fractures and pulmograms
    C. angiograms and G.I. studies
    D. angiograms and myelograms

13. Assume that the radiologist in your department requires two views for each simple fracture case. You are instructed to keep on hand as a supply of x-ray film for these simple fractures 1/3 of the total number which was required for the previous year.
    The number of films which you should have on hand at all times is MOST NEARLY

    A. 4,440   B. 9,064   C. 12,404   D. 18,128

14. A new x-ray technician has just reported to you for work. You should FIRST

    A. assign him to do only darkroom work for the first three weeks until he becomes familiar with the procedures
    B. let him start work at once so that you may observe whether he needs additional training
    C. tell him what his general duties are, introduce him to the other workers, and show him the work facilities
    D. train him in the first specialized techniques to which he will be assigned

15. In any on-the-job training program, after instruction has been given, follow-up is an important responsibility of the supervisor.
This means that, in conducting an on-the-job training program for technicians, you should

    A. give all technicians close supervision at all times
    B. check to see whether the technicians use the training given them
    C. repeat training at frequent intervals
    D. keep in touch with new developments in x-ray techniques

15.____

16. Suppose that one of your experienced technicians who has been doing the more difficult studies is resigning. Of the following, the LEAST appropriate way to select a replacement for this assignment is to

    A. ask the more skilled members of your staff individually if they are interested in this assignment
    B. review the educational backgrounds of present staff members
    C. consider the work performance of the present staff
    D. call a staff meeting and ask for a volunteer for this assignment

16.____

17. Assume that an x-ray technician is assigned to do a lumbo-sacral series of films on a patient. For the x-ray technician to tell the patient how many radiographs will be taken is

    A. *good,* because the patient will be less worried if he knows what to expect
    B. *poor,* because all information should be given to the patient by the physician
    C. *good,* because the patient will have confidence in the technician's ability
    D. *poor,* because it will make the patient nervous

17.____

18. Suppose that you find that you must correct the work of one of the technicians. Of the following, the BEST reason why this criticism or correction should be done in private is that

    A. this will not take the time of other technicians who do not need correction
    B. the technician will not feel that he has lost face with the other technicians
    C. you will not lose prestige if you are wrong in your criticism
    D. the other technicians will not worry about making mistakes

18.____

19. You have been given certain procedures by the radiologist which he expects you to have the technicians follow. Some of the instructions are not clear to you. Of the following, the action you should take is to

    A. ask one of your subordinate technicians what he thinks the procedures should be
    B. carry out the directions as best you can
    C. ask the radiologist to explain the procedures
    D. disregard the instructions and wait until they are given again

19.____

20. Of the following, the one which will BEST demonstrate your supervisory skill is the

    A. absence of any complaints about your method of supervision
    B. development of the abilities of the technicians to the highest degree possible
    C. willingness of the technicians to follow procedures
    D. high degree of cooperation between technicians and other employees of the hospital

20.____

21. While in charge of an x-ray department, you may be required to be away from the hospi-   21.____
tal for several days.
It is BEST for you to provide beforehand for such days by

    A. directing the technicians to call you to get instructions on how to proceed
    B. directing the technicians to get all their instructions from the radiologist
    C. working out written standardized procedures which the technicians are to follow
    D. telling the technicians to do the best they can, postponing difficult procedures until
       your return

22. Assume that two patients have had chest films on the same day and the identification of   22.____
both patients' films cannot be riade out with certainty. As the technician in charge, you
should

    A. attempt to sort out the films on the basis of the history and physical findings
    B. repeat one patient's films and determine identification by comparison with the orig-
       inal films
    C. repeat both examinations, making sure the films are adequately marked
    D. try to determine the approximate time each patient was examined

23. Suppose that you are responsible for scheduling all patients for radiography in your hos-   23.____
pital. One of the clinic patients, who is to have a G.I. study, has been given the first morning appointment for the next day. He asks if he can have the last afternoon appointment
instead.
Of the following, the BEST action for you to take is to

    A. deny his request unless the radiologist approves
    B. schedule the appointment as requested
    C. deny his request since he is a clinic patient
    D. tell him he can be taken if the technician is not busy in the afternoon

24. In order to avoid running short of necessary x-ray supplies, it is BEST to   24.____

    A. order the same amount of all supplies at the beginning of each week
    B. determine how much of each item is used in the average week and order when the
       supply reaches a minimum level
    C. see that all the supplies are used in the order in which they are delivered
    D. count the supplies on hand at the end of each week

25. Before an intravenous pyelogram may be scheduled for a certain time, it is MOST impor-   25.____
tant to

    A. determine the length of time such studies usually take
    B. know whether any other contrast studies are scheduled for the same day
    C. see how many technicians are scheduled to be on duty
    D. make certain a doctor will be available to give the intravenous injection

KEY (CORRECT ANSWERS)

1.	A		11.	C
2.	D		12.	B
3.	C		13.	B
4.	B		14.	C
5.	D		15.	B
6.	B		16.	D
7.	C		17.	A
8.	D		18.	B
9.	B		19.	C
10.	A		20.	B

21.	C
22.	C
23.	A
24.	B
25.	D

BASIC FUNDAMENTALS OF X-RAY EXAMINATIONS

CONTENTS

BASIC FUNDAMENTALS OF X-RAY EXAMINATIONS

I. BASIC PRINCIPLES

Recent investigations of x-ray use in the United States showed that approximately 60 percent of all diagnostic radiologic studies are now supervised by radiologists; however, almost all physicians are involved in making decisions to perform radiological examinations. This guide emphasizes the considerations necessary in deciding to perform an x-ray examination; it also reviews principles of good practice in the use of x-ray equipment. These considerations and principles do not interfere with the prerogative of the physician but they do require his cooperation if optimal good for the individual patient and for public health are to be achieved.

The basic principles may be summarized as follows:
1. In almost every medical situation, when a physician feels there is a reasonable expectation of obtaining information from a radiological examination that would affect the medical care of an individual, potential radiation hazard is not a consideration.

2. In diagnostic radiology, the goal is to obtain the desired information -- using the smallest radiation exposure that is practical.

3. Emphasis should be given to the technical means (collimators, filters, gonadal shielding, and so forth) by which radiation dose can be reduced without impairment of the medical value of the procedure.

4. Each physician should give due consideration to the potential somatic consequences of radiation exposure to the patient, and to the genetic effects upon mankind, as part of his responsibility toward public health.

5. The physician should retain complete freedom of judgment in the selection of radiographic procedures, and he should conform with good technical practice.

Equipment manufacturers, radiation safety experts and inspectors, technologists and others make important contributions to the efficient use of radiation in medical diagnosis, but the ultimate responsibility rests with the attending and consulting physicians. This guide is intended to aid physicians in exercising appropriate judgment.

II. BASIC INFORMATION

X-ray examinations are important in the diagnosis of most patients with serious illness or the potentiality of such illness. They have been of proven importance in preventive medical programs such as mass chest surveys and probably have a place in periodic health examinations.

Even if the examination is actually performed by a specialist in radiology, the attending physician usually decides when to refer individual patients for diagnostic x-ray procedures. His clinical judgment largely determines their frequency and influences the kinds of procedures and their comprehensiveness.

This part is designed:

To provide the attending physician with basic information concerning the factors involved in x-ray diagnosis of his own patients.

To provide information that every physician should have as part of his responsibility to public health -- particularly in reference to *third party* situations such as mass x-ray survey programs and pre-employment radiological examinations.

Two broad considerations are involved: why human radiation exposure is important generally, and specific situations in which there is need to be especially concerned.

A.   *WHY BE CONCERNED ABOUT RADIATION EXPOSURE GENERALLY?*

1. Possible genetic effects

Sound theoretical considerations suggest that even small amounts of radiation exposure to the gonads can adversely affect the genetic inheritance of future generations. This has led to the widely accepted principle that no amount of gonadal exposure is as small as to be dismissed as harmless.

2. Possible effects on the patient

Although no significant somatic change has been demonstrated in adults as a result of the low doses incurred in diagnostic radiology, there is laboratory evidence that even less levels of radiation may affect some cells; however, several epidemiological studies suggest that special consideration must be given to the relatively high radio sensitivity of the fetus in utero, particularly during the early phases of gestation.

3. Increasing need -- increasing use

The increased personnel and social resources available in recent years for health care, together with improvement in the versatility and precision of diagnostic radiology, have brought a steady increase in x-ray examinations -- amounting to an increment of about 7 percent annually. This trend is likely to continue. Naturally, there has been and will be a corresponding potential for more radiation exposure.

B.   *WHEN TO BE ESPECIALLY CONCERNED*

In almost every medical situation, when a physician feels there is a reasonable expectation that radiological examination will benefit the health of an individual, radiation hazard is not a contraindication.

The principle applies even in the case of pregnant women. The amount of previous medical radiation exposure to the nonpregnant patient is not relevant in deciding whether a procedure should be performed.

In each case, the physician may judge whether there is a reasonable expectation of useful information from a proposed examination. In making that judgment, he must take into account the theoretical risk involved. Consultation with the radiologist on the medical problem of a specific patient often leads to selection of the most appropriate procedure and also minimizes unproductive exposure. Examinations can sometimes be abbreviated without loss of diagnostic information. The potential hazard, however small, varies with the age of the patient and the part of the body being examined. Particular categories of individuals also require special consideration. Examples are given below.

1.   The parents of future generations

(a) Young Males
     A recent national x-ray survey by the United States Public Health Service included a study of genetically significant doses of radiation received by the United States population. The data showed that the largest contribution is from examination of males in the 15 to 29 age group. Most of this dose is received from studies of the abdominal and pelvic regions, where the gonads may be included in the primary beam. Examinations of these regions in young males should be performed only when there is clear clinical need. Optimal technical conditions are required, including beam area restriction and gonadal shielding whenever it does not interfere with the examination. For any complex symptoms involving these areas, it is often advisable to perform an initial study and evaluate the information obtained rather than to request three or four procedures simultaneously. Consultation with the radiologist is valuable here.

(b) Young Females
     The same considerations apply to potentially procreative females as to males since the genetic consequences of radiation are comparable. Practically, however, gonadal shielding is far more difficult to achieve for females without seriously compromising the examination. On the other hand, the natural shielding of the ovaries by overlying tissues result in a substantially smaller gonadal dose for females than for males for several types of lower abdominal area examinations. Closer attention to beam area restriction and specific gonadal shielding is nevertheless highly desirable.

(c) Pregnant Women (and Women Who Might Be Pregnant)
     The concern here is with the unborn child. X-ray procedures that include the uterus of women who are, or who might be, pregnant require particular guidelines in selection and timing. Examinations of other parts of the body maybe done at any time provided such examinations are conducted under conditions limiting the radiation exposure to the amount necessary for adequate examination.

In all women of childbearing age who may be pregnant, the period of choice for examinations involving the abdomen and pelvis is the first 14 days after onset of a menstrual period. In the remainder of the menstrual cycle of women who may be pregnant, the physician should consider whether he would still ask for the examination if the woman were known to be pregnant.

If the physician considers the examination necessary for immediate patient care, it should be conducted in accordance with good technical practice, even if the patient is pregnant. If he considers the examination useful but not necessary for immediate care, he should consider postponing it.

In the event that an examination is postponed because of the possibility of pregnancy, and the woman does prove to be pregnant, then a new decision is necessary as to whether further postponement is allowable. This situation is responsible for the recommendation that the ONLY examinations which should be considered for postponement are those which could be further postponed until at least the latter half of pregnancy, without seriously compromising the proper medical care of the patient. The reason for such further postponement, if possible, is that the relatively higher radio sensitivity of the fetus is greater during the first trimester as compared to a later trimester of prenatal life.

(d) A Practical Policy for X-ray Examinations of Pregnant Women

The need for an x-ray examination of abdomen and pelvis varies in its importance for the patient's benefit, and the physician must apply a broad scale of urgency, not susceptible to precise definition. At one extreme would be the example of a patient thought to be pregnant and who had relatively minor gastrointestinal or urinary tract symptoms of the type that frequently occur during pregnancy. In this case, there probably is not sufficient indication for a gastrointestinal examination or an excretory urogram. If, on the other hand, the patient has unexplained hematuria or melena, there would be adequate indication for proceeding with such a study, even in the case of confirmed pregnancy in the first trimester. In such circumstances, the radiologist should be informed of the pregnancy so that, if possible, the examination could be modified to reduce the radiation dose to a level even lower than usual.

If an x-ray examination is performed before the patient's pregnancy is discovered, there is normally little cause for concern. In most procedures, the radiation exposure is so small that the risk of interference with fetal development is negligible. Such radiation exposure alone should not be used as a justification for interruption of the pregnancy. In very unusual circumstances when it is suspected that a diagnostic procedure or combination of procedures may have resulted in an uncommonly large exposure, efforts should be made to determine the fetal dose and experts should be consulted about the possible hazard.

2.   Group and survey studies

(a) Survey Programs

Many physicians are asked to advise public agencies or other organizations interested in health surveyor screening programs. Such survey programs which involve radiographic examinations of healthy persons should be assessed for productivity. Only those programs that result in significant case finding are defensible. Most survey programs employ photofluorography of the chest. The main target is tuberculosis, which has not been completely overcome as a health problem in the United States.

Such activities must be justified in terms of detecting previously undiagnosed and unsuspected cases of active tuberculosis and thus, in most instances, should be limited to areas of high population density and low economic status where the incidence is greatest. Health authorities have suggested two or three cases or more per 10,000 examinations as a reasonable yield in terms of health benefits gained as opposed to the risk associated with subjecting large numbers of people to radiation exposure, small though that exposure may be to each individual.

Furthermore, real benefit from the programs, even those that attain high productivity in case finding is contingent upon effective follow-up of positive findings.

(b) Children's Chests

As an initial screening procedure for tuberculosis in infants and children, the tuberculin test is preferable to large-scale x-ray survey programs. Subsequent chest x-ray examinations are usually indicated only for positive findings.

(c) Mother's Chests

Prenatal survey programs are worthwhile where the incidence of tuberculosis may be relatively high because of socioeconomic or other factors. This is particularly so because undetected tuberculosis is especially hazardous for pregnant women. Properly done radiographs, and even photofluorograms, involve such minute doses that they represent an acceptable hazard for the fetus when there is expectation of a high yield of active tuberculosis.

(d) Hospital Admissions

Justification for performing chest x-ray examinations of all persons admitted to a hospital also depends on the yield of cases of tuberculosis. In turn, yield may depend upon the kind of hospital or service and the socioeconomic characteristics of the population the institution serves. If such programs are undertaken, they should include mechanisms for rapid interpretation, prompt follow-up of positive findings, and periodic reappraisal of productivity. The yield is always the primary factor. It tends to be higher from hospital admissions than from community surveys.

(e) Medical and Paramedical Personnel

This group is at high risk for tuberculosis. In most hospitals and clinics, the case yield will be such as to justify periodic chest x-ray examinations of personnel dealing directly with patients.

(f) Service Groups

In view of the potential tuberculosis hazard to the community, groups such as food handlers, barbers, beauticians, teachers, and others rendering personal service should have a chest film at least annually.

(g) Periodic Health Examinations

Health authorities are not in agreement on the value of periodic health examinations as a whole or on the value of chest x-rays in such programs. The radiation hazard of a chest radiograph obtained with good technique is minute with an estimated mean annual genetically significant dose contribution of 0.7 mrad.

(h) Special Occupational Groups

Periodic chest x-ray examinations are recommended for persons engaged in occupations with special pulmonary disease hazards such as miners and workers who have contact with beryllium, asbestos, glass, silica, and so forth. The premise that discovery of these special occupational illnesses in the recognizable but still asymptomatic phase has a beneficial effect upon the outcome is now generally accepted.

(I) Pre-employment Lumbar Spine Examinations

With this type of procedure, selected groups of healthy people are exposed to pelvic irradiation without clear-cut clinical indications. Protection of the public at large is less significant than in tuberculosis surveys. The practice cannot be categorically condemned, however, since it is based on a desire to obtain evidence of the likelihood of aggravating a pre-existing condition. It is not yet established whether the yield, in terms of prevention of injury, justifies the procedures. The gonadal region is involved, and the subjects are mainly young males. Since there is no urgency in the procedure, the very best technique can always be used in performing the examinations. Gonadal shielding should always be used.

III. BASIC PRACTICES

X-ray usage for most physicians and technicians should involve only radiography. Unless he has had special training in fluoroscopy, the nonradiologist should not use this procedure. Fluoroscopic examination has advantages only, when the dynamics of the body are to be studied. Fluoroscopy involves much greater radiation exposure than radiography. Considerable special training is required to do it well and with minimal radiation exposure. In no circumstances should fluoroscopy be used as a substitute for a procedure in which radiography is clearly indicated.

Guidelines to good radiography include:

A. *EMPHASIS ON QUALITY*

The value of a radiographic examination is directly related to the quality of the radiograph produced. Many of the technical factors that combine to produce good radiographs also tend to minimize radiation exposure. Good technique also reduces exposure by reducing the number of radiographs that must be repeated.

If a nonradiologist decides to undertake x-ray examinations, he should prepare himself properly. He should obtain equipment suitable and adequate for the types of examinations he plans to perform. He may delegate some aspects of the examination to an assistant, but the responsibility for quality control cannot be delegated. The physician himself must make sure that examinations are done properly and without unnecessary exposure. He should attain and maintain through postgraduate education, competence to interpret the radiographs.

B. *CHOICE OF EQUIPMENT*

Planning the installation involves the purchase of equipment and the design of an adequate radiographic room and darkroom. The selection of an x-ray machine appropriate for the proposed examinations can be made by consultation with radiologists and radiological physicists and also by reference to various resource publications.

C. *INSTALLATION*

The installation of an x-ray unit is usually apart of the sales contract. During the course of such installation, it is generally necessary to provide shielding for walls, floors, and ceilings against which the x-ray beam might be directed. The required degree of protection can be derived from various resource materials. In most instances, the physician will want to consult a suitable expert, usually a radiological physicist, to help with selection of equipment, planning of protection factors, and inspection and calibration of the equipment after installation. The physicist can also advise on the establishment of a film badge or other personnel monitoring system as a continuing check of the radiation protection measures and practices of the physician and technologist.

In some states, there will also be pertinent regulations and inspections. The physician should familiarize himself with these at an early stage of planning.

D. *FILTERS*

Even at high kilo voltage settings used in modern radiographic techniques, the x-ray beam always contains, some rays of low penetrating power that have no value in medical examinations. These add to the patient's absorbed dose without contributing to the diagnostic information. A large proportion of these useless rays are filtered out of the beam if the tube aperture is covered with at least 2 millimeters of aluminum or equivalent. Although most modern machines are equipped with such filters, this should not be assumed. The type of filter provided by the manufacturer or vendor should be clearly stated at the time of purchase. If a removable filter is provided, it is important to make sure that the filter is in place each time the machine is used.

E. *BEAM RESTRICTORS*

Only that part of the x-ray beam that falls on the film can provide useful information. The rest contributes nothing to diagnostic information, but adds unnecessarily to the patient's radiation dose and may contribute to the unintended exposure of other persons in the vicinity. Failure to limit the beam area properly is one of the most frequent causes of unnecessary radiation exposure.

Most x-ray machines can be purchased or equipped with adjustable collimating devices that can be used to restrict the size and shape of the x-ray beam. It is usually best for collimators to be equipped with a light localizer, which provides a visual indication of size and location of the radiation beam at any distance. The machine operator must adjust the opening of the collimator, for each examination performed, to the dimensions appropriate to the area being examined. Automated collimators are expected to be standard equipment on all machines produced beginning in 1972.

Before development of the adjustable collimator, the standard method of restricting the beam area was to place a non-adjustable cone or diaphragm over the aperture of the x-ray tube. Several cones or diaphragms were usually needed to allow for different film sizes. This method can still be used if varied sizes are provided and if the operator is conscientious in using the cone or diaphragm appropriate for the examination and the film size. Test radiographs should be made after installation to determine the effectiveness of collimating devices.

All these devices have an important function in addition to limiting patient dose. They improve the contrast and detail of the radiographic image by reducing the amount of scattered radiation reaching the film. If two radiographs are made under identical conditions, except that one is done with collimation and the other without, the one with collimation will show a decided superiority in image quality.

F. *GONADAL SHIELDS*

Suitable protective devices (usually lead) should be provided to shield the gonads of patients who are potentially procreative when the gonads cannot be excluded from the beam by collimation. Gonadal shields are not used when their presence would obscure important areas or otherwise interfere with the examination.

The use of special shields for the gonads during diagnostic radiology is still a developing art, and equipment for this purpose has not become standardized. The testes can usually be covered by some radiation barrier material with ease. In addition, careful attention to proper collimation will exclude them from the primary beam in most examinations. Conversely, the ovaries lie within the area that the primary beam must traverse for a number of common examinations. Shielding them without loss of needed diagnostic information may require considerable ingenuity and is frequently impracticable.

Gonadal shielding is new to most patients. It may not be readily accepted. To the patient, the use of a shield implies that there is danger to his or her reproductive system in the examination. Such apprehension can be very difficult to allay, and patients may refuse examinations that are urgently needed for their immediate health benefit. It is important, although not always easy, to convey the concept that the exposure hazard to the individual is statistically negligible, but that protection is indicated because of the millions of exposures sustained by the genetic pool of the species.

G. *FILMS AND SCREENS*

Nearly all x-ray examinations other than those of extremities are made with intensifying screens, which are placed in contact with the film. The x-ray beam causes the fluorescent crystals of the screen to emit light. As much as 95 percent of the darkening of the film may result from light produced by the screens.

Manufacturers of films and screens offer a wide range of sensitivities. In general, the most sensitive systems are leasable to record fine detail. A film-screen combination should be chosen for the type of examinations to be conducted to combine detail rendition and sensitivity required for optimum information content. Screens should be kept free of dirt and scratches.

H.   *FILM PROCESSING*

Even the best x-ray equipment, carefully used, will not produce satisfactory radiographs unless the darkroom equipment and techniques are comparable in quality and precision. The darkroom should be planned with the same care as the x-ray facility. It should be inspected for light leaks following construction and periodically thereafter. Proper temperature control of the processing solutions is essential. Storage of solutions should be planned to avoid contamination. Unexposed film should be checked periodically for fogging. The presence of fogging may indicate excessive age or a need for greater protection from light, heat, certain fumes, or radiation during storage. The safelight should be carefully chosen to match the film manufacturer's specifications and should be used only with a lamp of the specified wattage.

Manufacturers of x-ray films provide processing instructions and recommend suitable chemicals. The processing solutions should be kept fresh and maintained at adequate strength. Their temperature should be regulated as recommended; in general, manufacturers recommendations and technique charts should be followed. Experienced technical representatives routinely check darkroom solutions and procedures as possible causes of poor radiographs before examining the x-ray machines and controls.

I.   *TECHNIQUES FOR EXAMINATIONS*

Technique charts for proper exposure of the radiographs should be obtained and followed carefully. The use of an automatic exposure timer is helpful in improving the quality of films and in reducing the number of repeat examinations.

When the film is developed and dried, it should be displayed on a view box with sufficient brightness to permit observation of fine detail. Viewing in a partially darkened room enhances perception of details. A high-intensity light is necessary for examining dark areas of the radiograph.

J.   *INTERPRETATION*

The ultimate value of a radiographic examination to the patient necessarily depends upon the skill with which it is interpreted. Radiographic interpretation is the subject of many textbooks, and its study is a lifelong career for some physicians. Discussion of interpretative technique is beyond the scope of this manual; however, consultation is appropriate in any radiological examination. Radiologists, or other physicians, may be called upon to review radiographs. Better still, when feasible, the initial consultation should precede the examination for guidance in the selection of techniques for the particular clinical problem.

———

PRINCIPLES OF RADIOGRAPHIC EXPOSURE

SECTION A—INTRODUCTION

6-1. Introduction:

a. The purpose of an X-ray examination is to procure diagnostic information. The radiograph constitutes the record; it must depict all anatomical details of the body part being examined in such a way as to facilitate diagnosis. Making a radiograph is essentially a photographic procedure. The exposure and processing of the X-ray film involves complex physical and chemical changes that result in the formation of the silver image. Standardization of the several operations in the production of the image greatly simplifies the procedure (figure 6-1).

b. Radiologic technology entails the use of standardized apparatus and technique so that all operations will consume a minimum of time and yield radiographs of the best quality. The purpose of this portion of the manual is to describe the principles of radiographic exposure by means of theory, experiment, and application.

c. Radiographic results usually are unintelligible to the student technologist. For that reason he must be made acquainted early with the kind of radiograph that is most useful to the radiologist—one that possesses correct diagnostic quality. The student cannot acquire that knowledge except by actually making radiographs under guidance and then, during a film clinic, having demonstrated to him why the quality is satisfactory. This type of instruction gives the student self-confidence in his ability to produce good work— an invaluable asset. To facilitate training, a simple, exact exposure system, based upon proven fundamental theories and practices, is presented. Wherever possible, the exposure factors have been reduced to constants, thereby eliminating many sources of error. This system permits the student to become acquainted quickly with above average quality radiographs.

6-2. The X-Ray Beam:

a. Primary Radiation (PR) (figure 6-2) is confined to the portion of the X-ray beam emitted from the focal spot (FS) of the X-ray tube. Because of the inverse square law its intensity is reduced as the distance from the FS increases. The average wavelength is also shortened because of the absorption of some of the longer wavelengths of radiation

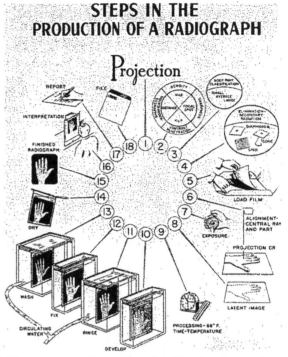

STEPS IN THE PRODUCTION OF A RADIOGRAPH

Figure 6-1. Steps in the Production of a Radiograph.

by the glass envelope surrounding the tube and by aluminum filtration.

b. Remnant Radiation (RR) is that portion of the PR that emerges from the body tissues to expose the X-ray film and record the radiographic image. It is the image-forming radiation. Remnant radiation is intermingled with secondary and scatter radiation (SR) from the tissues, the amount depending upon its wavelength and the manner in which it is controlled.

c. Central ray (CR) is the center of the X-ray beam. The term is employed in describing the direction of the X-rays in a given projection. The course of the CR extends from the FS of the X-ray tube (perpendicularly from the tube housing) to the X-ray film.

(1) The entire distance traversed by the CR is known as the focus-film distance (FFD).

(2) The distance from the object or body part to the X-ray film measured along the course of the CR is known as the object-film distance (OFD).

d. Secondary radiation is radiation emitted by atoms that have absorbed X-rays (*for example*, characteristic radiation). Secondary radiation has longer wavelengths than the PR that causes it. Scatter radiation refers to those X-ray photons that have undergone a change in direction after interacting with atoms. (It may also have been modified by an increase in wavelength.) In this text secondary and scatter radiation are normally considered together and abbreviated (SR). Since SR is unfocussed and may come from any direction, its action on the radiograph may cover the entire image with a veil of fog unless it is controlled by certain accessories.

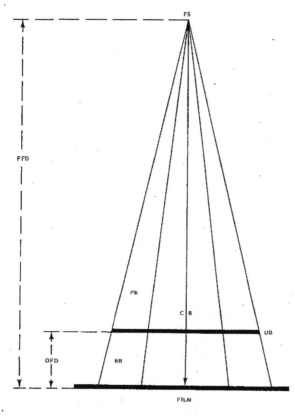

Figure 6-2. Various Components of an X-ray Beam.

6-3. X-Ray Exposure Terms:

a. The nomenclature of X-ray exposure comprises some electrical and sundry terms commonly used under the general designation of radiographic factors. Each factor listed below influences the character of the radiographic image. These terms and their symbols should be memorized.

Radiographic factor	Symbol
Central ray	CR
Focal spot	FS
Focus-film distance	FFD
Kilovolts peak	kVp
Milliamperes	mA
Milliampere-seconds	mAs

Radiographic factor	Symbol
Object-film distance	OFD
Primary radiation	PR
Remnant radiation	RR
Secondary and scatter radiation	SR
Time of exposure in seconds	sec

b. Several items of apparatus, when used, have a definite influence on the radiographic image. Through usage, these accessories are usually considered together with the actual exposure factors.

(1) X-ray intensifying screens in cassettes are used to augment the exposure effect of the X-rays.

(2) The beam restricting device limits the size of the X-ray beam irradiating the body part.

(3) The stationary grid reduces the SR reaching the X-ray film.

(4) The Potter-Bucky (P-B) diaphragm is similar to the stationary grid, but it is mechanized to move during the exposure.

SECTION B—THE SILVER IMAGE

6-4. Image Characteristics. The radiographic image is composed of many deposits of black metallic silver on both surfaces of the radiograph. These deposits blend into an image to represent the anatomical structures examined. The image has two major characteristics—density and contrast—directly influencing the diagnostic quality of the radiograph.

a. Radiographic density is the resultant deposit of black metallic silver on an X-ray film after exposure and processing. Details of the tissue elements examined are rendered as densities of varying concentration. During passage through a body part, the X-rays are absorbed by tissue components, resulting in a number of different silver deposits on the radiograph. The degree of silver concentration determines the brightness or tone value of the densities when viewed on an X-ray illuminator. The tonal relationship between one density and another enables image details to become visible. The greater the number of tones present (correct tone rendition), the greater the number of structural details that can be visualized in the image. The range of tones in an image is photographically known as the "gray scale."

b. Radiographic contrast exists when two or more radiographic densities are present; it provides differentiation between translucent radiographic densities to reveal all possible anatomical details when viewed on an X-ray illuminator. In figure 6-3 (left), contrast does not exist—there is only one radiographic density; in figure 6-3 (right), contrast exists—the image has numerous densities of different tone value.

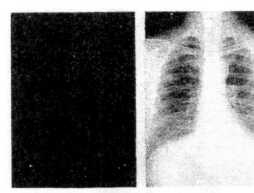

Figure 6-3. **Radiographs: Showing a Single Radiographic Density and Many Radiographic Densities.**

(1) Factors Influencing Contrast. The scale of densities determining contrast and visibility of details is influenced by X-ray wavelength which, in turn, is regulated by kVp. The exposure factor of kVp can be used as the active variable in altering radiographic contrast (Section D). Generally, visualization of details depends upon the degree of contrast and/or sharpness rendered. The contrast inherent to the X-ray developer, the type of film, the X-ray intensifying screens, and the type of tissue contribute to the sum total of radiographic contrast.

(2) Contrast Scale. The scale of contrast in a radiographic image is determined by the number and tone value of the various densities. Radiographic contrast may vary widely or within some acceptable average range depending upon the part being examined. A good radiograph possesses correct density balance over the entire contrast scale—good differentiation between tissue details of diagnostic interest without loss of detail in other areas of the image.

(a) Short-Scale Contrast. In this type of contrast the range of image densities is short and small in number, each density exhibiting a large tonal difference from its neighbor. In A, figure 6-4, long wavelength radiation is directed toward the step-wedge. It easily penetrates steps Nos. 1 and 2; RR is largely absorbed by the silver emulsion and an opaque density is produced. The radiation is greatly absorbed by step No. 3, and more so by step No. 4, resulting in RR of such low intensity that a translucent density with a

gray tone is produced in the former and a light gray tone in the latter. The radiation passing to steps Nos. 5 and 6 is totally absorbed, and the film is not exposed because there is no emergent RR. A representative image of the entire wedge was not recorded because of an inadequacy of RR. The differences between densities are wide and few in number, and the number of densities is insufficient to portray a complete image of the subject. This diagram illustrates that radiographic details of an object cannot be seen in the image unless there are discernible differences in tone value between densities, and that there must be a silver deposit on the film if a detail within the object is to be demonstrated.

(b) Long-Scale Contrast. In this type of contrast the range of image densities is wide and great in number, each density exhibiting only a small tonal difference from its neighbor. In B, figure 6-4, a short wavelength radiation is directed toward the step-wedge. The radiation penetrates all portions of the wedge, and the selective degree of absorption by each step permits RR to emerge with different intensities producing separate translucent densities of varying tone value. The transition between tones is gradual, each tone is distinctive, and the image is completely informative. Desirable long-scale contrast is produced when the kVp is adjusted to delineate all normal structures satisfactorily. In the case of human radiography, when the scale of densities representing a departure from the normal occurs, the image is open to suspicion from a pathologic or physiologic standpoint. The criterion of good diagnostic contrast is whether one sees all one expects to see.

(c) Short-Scale Versus Long-Scale Contrasts. The entire image exhibiting short-scale contrast is invariably incomplete, for details representing the thinner and thicker portions of the body part are not always shown. Only those details in the image produced by exposure factors optimum for the area are rendered with maximum visibility. Short-scale contrast is useful only as a special procedure in more adequately visualizing details of *small* tissue areas. Typical examples of short-scale contrast are shown in figure 6-5. Long-scale contrast makes possible the visualization of small variations of image density. To obtain the maximum diagnostic information in the survey film, a compromise must be made between the radiograph with short-scale contrast and that exhibiting the longer-scale contrast. Typical examples of long-scale contrast are shown in figure 6-6. Although long-scale contrast generally occupies one end of the contrast range and short-scale contrast the other, there is no definite point that separates the two scales. In other words, contrast is a relative measure of the differences in radiographic densities. Radiograph A may exhibit long-scale contrast when compared with radiograph B. However, if radiograph A were compared with radiograph C (which has a longer contrast scale than A), then radiograph A would exhibit short-scale contrast.

6-5. X-Ray Penetration. X-rays vary widely in penetrating human tissues. Each type of tissue absorbs radiation according to its own composition and thickness. Only a very small fraction of the original primary radiation is effectively utilized in an exposure because the bulk of the X-rays is either absorbed by the tissues or converted into SR. The greater the tissue absorption, the less intense the emergent radiation that can expose a film and record the image. To obtain a correct radiographic exposure, the X-radiation must be qualitatively and quantitatively adequate.

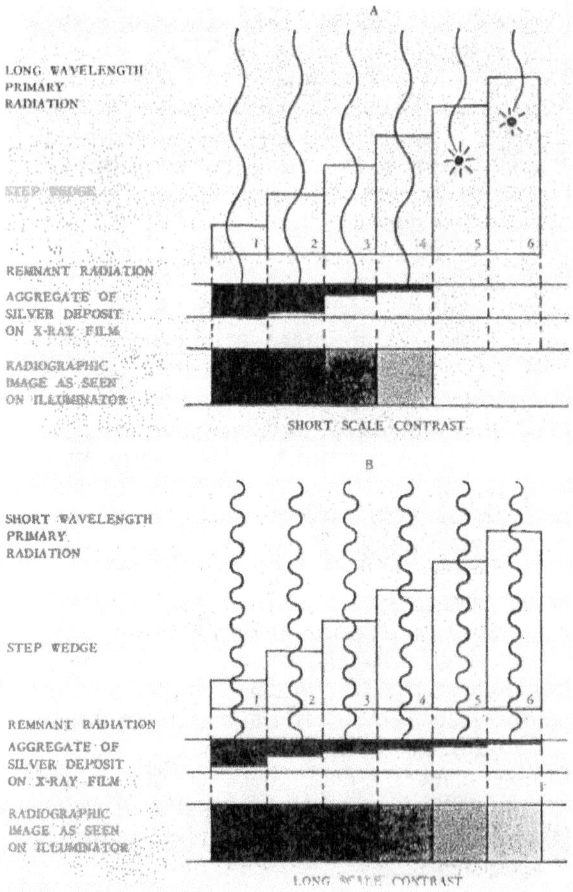

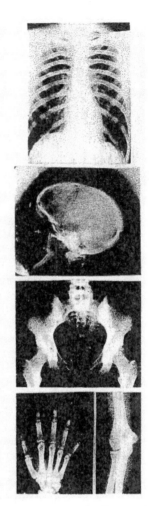

Figure 6-5. Typical Radiographs Exhibiting Short-Scale Contrast.

a. Factor of X-ray Wavelength. Satisfactory image densities result only when radiation penetrates the entire part. Attempts to penetrate the part by using high mAs and low kVp (relatively longer wavelength radiation) result in prolonged impractical exposures that seldom yield satisfactory images. When an impractically long exposure is employed, the shorter wavelengths create most of the image since the longer wavelengths are largely absorbed. Objections to such an exposure procedure include: lack of complete penetration; the patient reaches the MPD sooner; the patient may move during the exposure; and the latitude of exposure allows no margin for error. When the wavelength is shortened, the absorption properties of flesh and bone are brought closer together because of a more uniform penetration of the tissues.

LONG WAVELENGTH PRIMARY RADIATION

STEP WEDGE

REMNANT RADIATION

AGGREGATE OF SILVER DEPOSIT ON X-RAY FILM

RADIOGRAPHIC IMAGE AS SEEN ON ILLUMINATOR

SHORT SCALE CONTRAST

SHORT WAVELENGTH PRIMARY RADIATION

STEP WEDGE

REMNANT RADIATION

AGGREGATE OF SILVER DEPOSIT ON X-RAY FILM

RADIOGRAPHIC IMAGE AS SEEN ON ILLUMINATOR

LONG SCALE CONTRAST

Figure 6-4. Contrast Scale.

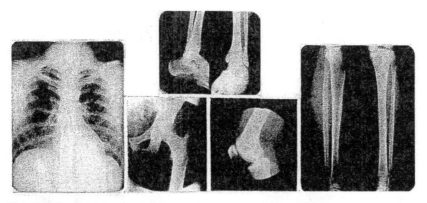

Figure 6-6. Typical Radiographs Exhibiting Long-Scale Contrast.

b. Absorption by Body Part. When long wavelength radiation is used, bone absorbs a large amount of radiation and few osseous details may be shown in a radiograph, yet soft tissue details are visible. The absorption properties between these two tissues under long wavelength radiation are exceedingly wide, and details of both tissues cannot be shown in a single image. A single radiograph recording both classes of tissue is preferable. The type of body part being examined has a decided bearing upon detail visualization, and the wide range of available kVp makes possible detail representation of any part of the body.

(1) When X-rays pass through human tissue, each type of tissue absorbs its proportion of radiation according to its own composition and thickness. For example, as X-rays pass through one thickness of flesh, then through a thickness of bone, and finally through another thickness of flesh or fat, the total absorption is the sum of the various degrees of absorption occurring in the different tissues (figure 6-7).

(2) Tissue contrast represents the relative differences in the tissue components of an anatomical part with respect to its X-ray absorption. The greater the absorption difference of a tissue with relation to adjacent tissue densities, the greater the tissue contrast; the lower the absorption difference, the lower the tissue contrast.

c. Absorption Variables. In radiography there are a number of unpredictable absorption variables in body tissues that are influenced by physiologic or pathologic changes, but they may be disregarded, in some measure, if the exposure system provides enough latitude. Generally, small deviations from the normal in tissue absorption or thickness can be ignored. Recognizable abnormal conditions may be easily compensated by adjustment of the variable exposure factors selected.

(1) Large Absorption Differences. When structural tissue details are widely different, each presents wide differences in absorbing power and, consequently, wide differences in tone value will exist in the radiograph. Where a body part contains thick heavy bone surrounded by a large quantity of muscle and fat, as in the lumbar vertebral region, X-ray absorption differences become relatively wide (figure 6-8). The image of a calcified body (figure 6-9) outlined by the darker adjacent densities of its containing tissues also exhibits great tonal differences and provides easy visibility. Such parts provide little difficulty in recording even

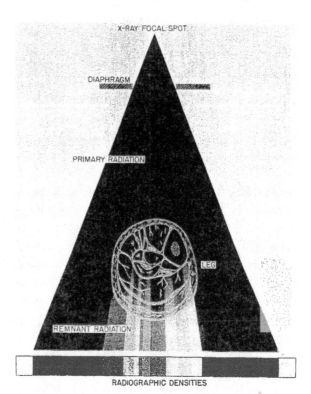

Figure 6-7. Penetration and Absorption of an X-ray Beam Traversing a Body Part.

though large errors in exposure may be made.

(2) Small Absorption Differences. At times, absorption differences between some tissues may be very small, and in such cases differentiation becomes difficult. The kidney, gall bladder, and liver areas are typical examples in which the X-ray absorbing power of the tissues is almost the same (figure 6-10). The tonal differentiation of a small portion of lymphatic tissue within its surrounding tissues, also, cannot be as distinctive against its background density as could a calculus because of the small tissue absorption differences. A shorter scale of contrast in the image would, therefore, be helpful and perhaps necessary.

from a given FFD; (2) the time that the X-rays act on the emulsion; and (3) the wavelength of the X-rays. If the X-rays do not penetrate the object or body part and reach the film, there is no exposure; hence, no emulsion response.

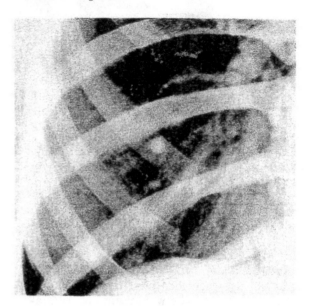

Figure 6-9. Portion of a PA Chest Showing a Calcification of High Contrast Against a Low Contrast Background Group of Densities.

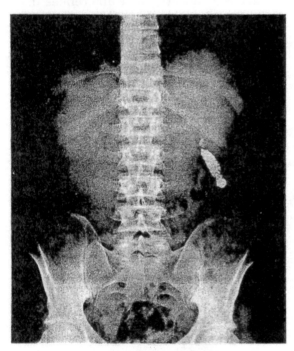

Figure 6-8. Radiograph of the Lumbar Vertebrae Showing Wide Absorption Differences.

6-6. Radiographic Exposure:

a. General. Radiographic exposure factors relating to image characteristics have two important aspects: photographic and geometric. The photographic aspect is related to quantity and distribution of silver deposited on the film (paragraph 6-4) and the geometric aspect is related to the form and sharpness of the image definition (Section H). Radiographic exposure denotes the sensitizing action of the silver bromide crystals within the film emulsion by X-rays. The action is based upon the combined effects of (1) the intensity of the X-rays reaching the film

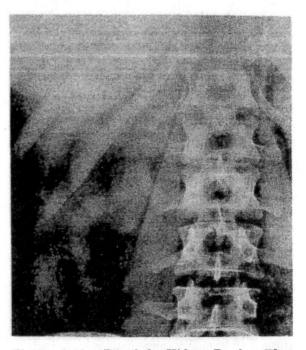

Figure 6-10. PA of the Kidney Region That Exhibits Small Differences in Density.

b. Value of Constants. To understand the many factors influencing the radiographic image, the function of each factor in the exposure system must be appreciated. The role of any factor must be determined by the use of the factor as a variable while all other factors remain constant. The influence of development on the radiographic image must also be known in establishing the whole processing procedure as a constant; any variations in radiographic quality may then be attributed to exposure variations rather than to development. For example, to determine the radiographic influence of kVp in the exposure system, it should be employed as the variable and all other exposure and processing factors should be constant. The establishment of an exposure system should be based upon the employment as constants of those factors that have the greatest influence on the quality of the image and selection of one factor that possesses only a single radiographic function as the variable.

SECTION C—THE EFFECT OF FOCUS-FILM DISTANCE ON DENSITY

6-7. Introduction. The FFD on the radiographic image influences radiographic density, the size and shape of the image of the part being examined, and the sharpness with which image details are rendered. Since intensity directly influences radiographic density, any change in distance will cause a change in density when other factors are constant.

6-8. Application of Inverse Square Law. Since X-rays diverge as they are emitted from the FS and proceed in straight paths, they cover an increasingly larger area with *lessened* intensity as they travel from their source. This principle is illustrated in figure 6-11. It is assumed that the intensity of the X-rays emitted at the FS remains the same and that X-rays cover an area of 4 square inches at the horizontal plane (C), 12 inches from FS. When the FFD is increased to 24 inches to plane D or twice the distance between FS and C, the X-rays will cover 16 square inches—an area four times as great as that at C. The intensity of the radiation per square inch on the plane at D is only one-quarter that at the level C. Thus, an adequate exposure at C must be increased four times in order to produce at D an equal radiographic density. (See the formula and example given in paragraph 6-9.) Table 6-1 may be used for determining the correct mAs multiplying factor when the FFD is changed.

6-9. Arithmetical Relation—mAs and FFD:

a. Rule. The mAs required to produce a given radiographic density is inversely proportional to the *square* of the FFD when the remaining factors are constant:

$$\frac{mAs_1}{mAs_2} = \frac{FFD_1^2}{FFD_2^2}$$

b. Example. If an exposure of 10 mAs (mAs_1) at an FFD of 25 inches (FFD_1) is used and the FFD is increased to 60 inches (FFD_2), what mAs (mAs_2) must be used to maintain the same radiographic density? mAs_1, FFD_1, and FFD_2 are known; mAs_2 is unknown.

$$mAs_2 = \frac{mAs_1 \times FFD_2^2}{FFD_1^2}$$

$$mAs_2 = \frac{10 \times 60^2}{25^2} = \frac{36,000}{625} = 57.6 \text{ mAs.}$$

To facilitate the mathematics involved, table 6-1 may be used to determine mAs values when common FFD values are changed. For example, under the column headed "Original Focus-Film Distance" find 25 inches. Find the vertical column headed by the new FFD of 60 inches. Where these two columns intersect will be found the mAs multiplying factor 5.76. Multiply the original mAs of 10 by 5.76. The answer is 57.6 mAs.

c. Cancellation of Constant Value. The original formula relating mAs and FFD may be altered slightly if either the mA or the sec is to remain constant. Thus the constant value will cancel from the numerator and denominator leaving the following two formulas:

$$(\text{Constant sec}) \quad \frac{mA_1 \times sec_1}{mA_2 \times sec_2} = \frac{FFD_1^2}{FFD_2^2} \text{ or}$$

$$\frac{mA_1}{mA_2} = \frac{FFD_1^2}{FFD_2^2} \quad \text{Formula 1.}$$

$$(\text{Constant mA}) \quad \frac{ma_1 \times sec_1}{ma_2 \times sec_2} = \frac{FFD_1^2}{FFD_2^2} \text{ or}$$

$$\frac{sec_1}{sec_2} = \frac{FFD_1^2}{FFD_2^2} \quad \text{Formula 2.}$$

SECTION D—FUNCTION OF KILOVOLTAGE

6-10. Introduction:

a. General. Of all the exposure factors, kVp has the greatest effect on the radi-ographic image when all other factors remain constant. It directly influences the quality of radiation reaching the film. This in turn determines the radiographic contrast and density. Kilovoltage is a major agent in the production of SR which must be controlled to prevent fogging on the film. Use of low kVp may result in images deficient in details; injudicious use of high kVp may result in fogged or high density images in which details are obscured by excessive silver deposits and a decrease in contrast.

b. Greater Exposure Efficiency by Use of Higher Kilovoltage:

(1) Anatomical details in all tissue thicknesses are rendered as translucent densities.

(2) Greater image sharpness is obtained because shorter exposures may be used with smaller FS.

(3) The radiation dose to patients is reduced because the body absorbs less radiation than at the lower kVp; therefore, more radiation can reach the film to expose it and exposures can be reduced.

(4) Heat production in the X-ray tube is reduced because smaller energy loads can be used, thereby increasing the efficiency and life of the X-ray tube.

(5) Greater exposure latitude may be secured because of the narrowed absorption range of the body tissues.

(6) More satisfactory radiography is possible when the source of electric power is variable or in a state of constant flux.

6-11. Kilovoltage and Density:

a. Experiment—Kilovoltage-Density Relation:

(1) Purpose. This experiment demonstrates the relation between kVp and radiographic density when a homogeneous absorber of varying thickness is used.

(2) Theory. When an absorber is placed on the film, the X-ray absorption properties of the material composing the absorber as well as its thickness are factors that cause variation in the radiographic densities.

(3) Procedure:

(a) A series of six radiographs of a long step-wedge containing a number of aluminum steps, 1 mm in thickness, should be made using the materials and exposure factors shown in table 6-2. The exposure of the first step is adjusted to obtain a light gray tone—a translucent density.

(b) Place step-wedge on 10 X 12 inch cardboard holder containing screen-type film. Directly expose each film in sequence

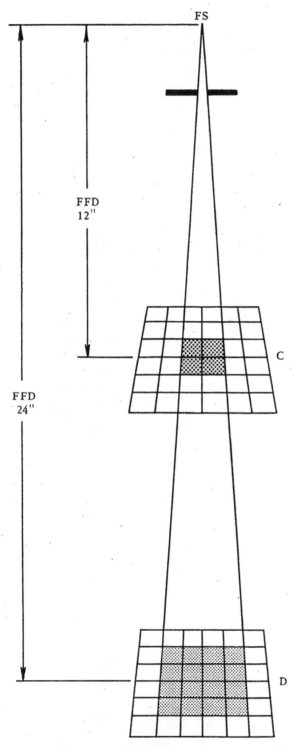

Figure 6-11. Change in Distance Influences Radiographic Density.

Table 6-1. mAs Conversion Factors for Changes in FED.

Original focus-film distance	New focus-film distance							
	20″	25″	30″	36″	40″	48″	60″	72″
20″	1.00	1.56	2.25	3.22	4.00	5.76	9.00	12.96
25″	.64	1.00	1.44	2.07	2.56	3.68	5.76	8.29
30″	.44	.69	1.00	1.44	1.77	2.56	4.00	5.76
36″	.31	.48	.69	1.00	1.23	1.77	2.77	4.00
40″	.25	.39	.56	.81	1.00	1.44	2.25	3.24
48″	.17	.27	.39	.59	.69	1.00	1.56	2.25
60″	.11	.17	.25	.36	.44	.64	1.00	1.44
72″	.08	.12	.17	.25	.31	.44	.69	1.00

until all exposures are completed. Process films.

(4) Comment. The quantity of silver deposit in each image representing the first step of the wedge is dependent in degree upon the quantity of RR emerging from the wedge to expose the film, and its wavelength (figure 6-12). The density of the first step in each radiograph increases with each advance in kVp indicating that greater image densities are obtained because of the greater penetrating quality of the radiation. The density of the sixth step in each radiograph differs widely as the kVp is advanced. It is here demonstrated that the thickness of any homogeneous object placed on the film has direct influence in decreasing the intensity of the radiation reaching the film. The variation in the intensities of the remnant beam reaching the film results in a series of radiographic densities of varying tone value that constitute a radiographic image of the entire wedge only at the higher kVp. At the lower kVp, an entire image of the wedge was not secured because the long wavelength radiation was absorbed by the thicker sections of the step-wedge and little RR reached the film to produce a satisfactory image. All

Table 6-2. Kilovoltage—Density Relation: Experiment.

Materials	Film	Screen-type, 10 X 12 inch.
	Exposure holder	10 X 12 inch cardboard holder.
	Cone	To cover exposure area.
Constant factors	Development	5 minutes. 68°F
	FFD	36 inches
	mA	10
	Time	2 sec
	mAs	20
	Filter	1 mm aluminum
Variable factor	Exposure No.	kVp
	1	40
	2	50
	3	60
	4	70
	5	80
	6	90

steps of the wedge are not shown in the 40 and 60 kVp images, but all steps show when 90 kVp is used because all portions of the wedge were penetrated.

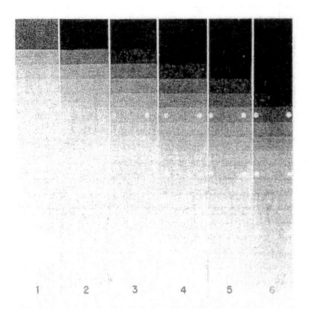

Figure 6-12.   Kilovoltage—Density Relation When an Absorber of Varying Thickness Is Used.

b. Illustrations of Small and Large Kilovoltage Changes:

(1) Small kVp changes have little radiographic effect since the wavelength is not appreciably changed.

(a) Figure 6-13 depicts a series of PA projections of the hand made on direct exposure in 1-kVp steps from 45 to 55 kVp; all

other factors were constant: 40 mAs; 36-inch FFD. Radiographs were developed for 5 minutes at 68°F in rapid developer. Comparison between the densities produced at 45 and 47 kVp shows no discernible difference; the densities produced at 45 and 50 and those between 50 and 55 kVp demonstrate visual differences. Changes in kVp of 1, 2, or 3 at this kVp range do not demonstrate definite visual density differences.

(b) Figure 6-14 depicts a series of PA screen exposures of the chest. A range of 75 to 84 kVp in 1-kVp steps was used; all other factors were constant: 2.5 mAs; 72-inch FFD. Comparison of the densities in the 75 and 76 kVp images and in the 83 and 84 kVp images shows little difference. A definite difference exists, however, between the 75 and 80 kVp and the 79 and 84 kVp images. A positive difference exists between the densities seen in the 75 and 84 kVp radiographs.

(2) Large kVp changes produce an increase in density. Figures 6-15, 6-16, and 6-17 exhibit the effect of large kVp changes when direct, screen, and grid exposures are made. The appearance of all the images is characteristic of the manner in which they were produced.

(a) Figure 6-15 depicts a series of direct exposure PA radiographs of the hand made in 5 kVp increments from 30 to 75 kVp; all other factors were constant: 45 mAs, 36-inch FFD. The increase in density between each increment of 5 kVp is appreciable between 30 and 55 kVp. The density change between increments above 55 kVp is small. As overexposure occurs by reason of the

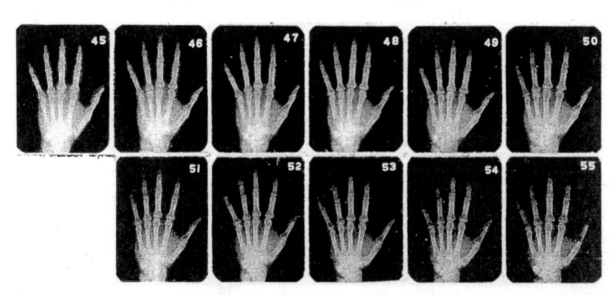

Figure 6-13.   Direct Exposure Radiographs of the Hand That Demonstrate the Effect on Radiographic Density With Small Changes in kVp.

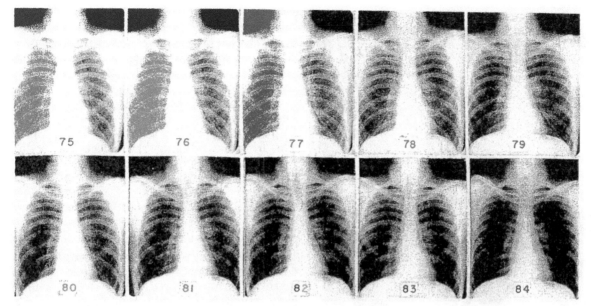

Figure 6-14. Screen Exposures of the Chest to Demonstrate the Density Effect With Small Changes in kVp.

accelerated density effect at the higher kVp (above 60 kVp), fogging of the image also occurs.

(b) Figure 6-16 depicts a series of screen PA chest radiographs made in increments of 10 kVp from 50 to 80 kVp; all other factors were constant: 10 mAs; 72-inch FFD; average-speed screens. The transition in densities is more exaggerated than in figure 6-15 because screen contrast was introduced.

At the higher kVp values (above 60 kVp) fog begins to appear because of overexposure.

(c) Figure 6-17 depicts a series of three grid radiographs of the shoulder made in increments of 5 kVp from 70 to 80 kVp with direct exposure film; all other factors were constant: 200 mAs; 36-inch FFD; P-B grid (8:1). The increase in density between the kVp increments in figure 6-16 for the density changes are due to the influence of

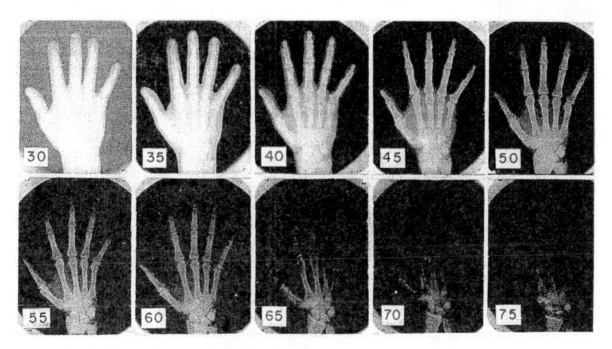

Figure 6-15. Demonstration of kVp-Density Changes.

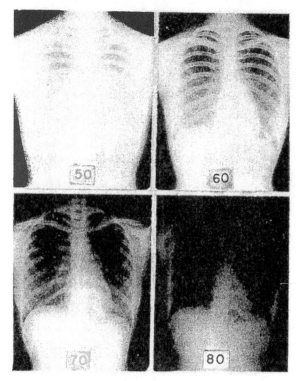

Figure 6-16. Screen Radiographs to Show Influence of Large kVp Increments on Overall Density.

kVp. Because a P-B grid was used, the low level of SR reaching the film contributed only a negligible amount of fog density.

c. Arithmetical Relation—kVp-mAs and Density:

(1) Radiographic density is influenced by kVp, and varies with the mAs and FFD used. In medical radiography, there is no simple mathematical method for determining kVp-mAs density ratios. Such factors as the thickness and density of the body tissues to be examined, the characteristics of the X-ray apparatus, and the use of intensifying screens exert pertinent influences. Close approximations between kVp and other exposure factors have been established by trial and error. There are two procedures that may be followed: one, to determine the approximate change in mAs for compensation of a change in kVp; the other, to determine the change in kVp required for a given mAs change.

(2) Based on measurements by Bierman and Boldingh, the density-producing effect of kVp varies approximately to the fifth power. The formula relating the effects of kVp, mAs, and FFD on the density may be expressed as:

$$\text{Density} = \frac{\text{mAs} \times \text{kVp}^5}{\text{FFD}^2}$$

Changing the kVp or mAs while keeping the density constant requires complex mathematical manipulations. Table 6-3 permits easy calculation of the new factors to be used. A nomogram form is used in this table because of its simplicity of operation.

(3) To change from one fixed kVp to another, lay a straightedge between the original mAs and original kVp values. Note the position of the straightedge on the reference line. Keeping the straightedge at the reference point, rotate the straightedge to the desired new kVp. The straightedge will cross the mAs line at the new value.

(a) Problem: If 80 kVp was used in making a PA of the chest using 10 mAs at an FFD of 72 inches, and it is desired to use 60 kVp to produce a higher contrast on the film, what mAs should be used to produce the same density as the original technique?

(b) Solution: Consult table 6-3. Lay a straightedge between 10 mAs and 80 kVp. Note the point at which the straight edge crosses the reference line; then rotate the straight-edge about this point until it rests on 60 on the kVp line. At this point the straightedge will also cross the mAs line at 62. The answer is 62 mAs.

(4) Some mAs values derived from table 6-3 may require the use of a time value that is not within the practical scope of the timer.

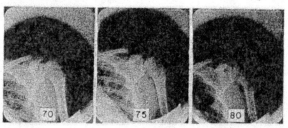

Figure 6-17. Direct Exposure Radiographs Made With a Grid To Show Influence of Large kVp Increments on Density.

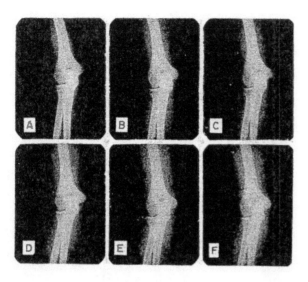

Figure 6-18. kVp—mAs Relationship. kVp and mAs (respectively) was: A-50, 75; B-60, 80; C-70, 50; D-80, 30; E-90, 20; F-100, 15.

It is then necessary to employ the nearest practical value. The resulting density difference is usually so small that it often is not recognizable.

(5) Table 6-3 may also be used to change from one mAs to another while keeping the density the same by adjusting the kVp.

(a) Problem: If 80 kVp is ordinarily used in making a PA of the chest employing 10 mAs at an FFD of 72 inches, and it is desired to examine a given anatomic structure using the same density but using an equivalent mAs of 50, what new kVp should be used to produce a density similar to that produced by the original 80 kVp and 10 mAs?

(b) Solution: Lay a straightedge between 80 kVp and 10 mAs. Note the point at which the straightedge crosses the reference line; then rotate the straightedge about this point until it crosses the mAs line at 50 mAs. The straightedge rests on 65 on the kVp line. The new kVp will be 65.

(6) Basically, the conversion of the factors just described, is nearly the same as the "50/15" rule. Using the 50/15 rule if the mAs is cut in half (reduced by 50 percent) the kVp is increased by 15 percent. By the same token if the mAs is doubled the kVp is decreased by 15 percent. For example, if 100 kVp and 20 mAs were used for a particular radiograph and it was necessary to reduce the mAs to 10, the new kVp would be 115.

d. Compensation for kVp-Density Effect:

(1) Accurate adjustment of the mAs cannot be established mathematically be-cause the thickness and tissue density of the human body exercise an unpredictable absorption influence. However, the new mAs as derived from table 6-3 produces a comparable density. As the kVp is increased, the mAs values are greatly reduced, thereby diminishing the radiation dose to the patient. The lower mAs values also contribute increased image sharpness since patient movement is virtually eliminated. Figure 6-18 depicts a series of direct exposure radiographs of the elbow, using screen-type film, made with a kVp range of 50 to 100 in 10-kVp increments and an FFD of 36 inches. By trial, the correct mAs value (80), was determined for the 60 kVp radiographs. The value 80 mAs was used as a basis for determining the balance of the mAs values to be used for all the other kVp. The overall image densities are approximately equal.

(2) No practical amount of mAs can compensate for insufficient kVp. Although the recognized technique for mammography is 20 to 30 kVp and many of the "high voltage" techniques are in excess of 120 kVp, most medical radiography is done within a range of 50 to 100 kVp. Excessive mAs values are dangerous to the patient. Figure 6-19 depicts a series of direct exposure PA radiographs of the hand on screen-type film and illustrates the futility of using an inadequate kVp. Factors used for the initial radiograph (A) were 30 kVp, 45 mAs, and an FFD of 36 inches. The mAs for each succeeding exposure was doubled, reaching 1,400 for the sixth exposure (F). By exposing the hand with 50 kVp, 50 mAs, and an FFD of 36 inches, a diagnostic image was obtained (G)—all densities are translucent and details in the entire image are clearly recorded.

e. Overexposure and Underexposure With Kilovoltage:

(1) Overexposure. When greater than necessary kVp is used, the overall density appears high, perhaps translucent, with SR fog (left, figure 6-20); the contrast scale is degraded, and detail is obscured. Usually, a reduction of 10 to 20 kVp will correct the appearance (right, figure 6-20). It may be necessary to adjust the mAs factor slightly. To avoid overexposure due to kVp, the optimum kVp for routine projections listed in table 6-8 should be adhered to.

(2) Underexposure. Use of inadequate kVp is characterized by blank transparent areas without silver deposit and other areas having high densities—few intermediate tones of density are present (figure 6-21). An increase of 15 to 20 kVp will usually produce sufficient penetrating radiation to obtain the

Table 6-3. Calculations of kVp-mAs Adjustments.

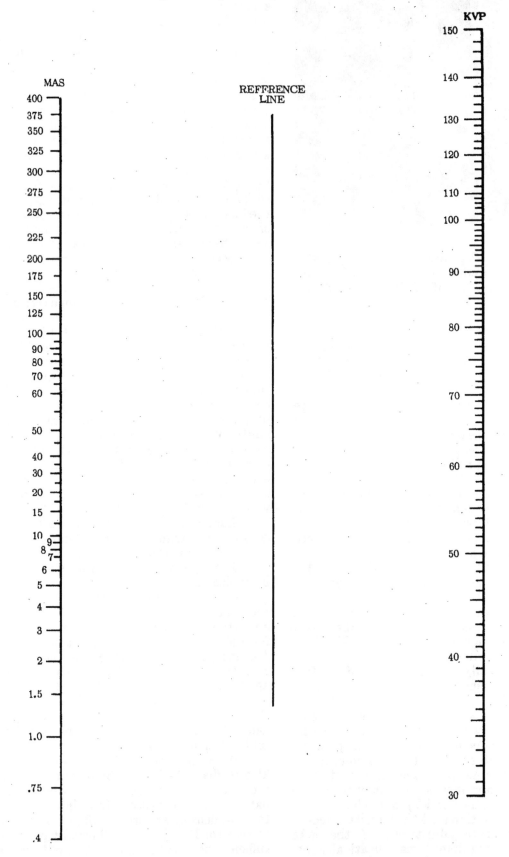

necessary detail, provided the mAs is also adjusted.

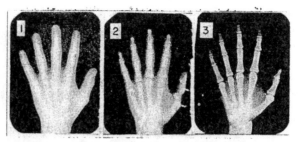

Figure 6-21. Low kVp Films. 1-120 mAs; 2-240 mAs; 3-480 mAs.

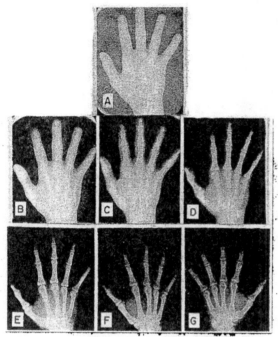

Figure 6-19. Direct Exposure Radiographs to Demonstrate That Insufficient kVp Cannot Practically Be Compensated by mAs.

b. Contrast Without Fog:

(1) Figure 6-23 consists of a series of radiographs of a dried skull and illustrates the influence of kVp on contrast. The absence of fluids in the specimen eliminates in large measure the influence of SR on the image. The images, therefore, may be considered free of SR fog. The radiographs were exposed in 5 kVp increments from 45 to 100 kVp. The density effect of each kVp was offset by compensating mAs (table 6-3). As a guide in mAs compensation, a step-wedge was recorded in each radiograph—the density of its third step being used as a "control." This density was maintained constant for all kVp. The procedure made it possible to dem-

6-12. Kilovoltage and Contrast:

a. General. Since the visualization of detail is dependent upon radiographic contrast kVp becomes an important factor in detail delineation. Radiographic details cannot become visible unless the radiation is able to penetrate the part being examined. When the radiation is optimum for a given part, numerous details become visible because of the large number of small density differences (figure 6-22).

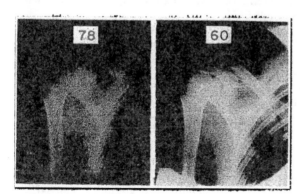

Figure 6-20. Radiographs Showing Effect of kVp Overexposure.

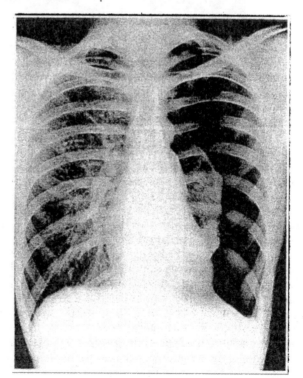

Figure 6-22. Radiograph of the Chest Demonstrating the Wide Range of Radiographic Densities Required for Diagnostic Purposes.

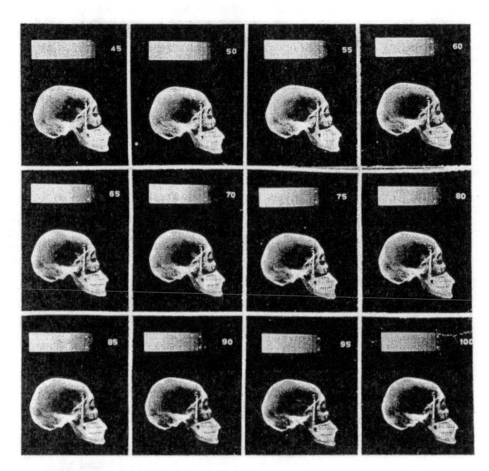

Figure 6-23. Direct Exposure Radiographs of a Dried Skull Demonstrating the Influence of kVp on Contrast and Its Relation to the Visualization of Detail.

onstrate the contrast characteristics of each skull image produced by each advance in kVp.

(2) In the 45 kVp film, there are very high image densities and also areas in which no details appear because of a lack of sufficient silver deposit. Penetrating radiation was needed to traverse the thicker and denser structures, such as the jaws, partes petrosae, and superior portions of the vault. With an increase in kVp, some details in these latter structures appear. At 90 and 100 kVp, all structures were thoroughly penetrated and all radiographic details are visible. In comparing the 45 kVp and 100 kVp radiographs, a difference in "brightness" of the images is manifest. The lower kVp film attracts the eye at once because of its brilliance; short-scale contrast exists. The eye ignores the absence of a large number of details representative of the anatomy. The few details adequately recorded are composed of rather heavy silver deposits and a rapid fall-off in image density occurs in areas representing the thicker or denser anatomical structures. Also, the distribution

in densities is unequal at 100 kVp, there is a uniform distribution of translucent densities over the entire image. This radiograph has a lower level of "brightness," but the image contains an abundance of details which are so necessary for diagnostic purposes; long-scale contrast exists. The contrast scale lengthens as the kVp rises. Examples of long-scale contrast radiographs are shown in figure 6-24.

(3) This does not mean that low kVp always produces radiographs of inferior quality. Some soft tissue examinations, for example mammography, require low kVp for differentiation of tissues. (See section on mammography elsewhere in the text.)

6-13. Kilovoltage and Exposure Latitude:

a. General. Exposure latitude varies with the kVp applied and is the range between minimum and maximum that will produce a diagnostically acceptable scale of translucent densities. Exposure latitude is an important element in any standardized exposure system. Depending upon the kVp used, the term "correct exposure" may mean that

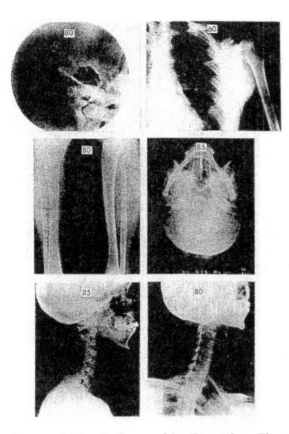

Figure 6-24. Radiographic Examples That Exhibit an Abundance of Details Made Possible by the Use of Optimum kVp for the Part.

many different exposures can be used to yield diagnostically acceptable radiographs. Use of an optimum kVp technique is more likely to produce greater uniformity of radiographic results than does the use of rela-

tively low variable kVp techniques. A general rule is: The longer the scale of radiographic contrast, the greater is the exposure latitude.

b. Wide Exposure Latitude:

(1) When optimum kVp values are used, the exposure latitude is wide because long-scale contrast is produced in the image which can compensate at times for wide errors in mAs. The large number of densities of small tonal differences produced by the more penetrating radiation serves to retain image details in the thin and thick portions of the part.

(2) Figure 6-25 depicts a series of AP direct exposure radiographs of the elbow in which the optimum kVp was 60, the FFD 30 inches and the mAs varied in steps of 15 mAs from 30 to 165 mAs. The exposure latitude may be considered to range between 60 and 150 mAs because visualization of all required details was attained in the images although they possessed varying degrees of density. The extremes in density shown in this range, however, are not recommended for routine radiography. Selection of the optimum density may be made by choosing three adjacent radiographs in the series that approach nearest to the required density—75, 90, and 105 mAs. A desirable density may be considered as produced by about 90 mAs.

c. Narrow Exposure Latitude:

(1) Exposure latitude is usually narrow when short-scale contrast prevails, as produced by the lower kVp. The small number of usable densities present requires that exposure be more nearly correct to obtain densities representative of the thinnest or the

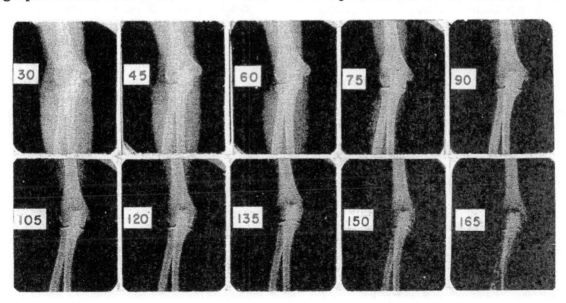

Figure 6-25. Direct Exposure Radiographs of the Elbow Demonstrating Exposure Latitude.

thickest portions of the part. The scale of contrast, however, is seldom such that all desired tissues are shown in the same image, particularly of a subject that contains structural details of widely different tissue densities. Also, the mAs values required are usually so great as to be impractical in application.

(2) Figure 6-26 depicts a series of three screen-grid lateral radiographs of the skull, made with 55 kVp, 36-inch FFD, and 50, 100, and 150 mAs. The 50 mAs image is underexposed (the image of the vault contains little silver); the 100 mAs radiograph shows the facial bones with excessive silver deposits although the partes petrosae are not penetrated; and the 150 mAs image shows opaque silver deposits in the facial area, the vault is well shown but the partes petrosal area was not recorded. The extremes of short-scale contrast are exhibited in this image—opacities and transparencies that make only a small portion of the image fully informative.

SECTION E—FACTORS INFLUENCING SECONDARY RADIATION FOG

6-14. Introduction. Secondary radiation fog, a supplemental density, is a fairly uniform veil of silver overlying the image density produced by RR. Caused by SR action, SR fog affects the visualization of detail—the quality of the image is degraded. By controlling the amount of SR reaching the film, details become more pronounced with resultant improvement in image quality. Figure 6-27 consists of radiographs that exhibit SR fog —the images have a dull gray appearance and lack important details.

6-15. Influence of Tissues:
a. The quantity of SR emitted by human body tissue depends upon:
(1) Tissue Thickness. The radiation emerging from a tissue thickness of 6 inches may assume a ratio of SR to RR of 5 to 1— and with greater thicknesses it may rise to 10 to 1. Relatively little SR fog will appear on radiographs of thin parts of the body (such as the hand, wrist, elbow, foot, and ankle).

(2) Tissue Density. The greater the fluid content (hydration) of a tissue, the larger the amount of SR emitted.

(3) Kilovoltage Used. See paragraph 6-16.

b. Since the structural composition and thickness of a normal body part are relatively constant, the amount of SR emitted may be considered as a constant for a given kVp. Wherever there is a physiologic departure from the normal, the possible adverse effects of increased SR must be considered. For example, as a result of injury or disease, an invasion of fluid into a knee joint would produce a larger quantity of SR than would a normal knee. Exposure factors and use of SR-controlling accessories (beam restricting devices and grids) must be varied to compensate for the change in tissue density.

6-16. Influence of Kilovoltage:

a. General. The characteristics of PR can be changed by kVp, resulting in control of SR fog and favorable image quality. As the kVp is increased, the quantity of fog produced may reach a point where it exceeds the density produced by RR, which, then, i almost completely hidden because of the predominance of fog.

b. Milliampere-Seconds Compensation for Kilovoltage:

(1) In figure 6-28 a series of chest radiographs illustrate that as kVp advances, radiographic density and fog increase. These radiographs were exposed with a range of 50 to 100 kVp in increments of 10 kVp; the mAs and all other factors were constant. The emitter of SR in this case is a human thorax. In the 50 and 60 kVp radiographs, no perceptible fog is shown in the images. In the 80 kVp radiograph the overall density increased, and the fog density can be visually separated from the density produced by RR.

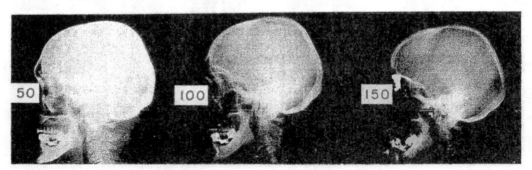

Figure 6-26. Lateral Screen-Grid Radiographs of the Skull at 55 kVp.

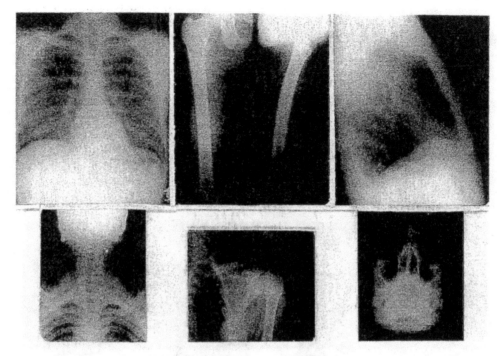

Figure 6-27. Radiographs That Exhibit Evidence of SR Fog.

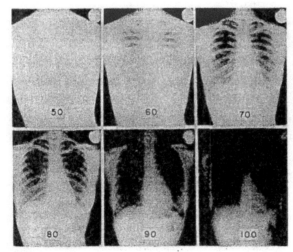

Figure 6-28. Series of Radiographs Demonstrating That as the kVp Advances and All Other Factors Are Constant, Radiographic Density Increases.

The combined densities rapidly gain in silver concentration as kVp advances. The fog density is obvious in the 90 and 100 kVp radiographs.

(2) To balance the radiographic densities and secure a satisfactory image, mAs must be changed to offset the density influence of increased kVp, along with measures to diminish the amount of SR. Figure 6-29 depicts a series of PA radiographs of the chest, with a range of 40 to 100 kVp in increments of 5. The overall density effect of kVp was compensated by using mAs values derived by the use of table 6-3. All the radiographs are relatively free from fog and the images more nearly in accordance with their true tissue-absorption pattern. Since the 90 and 100 kVp radiographs (K and M, figure 6-29) show a small amount of fog, 80 kVp (I, figure 6-29) seems to be the optimum value to use in PA chest radiography.

SECTION F—METHODS OF CONTROLLING FOG

6-17. Kilovoltage. When reducing the kVp as a means of reducing fog, image details distant from the film may still be fogged. Given correct exposure, structures nearer the film are usually rendered with satisfactory contrast because only a small amount of SR undercuts them. Use of lower kVp helps to increase the contrast of the nearer structures, but often results in insufficient penetrating radiation. Use of higher kVp is accompanied by appreciable amounts of SR depending upon the volume and density of the tissue irradiated. Therefore, in a given projection, there is a lower limit and an upper limit to the kVp that can be used and still secure good radiographs reasonably free from fog. Between these limits is an optimum kVp that assures penetration of the structures with a minimal acceptable fog level for

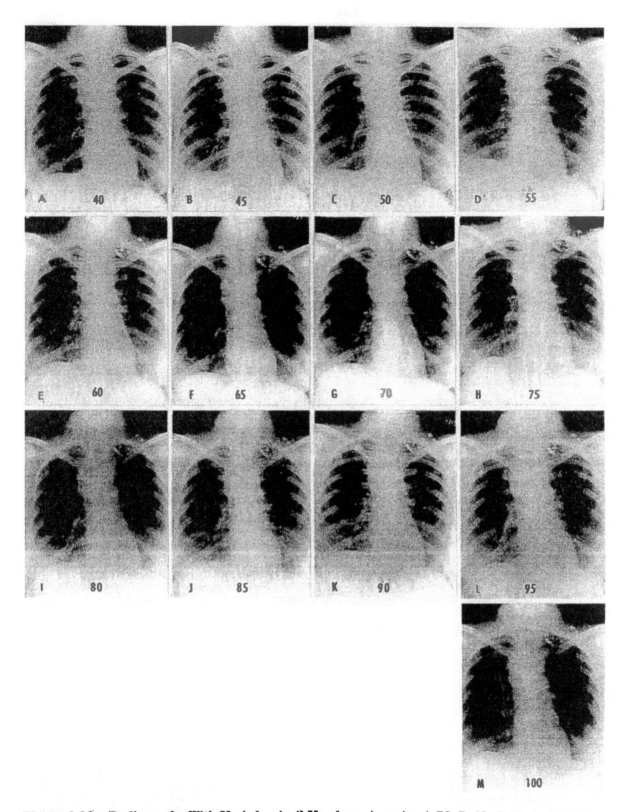

Figure 6-29. Radiographs With Varied mAs (kVp shown). mAs, A-70, B-40, C-20, D-10, E-8.3, F-6.3, G-5, H-4.1, I-3.3, J-2.5, K-2, L-1.6, M-0.6.

all thicknesses of a given part. These image characteristics are premised upon efficient control of SR.

a. Effects of Higher Kilovoltages. Radiographs made with the higher kVp often exhibit excessive densities (overexposure). The heavy densities in the image make it difficult to determine how much is due to overexposure by RR or by uncontrolled SR. Rather than disturb the basic contrast provided by the kVp employed, the easiest initial procedure to correct the high density is to halve the mAs, proceeding on the assumption that excessive fog is present. Thus, the density will be reduced to a value that may be correct or enable judgment of further adjustment; the excessive fog will have been decidedly reduced. The PA screen radiographs of the chest in figure 6-30 demonstrate a typical example of the condition described. Radiograph A was made with 80 kVp and 6.66 mAs; B, with 90 kVp and 5 mAs; C, with 100 kVp and 3.33 mAs; and all at a 72-inch FFD. Heavy densities are shown. When all the mAs values were halved and the kVp remained constant (D to F, figure 6-30), the overexposures were corrected and the high level of SR fog reduced to an acceptable level. By using this rule-of-thumb method of halving the mAs when overexposure occurs or of doubling the mAs when underexposure exists, an image more in keeping with the desired result can be obtained. If the quality is not satisfactory, an additional small mAs adjustment should usually provide the desired result. The kVp need not necessarily be reduced.

b. Effects of Lower Kilovoltages. When lower kVp is used, overexposure does not become complicated by excessive SR fog. It is only necessary to halve the mAs value to obtain the approximately correct density, or to make a further small adjustment of the mAs to secure the best quality. The kVp should not be changed. Figure 6-31 depicts two PA radiographs of the hand made with 50 kVp and 100 mAs (figure 6-31A) and 50 mAs (figure 6-31B). The image in A, figure 6-31, shows low fog level; by halving the mAs, a satisfactory image could be obtained.

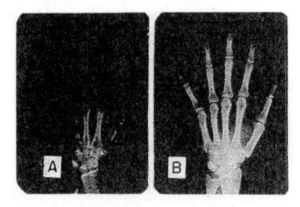

Figure 6-31. Two PA Radiographs of the Hand.

6-18. Grids. Secondary radiation is not only produced by the scattering of the primary beam by the atoms of the patient's body structures but also by the X-ray beam passing through the top of the X-ray table. In passing through the body, the primary beam sets up numerous centers of SR throughout the irradiated part (figure 6-32). The rays emitted from these centers within the body produce fog which covers the image on the film. The larger the volume of body tissue irradiated, the greater the fogging effect upon the film.

a. Function of Grids. The function of a grid is to absorb SR emitted by body tissues before it reaches the film. Although all SR cannot be absorbed by the grid, it can be greatly reduced. The two types of grids most commonly used are the stationary grid and the moving grid (P-B diaphragm); the basic principle and structure are the same.

b. The Stationary Wafer Grid:

(1) Description and Use. The stationary wafer grid is composed of alternate strips of lead and a radiotranslucent (X-ray transparent) substance, such as wood, aluminum, or a synthetic material. The strips are placed parallel to each other and form a very

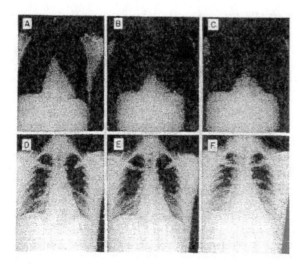

Figure 6-30. Series of PA Screen Radiographs Showing Typical Examples of Higher kVp.

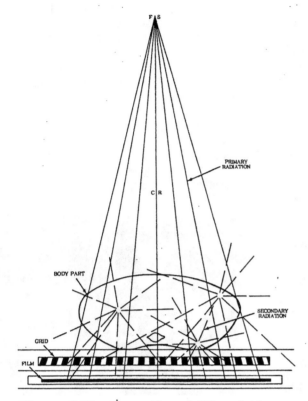

Figure 6-32. Formation of SR and Absorption of Same by Lead Strips in the Grid.

thin rectangular sheet the same size as the X-ray film. The grid is inserted between the patient and the cassette which contains the film so that the strips are lined up vertically beneath the patient's body. The PR emitted from the FS of the tube passes between the lead strips to reach the film. Since the direction of the SR cannot be controlled it is emitted in angles in all directions. Most of it strikes the lead strips at large angles and is absorbed, thus having little effect upon the film (figure 6-32). As much as 90 percent of the SR can be absorbed by the stationary wafer grid. The use of such a grid, therefore, greatly increases the diagnostic value of the radiograph because of the improved quality of the radiographic image. Although an image of the lead strips of the grid appears on the radiograph as evenly spaced thin white lines, they are not a disadvantage from the diagnostic standpoint. At the normal viewing distance of about 30 inches, the lines can seldom be seen. Normally, wafer grids are focused, that is, the lead strips are not parallel (c(2) below). Special care must be exercised in the use of this type of grid. If it is used at a very short FFD, the beam will be too widely divergent and the periphery (boundaries) of the radiograph will be under-

exposed because the outer rays will be absorbed by the lead strips. The beam must also be exactly perpendicular to the center of the grid, for if it is tilted across the length of the lead strips, more of the rays will be absorbed on one side than on the other; and the edge of that side of the radiograph will be lighter.

(2) Necessity for Increasing Exposure. When a grid is used, it is necessary to increase the exposure. The lead strips absorb a considerable amount of energy, and the exposure must be increased by adding kVp or mAs. However, because the grid is very thin, there is so little increase in the object-to-film distance (OFD) that there is little distortion of the radiographic image.

(3) Grid Ratio. The effectiveness of a grid in absorbing SR is determined by the grid ratio. The grid ratio is that of lead strip depth to radiolucent spaces width. If the radiolucent spaces between the lead strips in a grid average 0.25 mm, and the lead strips are 2 mm deep, the grid ratio is $2 \div 0.25 = 8$. Such a grid would be called an 8:1 grid, a common grid ratio. The efficiency of grids increases with increased grid ratio. For example, an 8:1 grid ratio is more efficient than a 5:1 ratio. With the lower grid ratios, less fog is eliminated, but there is the advantage of more latitude in positioning and in selecting FFD.

(4) Use with Cassettes. Grids are available in varying sizes and are used according to the size of the cassette to be covered. However, if a cassette is smaller than the grid to be used, a wooden frame is placed around the cassette to support the grid. As the grid is quite thin, it would be bent if it were not supported in this manner when a heavy body part is positioned over it. The lightness of the grid makes it particularly suitable for use with portable equipment and in making radiographs of thick body parts in an upright position. Intensifying screens normally are used with the grids so that heavy exposures will not be necessary. Some body parts, however, can be X-rayed using the grid without a screen, particularly in radiography of the ribs, shoulders, or knees. In these instances, excellent detail and contrast can be produced without use of the screen, but at the sacrifice of giving the patient a large dosage of radiation. Grid cassettes containing a built-in grid in the front of the cassette are available.

c. The Potter-Bucky Diaphragm:

(1) The "Potter-Bucky diaphragm" is a grid which moves across the film during the

time of the X-ray exposure. It is placed between the patient and the cassette. The strips of lead and radiotranslucent substance composing the P-B diaphragm may be thicker than those of the stationary grids because the movement of the grid while the exposure is being made keeps the shadows of the lead strips from appearing on the radiograph.

(2) The P-B diaphragm in general use is a focused grid—the lead strips are inclined at such angles that if they were extended into space they would meet at a point (the "grid focus"). Ideally, the X-ray tube should be placed at this point (figure 6-33). The vertical distance between the grid focus and the center of the grid is the grid radius (R, figure 6-33). An 8:1 grid will be efficient if the FFD is not changed by more than plus or minus 25 percent of the grid radius; distances either more or less result in a proportionate decrease in density around the margins of the radiograph because of relatively increased absorption around the periphery of the beam (figure 6-34). The beam must not be tilted across the direction of the lead strips because it will decrease the density along the edge of the film. However, tilting the beam parallel to the long axis of the lead strips does not cause a variation in the density of the radiograph produced. (NOTE: When using a crosshatch grid, which is two linear grids placed one on top of the other, the CR should not be angled at all.) Since the P-B diaphragm is positioned under the top of the radiographic table with the lead strips parallel to the long axis of the table, the beam may be tilted along the table's long axis but must not be tilted across the table (b(1)

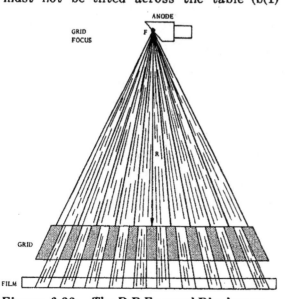

GRID FOCUS

ANODE

F

R

GRID

FILM

Figure 6-33. The P-B Focused Diaphragm.

above). To obtain the highest degree of grid efficiency, care must be taken to direct the tube toward the center of the grid. The decrease in the efficiency of a focused grid caused by an off-center position of the tube is in effect the same as angling the tube (figure 6-35).

(3) It is important that a focused grid, which has a "film side" and a "tube side," be placed correctly, with the film side toward the film and the tube side toward the target of the tube. Little or no exposure of the outer edges (peripheral regions) of the radiograph will result if the grid is inverted.

(4) In the P-B diaphragms, the 8:1 and 12:1 grid ratios are most commonly used. When changing from grid to nongrid, nongrid to grid, or from one grid ratio to another, appropriate changes in the technique must be made.

(a) One conversion system is outlined below:

Ratio	Nongrid to Grid	Grid to Nongrid
5:1	+ 15 kVp or 2.5 X mAs	− 15 kVp
6:1	+ 15 kVp or 2.5 X mAs	− 15 kVp
8:1	+ 20 kVp or 3.5 X mAs	− 20 kVp
12:1	+ 25 kVp or 4.5 X mAs	− 25 kVp
16:1	+ 30 kVp or 5.5 X mAs	− 30 kVp

(b) Another conversion system is as follows:

Ratio	Nongrid to Grid	Grid to Nongrid
5:1	+ 10% of kVp	− 10% of kVp
8:1	+ 15% of kVp	− 15% of kVp
12:1	+ 20% of kVp	− 20% of kVp
16:1	+ 25% of kVp	− 25% of kVp

NOTE: The system in this paragraph represents a change of 5 percent per ratio grid change.

(c) The different conversion systems given in (a) and (b) *above* represent two schools of thought. In (a) the nonlinear aspects of kVp are not considered important in this type of technique conversion. In (b) the nonlinear aspects are taken into consideration; consequently the kVp changes are in percentages. Both systems are expected to produce adequate results; however, additional compensations must be made if there is a change in the lines per inch of the grids.

(5) The movement of the P-B diaphragm during the X-ray exposure is accomplished

OFF DISTANCE CUT-OFF

A 24 INCH FFD

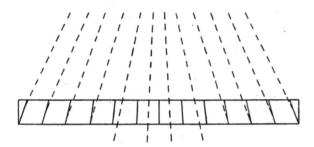

B 72 INCH FFD

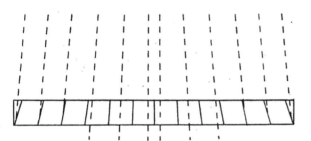

Figure 6-34.   The P-B Diaphragm—Effect of FFD.

OFF ANGLE CUT-OFF

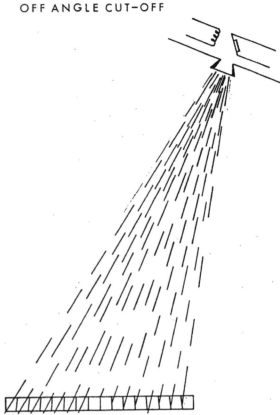

Figure 6-35.   Effect of Angled CR.

by a mechanism which moves the grid between the patient and the film. There are two general types of P-B diaphragms in use:

(a) The manual cock-type utilizes a spring which moves the grid across the film. Because the motion can be in but one direction and for only a limited distance, each time the grid is to be used the spring must be stretched by a cocking device and the grid held in place by a releasable catch. A hydraulic timing device is used to determine the speed of the grid motion. The speed should be slightly longer than the exposure time to insure motion of the grid during the whole exposure. The difference in grid time and exposure time should not be extreme, because if the grid moves too slowly the grid strips may remain in some areas for a longer period of time than in others. This will cause grid lines (shadows of the lead strips) to appear on the film. Just prior to exposure the grid is released by a manual or an electrical remote control switch. A bell is so placed as to ring upon completion of the grid motion

Ordinarily, the manual cock-type Bucky diaphragms should not be used for exposures shorter than 3/4 sec.

(b) The reciprocating grid utilizes an electric motor to move the grid back and forth above the film. The device that moves the grid is so designed that the time during which the grid stops at each end of its sweep is made as short as possible. No consideration need be given to the speed of the grid motion since that motion automatically starts at the beginning of the exposure and stops at its completion. Reciprocating grids may vary from one manufacturer to another; some have a grid speed that is identical in both directions, while others may have a slow sweep in one direction and a rapid sweep in another. Reciprocating grids may be used for exposures as short as 1/20 sec, however, some high-speed grids may be used for exposures of even shorter duration.

(6) The appearance of grid lines on the film when the Bucky is utilized is usually caused by the following errors:

(a) The exposure is started before the grid is travelling at full speed.

(b) The exposure is prolonged after the grid has stopped moving or the movement has slowed down.

(c) There is irregularity in the movement of the grid (may occur if anything rubs against the grid and restrains its motion).

(d) The tube target is not aligned with the center of the diaphragm.

(e) There is synchronism between the movement of the grid strips and pulsations in the tube current. If the speed of the grid is such that succeeding lead strips are always above a given point on the film at the same instant that the pulsations of the current produce X-rays (when a kVp is reached), images of the grid will appear on the film.

(7) The P-B diaphragm is especially useful in making radiographs of thick parts of the body. For such radiographs, cassettes with intensifying screens should be used because relatively heavy exposures are necessary. The P-B diaphragm normally is not to be used with cardboard holders.

6-19. Cones, Cylinders, Diaphragms, and Collimators:

a. Modification of the Primary Beam. SR can be reduced by modifying the primary beam. In the use of conventional equipment, *the amount* of SR is increased if the kVp is increased to a high value. To keep the SR as low as possible, the kVp should never be excessively high unless heavier filtration of rays and grids with a high grid ratio (12:1 or 16:1) are used. If the volume of irradiated tissue is kept as small as possible, the quantity of SR will be reduced in proportion. For this reason, the size of the field of entry of the X-ray beam must be limited to the smallest possible area that will cover the body area of diagnostic interest. The X-rays that strike the body area being exposed should be limited to a field no larger than the film that is used. The size of the field of entry is restricted by placing beam restricting devices: cones, cylinders, diaphragms, or collimators in the path of the primary beam. Figure 6-36 shows a cone, a cylinder and a diaphragm.

b. Cones, Cylinders, Diaphragms, and Collimators. Besides reducing the amount of SR produced (figure 6-37) and thereby improving the quality of the final film, these devices also reduce radiation damage to the patient by reducing the volume of tissue irradiated. These devices are placed as close to the X-ray tube as its housing will permit; in this way, they absorb the wide angle radiation that would not form a useful image on the film. Cones, cylinders, diaphragms, and collimators do not focus or bend the X-ray beam

—they absorb the unwanted part of the beam instead.

(1) Cones. A cone-shaped metal tube which absorbs the unwanted divergent rays from the X-ray beam (A, figure 6-36). The purpose of the cone is to produce a limited beam of radiation, so that a specific size film is completely covered.

(2) Cylinders. A cylindrically shaped metal tube which absorbs the unwanted part of the beam (B, figure 6-36). The cylinder differs from the cone in that the cylinder is designed to project a small beam of radiation to the center of the film. The cylinder is usually adjustable; an extension cylinder may be extended in length. As the cylinder is lengthened, the cone field becomes smaller; as it is shortened, the cone field becomes larger.

(3) Diaphragms. A diaphragm consists of a piece of lead with a small hole cut into it (C, figure 6-36). Unwanted radiation is absorbed by the lead, while useful radiation passes through the hole to the film. The diaphragm usually is used only when cones or cylinders are not available. Diaphragms may be made to produce almost any size cone field desirable.

(4) Collimators. The best all around device for restricting the primary beam is the collimator. It has a series of adjustable shutters which provide a variety of square and rectangular shaped X-ray fields. In addition, the collimator projects a light which indicates the actual x-ray field.

(a) Collimators should be checked periodically to make sure the "light" field coincides with the "radiation" field. This test can be done by marking the boundaries of the light field on a cassette with some opaque markers, and making an exposure. If the light field and the radiation field do not coincide, the discrepancy will show up on the processed film and appropriate adjustments can be made on the collimator. See the manufacturer's brochure before making adjustments.

(b) Some collimators are automatic; that is, they automatically adjust to the film size when the Bucky tray is used.

c. Geometry of Film Coverage. Using the principle of similar triangles, the size of the cone field can be determined for cones, cylinders, or diaphragms. The factors which determine the size of the exposed area on the film (diameter of the cone field—DCF) are: (1) FFD, (2) the distance from the anode to the

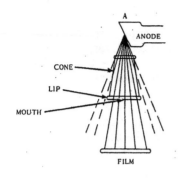

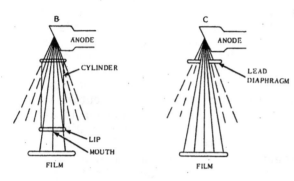

Figure 6-36. Cone, Cylinder, and Diaphragm.

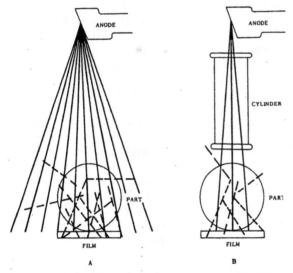

Figure 6-37. Effect of Cylinder on SR Formation.

lip or bottom of the cone (anode-lip distance —ALD), and (3) the diameter of the mouth of the cone (diameter of the cone—DC) (figure 6-38). Mathematically the relationship may be expressed as:

$$\frac{FFD}{ALD} = \frac{DCF}{DC}$$

When used with cones, the unknown factor is the DCF, in which case the FFD, ALD, and DC are dictated by the situation. When used with a cylinder, the FFD, DCF, and DC are always known, and the unknown factor is the ALD (the degree of extension of the cylinder). In this case, the ALD must be adjusted to produce the desired DCF. In making a diaphragm, the ALD is determined by the position of the filter slot in the tube head where the diaphragm is to be placed. If the FFD is fixed, a hole has to be cut that will produce the specific sized cone field. The size of the hole to be made can be found by solving for DC.

d. Ratio of Secondary Radiation to Remnant Radiation. The ratio of SR to RR emitted by thin parts is small, irrespective of the size of the field, because of the small amount of tissue irradiated. However, this does not hold true for the thicker and more dense structures, such as are shown in a series of PA screen radiographs (figure 6-39) of the frontal sinuses which were all exposed with the same factors. Radiograph A was made without a cone; the high image density is largely attributable to fog. Radiograph B was made with a large cone, and the fog is somewhat reduced. Radiograph C was made with a smaller cone, and the level of fog has been greatly reduced. Radiograph D was made with a cone of correct size, and the image contains all anatomic details clearly and with a minimal level of fog. When the entire area of a film is to be exposed, the x-ray beam should be limited to the film size if a collimator is used. If a cone, cylinder, or diaphragm is used, the diameter of the cone field should be no larger than the film diagonal.

SECTION G—FUNCTION OF MILLIAMPERE-SECONDS

6-20. Introduction. The mAs directly influences radiographic density when all other factors are constant. Either the mA or sec may be changed to conform to required radiographic exposures as long as their product —mAs—remains the same. This holds true on all direct X-ray exposures. However, intensifying screen exposure may show some loss in radiographic density when the exposure is exceedingly long because of failure of the reciprocity law. The mA is seldom changed for a given projection and may usually be considered as a constant; the sec can be readily changed and should constitute the variable in the mAs. For ease in computation, the mAs may be employed for a given projection rather than its components.

6-21. Rule of Thumb for Density Changes. It requires at least a 35 percent increase in

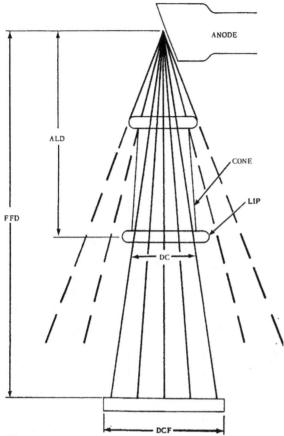

Figure 6-38. Determination of Film-Coverage Using a Cone.

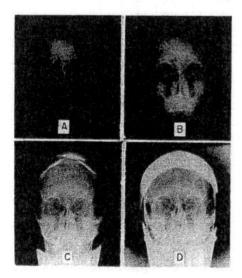

Figure 6-39. PA Screen Radiographs of the Frontal Sinuses Which Were All Exposed With the Same Factors.

mAs to produce a discernible increase in density. To produce a worthwhile increase or decrease in density, a rule of thumb can be employed to effect density changes in an or-

derly and easy manner. When the kVp and processing are constant, to change density, either double or halve the initial mAs value, depending upon the requirements. If further alteration is necessary, an intermediate change either way from the last mAs used should produce the desired density, or one so close that only a slight adjustment of the mAs value is needed.

6-22. Reciprocity Law. An important photographic law formulated in 1875 states that the reaction of a photographic emulsion to light is equal to the product of the intensity of the light and the duration of exposure. This phenomenon occurs in radiography only when direct exposures are made. When intensifying screens are used, the law does not strictly hold true, because exposure of the film under these circumstances is chiefly caused by the fluorescent light emitted by the screens and very little by the direct action of X-rays. Failure of this law may be observed when the radiographic density is greater upon short exposure with a large quantity of fluorescent light than that produced by a long exposure and a small amount of fluorescent light even though the total quantity of X-radiation exposing the film remains the same, that is, mAs. It is not necessary to be concerned about this effect in routine work, for it is seldom encountered because of the speed of the X-ray film emulsion; therefore, the mAs value may be considered reliable for use as an exposure factor in general radiography. For example, approximately the same radiographic density will be obtained whether 50 mA is used for 1/10 sec or 10 mA for 5/10 sec—both conditions entail the use of 5 mAs.

6-23. Tables of Milliampere-Second Values:

a. Tables 6-4 and 6-5 make possible rapid determination of mAs values when the sec and the mA are known. Table 6-4 lists the common fractional exposures and the number of impulses employed for short exposures. Table 6-5 lists exposure times of longer duration. The mA values in each table are identical. To use the tables, find the exposure to be used in the left-hand vertical column; then, in the horizontal row at the bottom of the table, find the mA value to be used. The required mAs value is found at the point where these two columns intersect.

b. In computing mAs values, it is often convenient to use the decimal equivalent of the exposure time fraction. Table 6-6 lists decimal equivalents of commonly employed exposure fractions. The numerators of frac-

Table 6-4. mAs Values Derived by Multiplying Specific mA and Time Values (Impulses (1/120 sec) and Time Fractions).

Milliampere seconds

Impulses	Time (seconds)	10	15	20	25	30	50	100	150	200	300	400	500
2	1/60	0.16	0.25	0.33	0.41	0.5	0.83	1.66	2.5	3.33	5.	6.66	8.33
3	1/40	.25	.37	.5	.62	.75	1.25	2.5	3.75	5.	7.5	10.	12.5
4	1/30	.33	.5	.66	.83	1.	1.66	3.33	5.	6.66	10.	13.33	16.66
5	1/24	.41	.62	.83	1.04	1.25	2.08	4.12	6.25	8.33	12.5	16.66	20.83
6	1/20	.5	.75	1.	1.25	1.5	2.5	5.	7.5	10.	15.	20.	25.
7		.58	.87	1.16	1.56	1.75	2.91	5.83	8.75	11.66	17.5	23.33	29.16
8	1/15	.66	1.	1.33	1.66	2.	3.33	6.66	10.	13.33	20.	26.66	33.33
9	3/40	.75	1.12	1.5	1.87	2.25	3.75	7.5	11.25	15.	22.5	30.	37.5
10	1/12	.83	1.25	1.66	2.08	2.5	4.16	8.33	12.5	16.66	25.	33.33	41.66
11		.91	1.37	1.83	2.27	2.75	4.58	9.16	13.75	18.33	27.5	36.66	45.83
12	1/10	1.	1.5	2.	2.5	3.	5.	10.	15.	20.	30.	40.	50.
13		1.08	1.62	2.16	2.77	3.25	5.41	10.83	16.25	21.66	32.5	43.33	54.16
14		1.16	1.75	2.33	2.91	3.5	5.83	11.66	17.5	23.33	35.	46.66	58.33
15	2/15	1.25	1.87	2.5	3.12	3.75	6.25	12.5	18.75	25.	37.5	50.	62.5
16		1.33	2.	2.66	3.33	4.	6.66	13.33	20.	26.66	40.	53.33	66.66
17		1.41	2.12	2.83	3.54	4.25	7.08	14.16	21.25	28.33	42.5	56.66	70.83
18	3/20	1.5	2.25	3.	3.74	4.5	7.5	15.	22.5	30.	45.	60.	75.
19		1.58	2.37	3.16	3.95	4.75	7.91	15.83	23.75	31.66	47.5	63.33	79.16
20		1.66	2.5	3.33	4.16	5.	8.33	16.66	25.	33.33	50.	66.66	83.33
21		1.75	2.62	3.5	4.37	5.25	8.75	17.5	26.25	35.	52.5	70.	87.5
22		1.83	2.75	3.66	4.58	5.5	9.16	18.33	27.5	36.66	55.	73.33	91.66
23		1.91	2.87	3.83	4.79	5.75	9.58	19.16	28.75	38.33	57.5	76.66	95.83
24	1/5	2.	3.	4.	5.	6.	10.	20.	30.	40.	60.	80.	100.
25		2.08	3.12	4.16	5.20	6.25	10.41	20.83	31.25	41.66	62.5	83.33	104.16
26		2.16	3.25	4.33	5.41	6.5	10.83	21.66	32.5	43.33	65.	86.66	108.33
27		2.25	3.37	4.5	5.62	6.75	11.25	22.5	33.75	45.	67.5	90.	112.5
28		2.33	3.5	4.66	5.83	7.	11.66	23.33	35.	46.66	70.	93.33	116.66
29		2.41	3.62	4.83	6.04	7.25	12.08	24.16	36.25	48.33	72.5	96.66	120.83
30	1/4	2.5	3.75	5.	6.25	7.5	12.5	25.	37.5	50.	75.	100.	125.
	Milliamperes	10	15	20	25	30	50	100	150	200	300	400	500

Table 6-5. mAs Values Derived by Multiplying Specific mA and Time Values (1/10 to 4 Seconds).

Time (seconds)	Milliampere seconds								
1/10	1	1.5	2	2.5	3	5	10	15	20
2/10	2	3	4	5	6	10	20	30	40
1/4	2.5	3.75	5	6.25	7.5	12.5	25	37.5	50
3/10	3	4.5	6	7.5	9	15	30	45	60
4/10	4	6	8	10	12	20	40	60	80
5/10	5	7.5	10	12.5	15	25	50	75	100
6/10	6	9	12	15	18	30	60	90	120
7/10	7	10.5	14	17.5	21	35	70	105	140
3/4	7.5	11.25	15	18.75	22.25	37.5	75	112.5	150
8/10	8	12	16	20	24	40	80	120	160
9/10	9	13.5	18	22.5	27	45	90	135	180
1	10	15	20	25	30	50	100	150	200
1 1/4	12.5	18.75	25	31.25	37.5	62.5	125	187.5	250
1 1/2	15	22.5	30	37.5	45	75	150	225	300
1 3/4	17.5	26.25	35	43.75	52.5	87.5	175	262.5	350
2	20	30	40	50	60	100	200	300	400
2 1/4	22.5	33.75	45	56.25	67.5	112.5	225	337.5	450
2 1/2	25	37.5	50	62.5	75	125	250	375	500
2 3/4	27.5	41.25	55	68.75	82.5	137.5	275	412.5	550
3	30	45	60	75	90	150	300	450	600
3 1/4	32.5	48.75	65	81.25	97.5	162.5	325	487.5	650
3 1/2	35	52.5	70	87.5	105	175	350	525	700
3 3/4	37.5	56.25	75	93.75	112.5	187.5	375	562.5	750
4	40	60	80	100	120	200	400	600	800
Milliamperes	10	15	20	25	30	50	100	150	200

Milliampere seconds

Table 6-6. Decimal Equivalents of Fractional Exposure Times.

	Decimal equivalents of fractional exposures												
	Numerators												
Denominators	1	2	3	4	5	6	7	8	9	10	11	12	Denominators
2	0.5	1.	1.5	2.	2.5	3.	3.5	4.	4.5	5.	5.5	6.	2
3	.333	.666	1.	1.33	1.666	2.	2.33	2.66	3.	3.33	3.66	4.	3
4	.25	.5	.75	1.	1.25	1.5	1.75	2.	2.25	2.5	2.75	3.	4
5	.2	.4	.6	.8	1.	1.2	1.4	1.6	1.8	2.	2.2	2.4	5
6	.167	.333	.5	.667	.835	1.	1.167	1.333	1.5	1.667	1.833	2.	6
7	.143	.286	.429	.572	.715	.858	1.	1.43	1.286	1.429	1.57	1.7	7
8	.125	.25	.375	.5	.625	.75	.875	1.	1.125	1.25	1.375	1.5	8
9	.111	.222	.333	.444	.555	.666	.777	.888	1.	1.111	1.222	1.333	9
10	.1	.2	.3	.4	.5	.6	.7	.8	.9	1.	1.1	1.2	10
11	.09	.18	.27	.363	.455	.545	.636	.727	.818	.090	1.	1.09	11
12	.083	.167	.25	.333	.415	.5	.583	.667	.75	.833	.917	1.	12
15	.067	.134	.2	.267	.333	.4	.467	.533	.6	.667	.733	.8	15
20	.05	.1	.15	.2	.25	.3	.35	.4	.45	.5	.55	.6	20
24	.042	.083	.125	.167	.208	.25	.292	.333	.375	.416	.458	.5	24
30	.033	.067	.1	.133	.167	.2	.233	.267	.3	.333	.367	.4	30
40	.025	.05	.075	.1	.125	.15	.175	.2	.225	.25	.275	.3	40
60	.017	.033	.05	.067	.083	.1	.117	.133	.15	.167	.183	.2	60
120	.008	.017	.025	.033	.042	.05	.058	.067	.075	.083	.092	.1	120

tions are listed horizontally at the top of the table, and the denominators are listed vertically in the columns to the left and the right.

The body of the table contains the decimal equivalents of various combinations of numerators and denominators.

6-24. Milliampere and Time Relation:

a. Rule. The mA required for a given radiographic density is inversely proportional to the time of exposure when the mAs is to remain constant. This rule may be expressed by the following formula:

$$mA_1 \times sec_1 = mA_2 \times sec_2$$
$$mA_1 = \text{original mA}$$
$$sec_1 = \text{original sec}$$
$$mA_2 = \text{new mA}$$
$$sec_2 = \text{new sec}$$

b. Problem. If 10 mA (mA_1) and an exposure time (sec_1) of 0.5 sec are employed in making a radiograph and it is desired to decrease the exposure time (sec_2) to 0.05 sec, what mA (mA_2) would be needed to assure comparable radiographic densities?

c. Solution. mA_1, sec_1, and sec_2 are known; mA_2, is unknown.

$$mA_2 = \frac{mA_1 \times sec_1}{sec_2}$$

$$mA_2 = \frac{10 \times 0.5}{0.05} = \frac{5}{0.05} = 100 \text{ mA.} \quad \text{Answer.}$$

6-25. Time-Density Relation.
When all other factors but time are constant, the quantity of X-rays emitted by the X-ray tube increases in direct proportion to the time of exposure. Thus, the quantity of X-rays applied in 1 sec is doubled when the exposure time is 2 sec. Since radiographic density is influenced by this action, increasing the time increases the density and vice versa (figure 6-40).

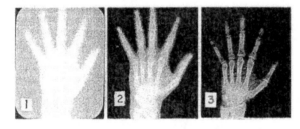

Figure 6-40. Influence of Sec on Density. #1-X Sec, #2-5X Sec, #3-10X Sec.

6-26. Experiment—Milliampere-Time Density Relation:

a. Purpose. The purpose of this experiment is to demonstrate the interrelation of mA and exposure time with respect to radiographic density when all other factors are constant.

b. Theory. The mA required for a given radiographic density is inversely propor-

tional to the exposure time when all other factors are constant.

c. Procedure. The mAs-density relation is demonstrated by three PA radiographs of the hand (figure 6-41), the materials and exposure factors being used are shown in table 6-7.

d. Comment. The radiographs (figure 6-41) demonstrate that as the mA is increased and all other factors but time are constant, time may be reduced to equalize radiographic densities. Since mA and time directly influence density, in actual practice the mA is usually established as a constant and the exposure time as a variable. Modern apparatus is usually calibrated with preset mA stations, and it is difficult to convert to manual control operation and accurately select all mA readings from the meters.

SECTION H—GEOMETRY OF IMAGE FORMATION

6-27. Shadows:

a. General. The formation of the radiographic image is dependent upon geometric conditions associated with its projection. Actually, the image is composed of various details that are renditions of the anatomical structures through which the X-ray beam passed. These details are defined by various degrees of sharpness and shape, depending upon the geometric conditions. "Definition" describes the sharpness with which the detail is recorded. Radiographic details are never points in the image but are minute areas of black metallic silver.

b. Shadows and X-ray Images. A shadow is a mass of darkness or shade produced on a surface by an object that intercepts a beam of light—it is a silhouette. An X-ray image is also a shadow, but it contains abundant details. Except for the physical laws for the formation of a shadow by light and those that make an X-ray image, there is no similarity between a shadow and an X-ray image. The shadow caused by light and the image produced by X-rays are very dissimilar in appearance. There is some resemblance between an image produced by a lens and that produced by an X-ray beam, but the means of production are entirely dissimilar. The laws governing the formation of a light shadow, such as size and shape of light source and its distance from the object and recording surface, have a definite influence on the size, shape, and peripheral sharpness of the shadow. This situation is comparable to the production of an X-ray image using such factors as an X-ray FS, FFD, OFD, et cetera.

Table 6-7. Mulliampere—Time Density Relation: Experiment.

Materials	Film	Screen-type, 8 X 10 inch.
	Exposure holder	8 X 10 inch cardboard holder.
	Cone	To cover exposure area.
Constant factors	Development	5 min. 68°F
	kVp	50
	FFD	36 inches
	Filter	1 mm aluminum
	mAs	50

Variable factors	Exposure No.	mA	Time
	1	10	5 sec
	2	50	1 sec
	3	100	1/2 sec

c. **Shadow Formation by Light:**

(1) *General.* When an enlarged though sharp shadow of the object is to be produced by means of light:

(a) The source of the light must be small.

(b) The source of the light should be at a practical distance to avoid objectionable enlargement.

(c) The recording card should be as close to the object as possible so as to avoid a great degree of enlargement.

(d) The light should be directed perpendicularly to the recording card.

(e) The plane of the object and the plane of the recording card should be parallel.

(2) *Illustration.* To demonstrate shadow formation by light, a source of light (LS), an opaque object (OB) to be projected by the light, and a recording card (RC) are needed. The plane of the object should be parallel to the plane of the recording card.

(a) *Point Light Source.* Assume that LS falls on the RC (A, figure 6-42), and the OB is interposed between LS and RC. A shadow (S) of the OB will be formed, the edges of which are sharply defined. The S naturally is larger than the OB. The degree of enlargement will vary according to the distance of the OB from RC and LS. When the OB is moved nearer the LS, the margins of the S are still sharply defined, but the S is larger (B, figure 6-42). When the OB is placed at the same distance from the RC, as shown in diagram B, but the distance from the LS is increased, the S is reduced (C, figure 6-42). In all these examples, the periphery of the S is sharply delineated because a point source of light was used; the size of the S, varied with the distance between the OB and the RC, as well as between the OB and the LS.

(b) *Area Light Source.* Assume another situation wherein the LS is a small area (D, figure 6-42) instead of a point. The relation of the OB to the RC is the same as shown in diagram B. Many points of light emanate from this source, and many light beams strike the OB; each, in turn, produces its S of the OB on the RC. The result of these combined S diffuses the margins of the image so that it is not sharply defined. The S produced in diagrams A, B, and C are umbras and their

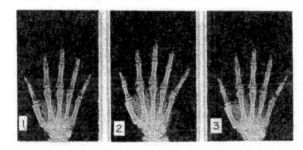

Figure 6-41. Effect of mA and Time on Radiographic Density When All Other Factors Are Constant.

margins are sharply defined. In diagram D, an umbra is present, but its margins are not sharp. The area of unsharpness is a penumbra (P). Some improvement in definition may be secured if the OB is placed nearer to the RC or if the LS is moved farther away.

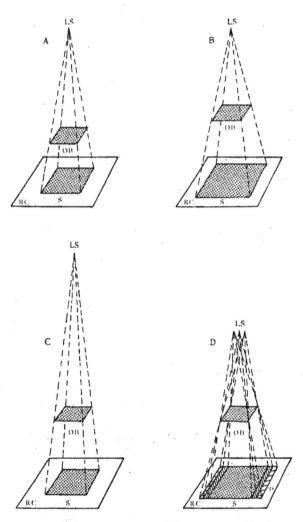

Figure 6-42. Diagrams Illustrating Shadow Formation by Light.

6-28. Image Characteristics:

a. General. Every radiographic image represents a projection on a two-dimensional surface of a number of body details disposed in a three dimensional medium. A spatial situation of this character produces distortions that are a departure from the actual situation; the depth factor is lost in some degree; and variations from the true shapes and sizes of the object occur. Consequently, the projection of the X-ray beam should be such that these image-degrading effects are reduced to a minimum. The source of the X-

ray beam is at the target in the x-ray tube, and it cannot be a point—it must be a small area. The size of the area varies with the electrical capacity of the tube. The radiographic image cannot ever be geometrically sharp because it consists of a large number of minute specks of silver located on both sides of the film base. The borders of the image are broken up into microscopic specks which the eye is not capable of seeing individually and which may seem to consist of diffused lines of configuration. The sharpness of detail is directly influenced by the width of the marginal diffusion.

b. Reduction of Unsharpness:

(1) Measures. Measures to reduce detail unsharpness to a minimum are:

(a) As small an FS as possible should be used, consistent with the safety limits of the electrical load on the X-ray tube.

(b) The FFD should be as long as possible, within practical working limits.

(c) The OFD should be minimal.

(d) The CR should pass through the center of the part and perpendicular to its major planes and that of the film.

(2) Influence of Factor Change. The effects of the above changes are illustrated in figure 6-43. In diagram A, an OB was placed so that the OFD was long; a large FS was used. The P as projected on the film was wide, indicating excessive image unsharpness that was also influenced by the relatively short FFD. The situation represents the worst sort of geometric relationship between image and OB. In diagram B, the same conditions prevailed as in A, except that a smaller FS was used. The narrower P indicates that less unsharpness was obtained. In diagram C, a long FFD was used with other conditions remaining as in A. The increased FFD narrowed the P, but not to the same extent as in B, where a smaller FS was used. In diagram D, the same conditions prevailed as in C, except that a small FS was used. The very narrow P indicates a decrease in unsharpness due to the use of a smaller FS. This condition should prevail when an appreciable OFD exists. Diagram E shows the OB close to the film; an average FFD and a large FS were used. A fair degree of sharpness was achieved, although a smaller FS as shown in diagram F, slightly improved the sharpness. Diagrams E and F illustrate that when the OB is close to the film, the size of the FS is, in a measure, immaterial when the thickness of the OB is within average limits. A large FS at a long FFD with the OB close to the film as shown in diagram G, produced a very narrow

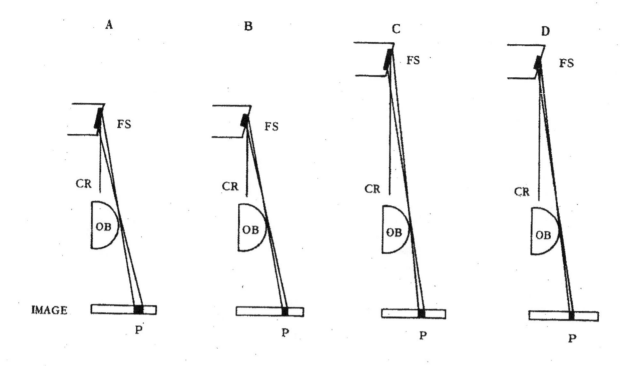

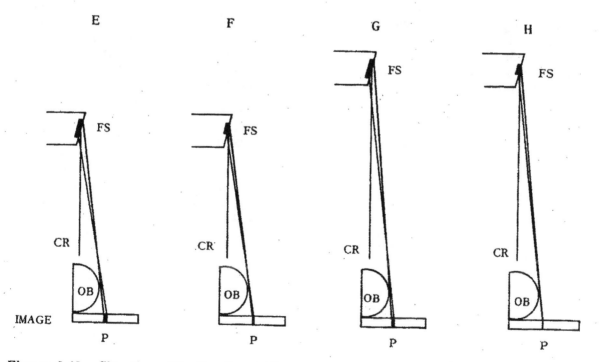

Figure 6-43.   Situations Affecting Image Sharpness.

P. By using a smaller FS under the same conditions as in G, the maximum sharpness was obtained as shown in diagram H. Of all the situations depicted in diagrams A through H, the image sharpness is at its maximum in H.

6-29. Types of Definition:

a. General. Definitions may be divided into three types: (1) geometrical unsharpness, which is influenced by the FS, OFD, or FFD; (2) motion unsharpness, which may be voluntary or involuntary on the part of the patient, or caused by vibration of the apparatus; and (3) screen unsharpness, which is influenced by the character of the screens and screen-film contact. All of these factors contribute to the total unsharpness. Correction of some factors may include unsharpness by some other factor. For example, if a radiograph were made without screens to ensure image sharpness, patient movement may cause blurring if a long exposure time is used.

b. Geometrical Unsharpness. Geometrical unsharpness is influenced by all factors of projection that alter the size, shape, and location of images of structures traversed by the X-rays.

(1) Influence of Focal Spot:

(a) The FS of the X-ray buse is comparable to the light source used in shadow formation. The influence of the FS on definition is confined to image sharpness. With all other factors constant, the smaller the FS, the sharper the definition. A large FS, although capable of withstanding high electrical energies, does not produce the sharpness of detail that is characteristic of tubes with a small FS. In some instances, a long FFD will aid in showing sharper detail when using a large FS, but it is generally advantageous to use a smaller FS with smaller tube capacities or a rotating anode tube. The relative unsharpness produced by a larger FS is immaterial when the object is close to the film.

(b) The site of the projected FS varies with the angle at which it is projected from the target (figure 6-44). When the projected FS is nearly perpendicular to the face of the target, it is large (4, figure 6-44), becoming smaller as the angle decreases toward the CR. The FS as projected at the CR (2, figure 6-44) is characteristic of the rated or effective focus of the tube. As the projected FS moves anode-wise from the CR, it becomes smaller (1, figure 6-44) until it reaches the limits of the anode side of the beam. At routine FFD, the differences in sharpness of

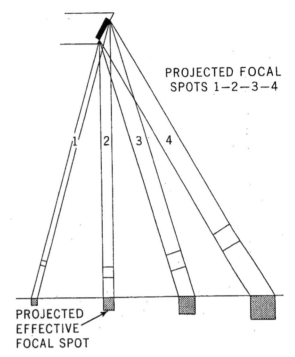

Figure 6-44. **Diagram Showing How the Size of the FS Varies With the Angle at Which It Is Projected From the Target.**

definition are minimal and difficult to determine visually.

(2) Influence of Object-Film Distance. When the object is at some distance from the film as shown in diagram B, figure 6-43, the sharpness is not as great as it is in F, figure 6-43, wherein the object is shown next to the film. The larger the OFD, the greater the unsharpness. The use of grids requires an increase in OFD, but the gain in contrast offsets the small amount of image unsharpness introduced. The effect of OFD is illustrated in figure 6-45. A series of four PA radiographs of a hand was made in which all factors were constant except the OFD. Radiograph A was made with the hand on the film; for B, the OFD was 2 inches; for C, 6 inches; and for D, 8 inches. As the OFD was increased, the size of the hand also increased.

(3) Influence of Focus-Film Distance. When a body part is placed on a film, image unsharpness is minimal, and its degree is directly attributable to the projected FS and the FFD. When a short FFD is used, the unsharpness increases. The image of the plane of the body part next to the film is always sharper than the image of the plane farthest away. At maximum FFD, definition is improved and the image is also more nearly the actual size of the body part. In all situations

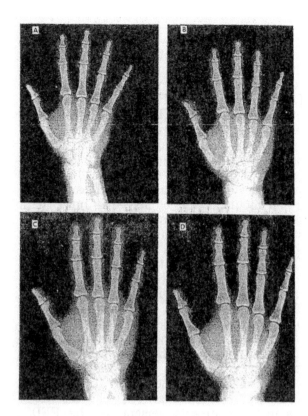

Figure 6-45. Radiographs With Various OFD.
A - no OFD; B - 2 in.; C - 6 in.; D - 8 in.

sharpness is improved as the FFD is increased. However, it is impractical to extend the FFD to the point where the unsharpness is less than the crystal size of the intensifying screens. Also, the greater the FFD, the greater the probability of introducing motion unsharpness because of the need for longer exposures. When a body part cannot be placed close to the film, the FFD should be increased beyond that normally used. A good beginning would be to double the normal value.

c. Motion Unsharpness. Motion of a body part being examined directly influences sharpness of image definition. The only means for controlling the effects of motion are (1) patient cooperation, (2) immobilization of the part being examined, and (3) short exposures.

(1) Voluntary Motion. Voluntary motion may take several forms. The noncooperative child who needs restraint is a common form. The patient who does not understand the manner in which he is to cooperate is usually the fearful one. An explanation of the procedure usually creates confidence. When in doubt, immobilize the part and use short exposures.

(2) Involuntary Motion. Involuntary motion is normally associated with the phy-

siologic activity of the body tissues. Respiration produces movement of the thorax and its contents so that short exposures are mandatory. The normal adult respiratory rate is 16 to 18 respirations per minute; in some pulmonary or cardiac lesions, the rate may be greater; in the newborn, it may be 30 to 40 per minute. Respiration also influences in some degree the viscera adjacent to the diaphragm. Movement of the heart and great vessels is an important radiographic factor. Functional activity of other abdominal viscera tends to produce motion.

(3) Effect of Motion on Image. The influence of motion in producing image unsharpness is shown in figure 6-46—the object moved during the exposure resulting in unsharpness in the margins of the image.

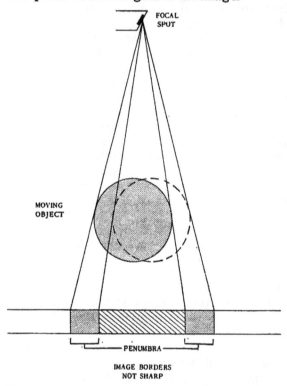

Figure 6-46. Diagram Showing the Influence of Motion in Producing Image Unsharpness.

(4) Immobilization. Immobilization is imperative in radiography, for differential diagnoses depend upon the visualization of sharp, undistorted images. Movement should be eliminated during the exposure to avoid blurring of details in the image.

(a) Composing the Patient. The X-ray technologist is responsible for keeping the body part immobile. Frequently, the patients are nervous and afraid; some may tremble. A few words of assurance will help put the patient at ease.

(b) Immobilization Methods:

1. Much of the success in obtaining a good radiograph is dependent upon the closeness and firmness with which the part is placed against the film-holder and the method of immobilization used. Even with short exposures immobilization is necessary. Proper immobilization assures comparison of symmetrical parts, for it also serves to prevent involuntary rotation of the part. The tube carriage should always be locked in position because its vibration is a common cause for blurred radiographs.

2. There are a number of good methods for immobilizing the body part, such as sandbags, compression bands, compression cones, and special clamps. Many of these devices for immobilization are found in the modern laboratory. An important aspect of immobilization is compression of tissues, particularly in the abdomen. By displacing some of the tissues, less SR is produced and better definition attained because of the improvement in contrast.

(c) An Advantage of Motion. Tissues in motion can in some instances serve diagnostic purposes, because their movement can be made to blur out undesirable details of superimposed structures. This can be effectively accomplished in lateral radiography of the thoracic vertebrae and the sternum.

d. Screen Unsharpness. The introduction of unsharpness when X-ray intensifying screens are used is discussed in Section I, this chapter.

6-30. Distortion:

a. General. Body parts are not always symmetrical since the body is an irregularly shaped object. Because of this, the radiographic image of a body part is sometimes misshapen, and the different portions of the area under exposure are not shown in correct relationship to each other. This untrue portrayal of the shape or size of a body part (or other object) in a radiograph is called distortion. There will be a certain amount of distortion in every radiograph, since the film upon which the radiographic image appears has only one plane, and the body part, or any other three-dimensional object radiographed, has many planes. There are two kinds of distortions: (1) magnified distortion, in which the image is larger than the object; and (2) true distortion, in which the image shape is different from the shape of the object.

b. Magnified Distortion:

(1) General. Magnification, or magnified distortion, in the radiographic image is a normal occurrence. The degree of enlargement is a function of the FFD and OFD. When the object is close to the film, enlargement is minimal. When the center of the part is traversed by the CR, normal magnification occurs. Whether the FFD is great or small, when a large OFD exists, the image will always be magnified to a degree. The use of a long FFD in these situations serves only slightly to increase the sharpness of definition and decrease the image size. Therefore, the film should always be placed as near the object as possible, even though some true distortion of the image may occasionally result.

(2) Effects of Magnified Distortion:

(a) Figure 6-47 illustrates the effects of magnified distortion. Two series of lateral radiographs of a dried skull were made in which the FFD varied. Radiographs A-D:A, 72 inches; B, 40 inches; C, 30 inches; and D, 20 inches. As the FFD was decreased, the images became larger. Radiographs E-H: FFD for E-H are the same as in A-D, but OFD was increased to 4 inches. Note the tremendous increase in enlargement as the FFD was decreased. The least enlargement is shown in each group at an FFD of 72 inches.

(b) Occasionally, an opaque object in the tissues may have a diameter less than that of the tube FS. If sufficient magnification is achieved by a reasonable OFD and a short FFD, the object may be visualized as a diffuse gray area. This condition is diagrammatically represented in figure 6-48, in which a small object (OB) at an extended OFD is shown projected by a larger FS (B, figure 6-48). If details composed the object, all image details would be blurred and indistinguishable, having only the gross shape of the object. If SR undercut the object, the blurred details would be superimposed by fog; any suggestion of image might then be entirely eliminated. In A, the object is shown projected by an FS smaller than the diameter of the object. The image would then contain details with small blurred margins.

c. True Distortion:

(1) General. Because the body is an irregularly shaped object, all body parts cannot be over the center of the film; nor can all tissue planes be parallel with the film. Some distortion of shape will always be present because some portions will be projected obliquely and their details distorted more than those in the center of the film. True distortion in a radiographic image is a variation from the true size and shape of a body part. It is most important that the size and shape of the image of various anatomical

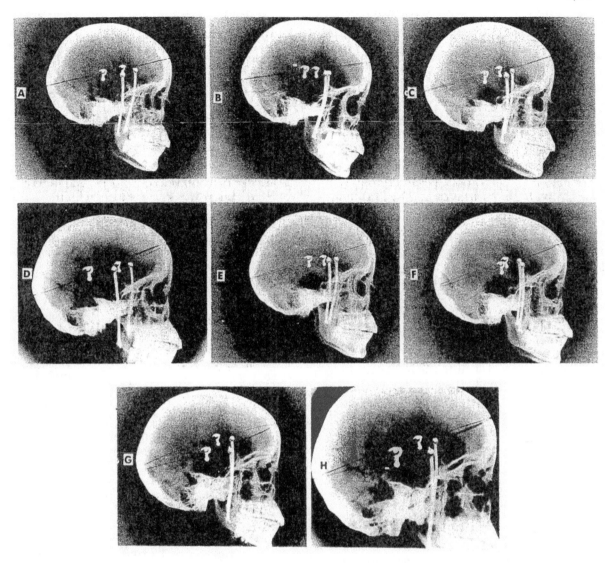

Figure 6-47. Lateral Radiographs of a Dried Skull Demonstrating the Influence of FFD and OFD on Magnification of the Image.

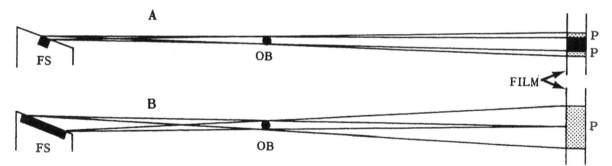

Figure 6-48. Effects of Magnification When the FS is Greater Than the Object.

structures be comparable to the original. There are occasions in which body parts are deliberately distorted to obtain more diagnostic information, as in PA radiography of the sinuses. In the main, however, the CR should be perpendicular to the plane of the film and the major planes of the object.

(2) Illustration of True Distortion. Figure 6-49, a series of radiographs of apertures made in a lead plate, illustrates the effects of true distortion. From left to right, the holes were numbered 1, 2, and 3. In diagrams A, C, and E, the FFD was 60 inches and in diagrams B, D, and F the FFD was 25

inches. An OFD of 2 inches was used. In all diagrams, the CR passed through the center of hole No. 1, and divergent portions of the X-ray beam passed through holes No. 2 and No. 3. Diagrams of the various positions assumed by the aperture plate with respect to the FS and film are shown. Below the diagrams are the radiographic images which were obtained under each set of conditions.

(a) Diagram A. All radiographic images exhibit magnified distortion because the 60 inch FFD permits projection of approximately parallel X-rays.

(b) Diagram B. Since the FFD was shortened to 25 inches, magnified distortion of the images resulted, although it is greater than that shown in diagram A. Some oblique radiation partially altered the shape of the No. 3 image.

(c) Diagram C. The aperture plate was tipped so that the right-hand edge rested on the film. The center of hole No. 1 was supported 2 inches from the film; the FFD was 60 inches. Besides magnification of all images, the horizontal image axis is foreshortened and true distortion of the original shape occurs.

(d) Diagram D. When the FFD is reduced to 25 inches, greater magnification and distortion are shown. Image No. 1 in diagrams C and D shows less distortion, because it is produced by the central portion of the beam containing the CR.

(e) Diagram E. The aperture plate was inclined in a reverse direction to that shown in diagram D, and at a greater angle to the film plane. The center of hole No. 1 is supported 2 inches above the film. An FFD of 60 inches was used. Magnification of the images in their vertical axes is shown in Nos. 1 to 3 but foreshortening of the horizontal image axes occurs, thereby producing true distortion.

(f) Diagram F. The FFD was reduced to 25 inches in this diagram, and the size and shape of image No. 1 is about the same as that shown in diagram E. However, because of the great angle at which holes No. 2 and No. 3 are inclined, considerable true distortion and magnification occur in image No. 2; No. 3 image assumes a more spherical form although greatly magnified.

SECTION I—X-RAY INTENSIFYING SCREENS

6-31. Introduction. X-ray intensifying screens are radiographically indispensable. Although they introduce some measure of detail unsharpness in the image, their value in radically shortening exposures and reducing motion unsharpness is of prime importance. Less than 1 percent of the X-rays exposing an X-ray film is absorbed by the emulsion, governing the formation of the latent image. A means for fully utilizing this small percentage of energy, without complicating the technical procedure, may be accomplished by the use of X-ray intensifying screens that serve to increase the effect of the X-radiation on the sensitized emulsion by means of fluorescence, thereby reducing the exposure. Certain chemicals have the ability to absorb X-rays and fluoresce or emit light. These chemicals are used in constructing intensifying screens.

6-32. Film Exposure Holders:

a. Direct Exposure Film Holders. Holders for X-ray film must have two characteristics: (1) protect the film from the light when taken to the X-ray exposure room, and (2) allow the film to be exposed to the X-ray beam to make the radiograph. The direct exposure film holder (usually referred to as cardboard or cardboard cassette) meets both of these requirements. These holders are made to fit the various film sizes. The cardboard holder has a light-proof envelope. The film must be placed in this envelope in the darkroom in the manner described in chapter 7. The front of the holder must face the X-ray tube, since there is a lead foil lining in the back of the holder to prevent fogging of the film by SR from the radiographic table (figure 6-50). Some direct exposure film holders are made of cardboard, and some are made of plastic. Those made of plastic are more durable and can be cleaned more easily than the cardboards.

b. Cassette. A "cassette" is a film holder about 1/2-inch thick with a metal frame (either aluminum or stainless steel), a front of bakelite, and a hinged lid with flat springs. It is used with two intensifying screens, one on either side of the film (figure 6-51). One screen is mounted on the inside of the lid, and the other on the inside of the bakelite front of the cassette. The lead foil backing in a cassette helps prevent fogging of the film by SR from below the cassette. The thickness of the lead is usually 0.025 inches unless the cassette is manufactured specifically for phototiming; then it is about 0.0025 inch. The cassette must also be loaded in the darkroom.

6-33. Intensifying Screens:

a. Intensifying screens are made by incorporating fine fluorescent crystals in a binding substance which is spread on one side of

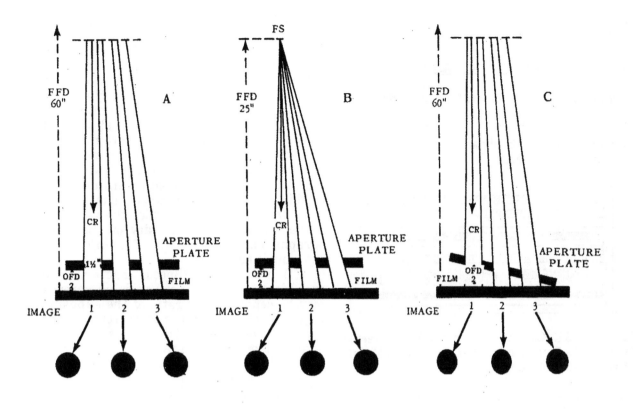

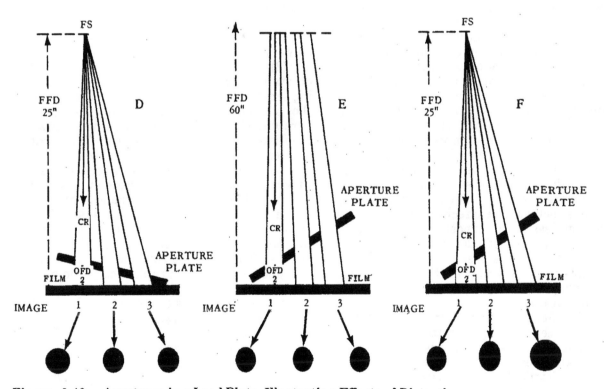

Figure 6-49. Apertures in a Lead Plate, Illustrating Effects of Distortion.

6-40

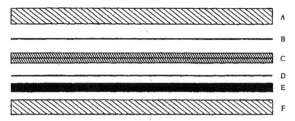

Figure 6-50. Cardboard. A—Front; B; D—Envelope; C—Film; E—Lead Foil; F—Back.

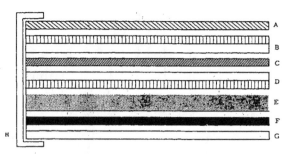

Figure 6-51. Cassette. A—Front; B; D–Screens; C-Film; E–Felt Cushion; F–Lead Foil; G-Metal Back; H–Metal Frame.

a piece of special cardboard. Calcium tungstate and barium lead sulfate are two such materials which emit light (fluoresce) when struck by X-rays. Either of these materials may compose the "active layer" of the intensifying screen.

b. Each of the numberless fine crystals on the intensifying screen emits light in every direction. When uniformly radiated, the intensifying screen appears to be uniformly bright. The film emulsion is sensitive to the blue light emitted by the fluorescent crystals. More than 90 percent of the density recorded on an X-ray film when intensifying screens are used is caused by the light emitted by the screens; the X-rays which strike the film directly cause less than 10 percent of the recorded density. Because intensifying screens increase the effect of the X-rays on the film, less X-ray exposure is required to attain the desired density. Intensifying screens have made possible the use of grid diaphragms, without which good quality radiographs of large anatomic areas could not be obtained.

c. The action upon the film of the intensifying screens of the cassette is effected in the following way. The X-rays pass through the translucent bakelite front of the cassette and strike the first intensifying screen. As the rays strike it, this screen emits light which affects the emulsion on the side of the film facing it. The X-rays penetrate to the film and sensitize it to a small degree. Some

of the X-rays also penetrate through the film, strike the back intensifying screen, and expose the emulsion on the side of the film facing it. It is for this reason that an X-ray film has coat of sensitive emulsion on both sides. Each side receives light from the intensifying screen which it faces. For maximum effectiveness intensifying screens should not continue to emit after the exposure has been terminated. This condition known as phosphorescence or screen lag is undesirable.

d. An intensifying screen is considered to be "high speed" or "fast" when a short x-ray exposure is needed to produce the required darkening of the film (density of the radiographic image) and "slow" if a long X-ray exposure is necessary.

(1) Intensifying (Speed) Factor. The speed factor of the two intensifying screens may be defined as the ratio of the exposure required without the use of screens to the exposure required with the use of the screens. Expressed as a ratio,

$$\text{intensifying (speed) factor} = \frac{\text{exposure without intensifying screens}}{\text{exposure with intensifying screens}}$$

Since the numerator is always greater than the denominator, the intensifying factor of the two screens is always greater than unity (one). Exposure with intensifying screens will be for a shorter time to produce the desired density in the radiographic image than without them.

(2) Crystal Size. The size of fluorescent crystals or grains used to coat an intensifying screen affect the speed of the screen and the sharpness of definition in the radiographic image. The larger the crystal size, the faster the speed of the screen. The light emitted grows broader as the size of the crystals increases. Therefore, a screen coated with the larger-sized crystals is a faster screen, but the detail and sharpness of definition of the radiograph are decreased. The smaller the size of the crystals, the slower the screen, but sharpness of detail is increased. There will be some decrease in the sharpness of the radiographic image no matter how small the crystals of an intensifying screen may be. This is true because the light emitted by a crystal is scattered by the adjacent crystals.

(3) Types of Screens. Intensifying screens commonly used are the slow speed (high detail), medium or par speed (medium detail), and fast or high speed (low detail). The effect of the crystal size on screen speed and on detail (definition) of the radiographic image is shown in figure 6-52.

(4) Screen Conversion Factors. Manufacturers of intensifying screens usually publish particulars for changing the technique from one screen to another. Dupont recommends the following for their Cronex* screens:

mAs Factor	Type of Screen
25	Medical film without screens
4	detail
2	fast detail
1	par speed
.5	hi-plus

For example, if 100 mAs were used with par speed screens and it was necessary to change to hi-plus screens, the new mAs would be 50 (100 X .5 = 50).

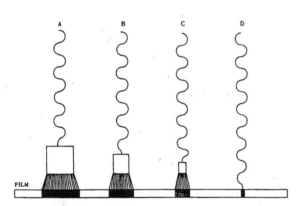

Figure 6-52. Effect of Large (A) and Small (C) Crystals on Speed and Detail. (D) Direct Exposure Is Slowest but Has Best Detail.

e. Perfect contact between the X-ray film and the two screens is required. The double-coated X-ray film must be evenly placed between the active faces of the two screens and must be in full contact with both. Any space between the film and the screen allows the rays emitted from the screen at that point to spread and produce blurring of the image at that location on the film (figure 6-53). Evenness of contact between the film and the two screens can be tested in the following way. A radiograph of a piece of wire screen is made. The screen is placed over the front of the cassette, and a film exposure is made using

*Registered trade mark of E. I. Dupont DeNemours & Co. (Inc)

50 kVp, 1.5 mAs, and 40 inch FFD. The image of the wire mesh will appear in sharp detail over the entire surface of the film if the contact is good. Wherever there is an area of poor contact, the image will be blurred.

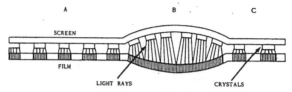

Figure 6-53. Screen Contact and Detail. A and C—Good Contact and Detail. B—Poor Contact and Detail.

6-34. Proper Care of Screens:

a. General. Because the intensifying screens influence the quality of the radiograph, it is very important that they be kept in good condition. Except when it is being loaded or unloaded, the cassette should be kept closed so as to keep the screen surfaces free of dust and protected from scratches.

b. Mounting. Only rubber cement or special adhesive tape should be used to mount intensifying screens. Do not use water-soluble paste. In older-type screens, one of the pair is thicker than the other; the thicker one is mounted on the lid of the cassette, and the thinner one in the front of the cassette.

c. Cleaning. Any foreign matter on a screen will absorb light during the exposure and cause white shadows to appear on the radiograph. For washable screens use cotton and a mild soap, rinse with wet cotton, and dry with dry cotton. Since the cardboard backing will absorb water and become warped do not use any more water than is absolutely necessary. Stand the cassette on its side, leaving it half open to dry in a room free from dust. There is one type of screen which may be cleaned with pure grain alcohol swabbed on with cotton (see the manufacturer's instructions); do not allow the alcohol to touch the letters appearing on the side of the screen as the printing may run and stain the surface of the screen. Whenever possible commercially produced antistatic cleaning solutions should be used.

d. Handling. Intensifying screens are very easily scratched, chipped, or nicked. They must be handled very carefully to keep them free of marks which will mar the radiographic image. Even the corner of a film brushing across the screen can scratch its surface. The technologist must be very careful not to scratch the screen with his fingernails in removing the film from the cassette.

6-35. Fluoroscopic Screen. Use of the fluoroscopic screen is based upon the same physical principles as the intensifying screen. However, the fluoroscopic screen not only fluoresces but also phosphoresces. Although phosphorescence is undesirable for intensifying screens, it is a necessary factor for fluoroscopic screens. The fluorescent material generally used to coat the active surface of a fluoroscopic screen is cadmium zinc sulfide. The fluoroscopic screen has a lead glass backing to protect the fluoroscopist.

SECTION J—STANDARDIZATION OF EXPOSURE

6-36. Radiographic Quality:

a. General:

(1) Uniform radiographic quality can only be achieved through complete control and standardization of exposure and processing procedures. The apparatus, X-ray tube, X-ray film, and processing chemicals have been scientifically designed to facilitate standardization. Sound judgment must be used when selecting the exposure factors and processing the exposed X-ray film. Also, a balance should exist in compromise between the exposure factors used, the clinical situation presented to the X-ray technologist, and the objective of the examination—the diagnosis. Radiographic quality should be evaluated along realistic lines. If the quality is not what the radiologist should reasonably expect, the practical reasons for failure should be investigated.

(2) Knowledge of the normal appearance of anatomic structures in the image and visual acuity in noting deviations from the normal are the tools which the radiologist uses in making his interpretations. Because an essential point in the radiographic diagnosis often appears in an inconspicuous portion of the image, a systematic analysis and evaluation of the entire image is necessary. This requires the entire image to be diagnostically informative and to have translucent silver deposits representative of the anatomic structures. The radiographic images must represent the true anatomic situation, and their appearance should always be fairly consistent. Standardized projections of an anatomic part always portray the structures in the same manner.

b. Criteria for Radiographic Quality:

(1) All image densities should be translucent when viewed before a conventional X-ray illuminator.

(2) All portions of the image should have some silver deposit. Areas devoid of silver deposit and those with excessive silver deposits are diagnostically useless.

(3) The part examined should be fully penetrated.

(4) The basic mAs factor should be selected so as to provide the best overall radiographic density for the patient whose measurement is within the average thickness range.

(5) Contrast should be such that differentiation between densities or details can be readily made.

(6) Image details should not be obscured by SR or chemical fog.

(7) Maximum sharpness and true shape of the image should be consistent with the clinical needs of the examination.

c. Contrast Extremes. To satisfy diagnostic requirements, there should be a good balance of densities. The extremes of the contrast scale in a radiogram—opacity and transparency—cannot reveal all the details of an image. Images that merely depict size, shape, or outline of the object are not satisfactory; there must be a multitude of gray tones to differentiate detail. There is, however, a limit to the number of tones necessary because differentiation between densities is difficult when the contrast scale is unduly lengthened. Through recognition of the value of long-scale contrast for a given projection, errors in the application of exposure factors can be corrected.

d. Contrast and Sharpness:

(1) General. Image contrast and sharpness are the basic factors in detail visibility. It is desirable to record with sufficient contrast slight variations in radiographic density of all details within the part examined and to show small differences over a wide range of tissue thicknesses in the same exposure. If all radiographic densities are translucent, there is, then, image representation of all tissue details because all elements within the part have been penetrated. The scale of contrast should not be shortened beyond the point where essential detail, when viewed before an X-ray illuminator, begins to be lost to the eye in the higher and lower densities of the radiograph; it is preferable to stop short of this limit so as to have sufficient latitude to allow for unavoidable density deviations that may occur because of unusual or unpredictable tissue absorption. As a rule, improvements in detail visibility of some body parts can be effected by increasing the contrast within limits. However, certain restrictions as to overall detail visibility are imposed. On occasion, small areas of image detail are rendered

brightly visible because the exposure factors may be optimum for the region. However, adjacent areas may be devoid of sufficient silver to produce a satisfactory overall image because the radiation did not penetrate all the tissues. Except for special cases, it is best to be satisfied with a lower image contrast and assured penetration that will reveal details in the overall image. The greater number of densities provided by long-scale contrast makes possible the visualization of a larger number of tissue components.

(2) Value of Total Impression. The evaluation of an X-ray image is dependent upon the distinctness of all the recognizable detail and not on contrast or sharpness alone. In the examination of unsatisfactory radiographs, these two qualities must be carefully evaluated. Generally, it is easier to correct unsatisfactory image sharpness by greater contrast, rather than the opposite. Figure 6-54 depicts a wide difference in contrast of two screen radiographs of the pelvis. Owing to the shorter exposure time for A, it is sharper than B and possesses a wide range of densities; however, the high contrast of B may create the impression of greater sharpness because of the exaggerated density values.

6-37. Formulation of a Standardized Exposure System:

a. Standardization Phases. The bulk of modern radiography is "production-line" effort. A standardized system for selecting and applying exposure factors must produce consistently good radiographic quality. In formulating a standardized exposure system, the ideal should establish all factors as constants with the exception of one as a variable. With kVp as the factor of penetration and radiographic contrast, mAs as the factor of radiographic density, and FFD and OFD as geometric factors influencing image sharpness, shape, and size, standardization of radiography revolves itself into four phases.

(1) Standardization of Processing Procedure—the reduction of time and temperature values to constants so that changes in radiographic density can be more properly attributed to exposure. Standardization of processing should normally be accomplished first.

(2) Standardization of Exposure Factors— the reduction of all exposure factors in a given projection to constants with the exception of one variable (mAs).

(3) Standardization of Exposure Techniques—the division of exposure techniques

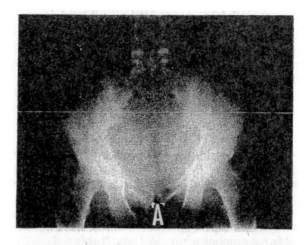

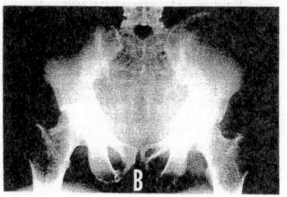

Figure 6-54. Differences in Contrast. A—92 kVp, 15 mAs; B—44 kVp, 400 mAs.

into three major classes: direct, screen, and screen-grid.

(4) Standardization of Projections— the establishment of a routine method for positioning the patient and projecting the CR for a given projection.

b. Optimum Kilovoltage Technique. The optimum kVp technique is based upon standardization of the processing procedure and the reduction of exposure factors to constants with the exception of one variable. In working out an optimum kVp technique, each projection must be considered individually.

(1) General Principles:

(a) By trial, a fixed or optimum kVp is established for an average tissue thickness range and for a given projection. For a given thickness of a particular body part, the X-ray wavelength used to penetrate the tissues must be adequate. The amount and kind of tissue— the relation of bone to soft tissue— and its penetrability by X-radiation must be evaluated. Measurement of the part must be made along the course traversed through the tissues by the CR, and the average range of measurements verified by checking many individuals. The kVp that thoroughly penetrates the part, irrespective of size, and produces satisfactory contrast is established as a constant. (Using kVp as a constant to establish contrast places the burden of providing sufficient silver in the image upon the mAs.) It should not be changed unless the conditions under which it was established are changed (table 6-8). Average thickness ranges are guides for establishing basic mAs values for various projections since approximately 80 percent of all patients fall within these ranges. Average thickness ranges and reliable optimum kVp's have been established for a number of projections (table 6-8). Using the principles advocated, kVp's for other projections may be easily made.

(b) With the kVp fixed, a basic mAs or density value must be established for the average thickness range of the part. In deriving mAs values for thicknesses outside the average range or for variations in the physiologic or pathologic state for the tissues, the rule of thumb for density changes is used.

(c) The FFD need seldom be changed and in most instances may be considered a constant. All other factors, including processing, are constants.

(2) Advantages:

(a) Less mAs permits more radiographs in a given projection before the radiation safety limit is reached. When the wavelength is optimum, a lower mAs value is usually more adequate for the exposure than that used for the same purpose with lower kVp.

(b) The overall radiographic density is uniform from case to case. Any differences from the normal density may be attributed to abnormal tissue changes.

(c) Duplication of results is easy to attain in follow-up cases.

(d) The technique may be used with any type of apparatus. Whatever the type of generator, the only variable to adjust is the mAs.

(3) Rules for Application. When all other exposure factors remain constant, the factors listed below function as described. Successful operation of the optimum kVp technique is dependent upon rigid acceptance and application of these data.

(a) Focus-film distance influences radiographic density, and image sharpness and magnification.

(b) Kilovoltage regulates radiation wavelength and the scale of radiographic contrast; determines the degree of tissue penetration, and exposure latitude; and influences production of SR fog, and radiographic density.

(c) Milliampere-seconds regulates the quantity of X-radiation emitted by the X-ray tube, and radiographic density.

c. Selection of Factors. The selection of factors that influence the image should be based upon consideration of all aspects that might have an eventual effect on radiographic quality.

(1) Focal Spot. The FS should always be selected so that the maximum image sharpness is obtained assuming that the exposure factors to be used conform to the rated capacity of the X-ray tube.

(2) Collimation. Collimation in some form should be used for all projections. The size of the field should be such as to exactly cover the size of film used at a given FFD. There are occasions when the field size should conform to the size of the anatomical area being examined. For example, a beam restricting device covers an 8 X 10 inch film, but is inadequate for delineating a very small area, such as the mastoid process; a smaller device (cylinder) is needed.

(3) Grids. Stationary or moving grids are used in examining the heavier tissue parts. The technologist should be familiar with grid ratios as well as the FFD used with the various grids. The higher the grid ratio, the greater the care in selecting the FFD and in centering the tube to the grid and part to avoid "grid cutoff". For best results, conventional moving grids of 8:1 or 12:1 ratio should be used with optimum kVp. The stationary grid of the Lysholm type is a very useful accessory when a moving grid is impractical.

(4) Focus-Film Distance. The FFD should be chosen to produce the most realistic geometric image pattern with satisfactory sharpness of definition. Once the FFD is selected for a specific projection, it should be established as a constant. If the distance must be changed for a given projection, the mAs can be adjusted so that the resulting radiographic density is approximately equal to the density obtained with the original FFD by applying the mAs-FFD relationship.

(5) Kilovoltage. The variety of effects that may be produced on the radiographic image by kVp makes it an important and influential exposure factor. Consequently, it should be closely controlled and established as a constant for a given projection. When a kVp provides an acceptable contrast scale in a given projection of a normal part, that

Table 6-8. Average Thickness Ranges and Approximate Optimum Kilovoltages for Making Non-Grid (PB) Exposures.

Region		Average thickness—CM				KVP
		AP	PA	Obl	Lat	
Thumb, fingers, toes		1.5–4		1.5–4	1.5–4	
Hand		2–4		2–4	7–10	50
Wrist		3–5		4–6	5–8	
Forearm		5–8			6–9	
Elbow		6–9			7–10	60
Arm		8–12			7–11	
Shoulder (PB)		11–15				
Clavicle (PB)			11–15			80
Foot		5–8		6–9	6–9	
Ankle		8–11		6–9	6–9	60
Leg		9–12			8–11	
Knee		10–13			9–12	65
Thigh (PB)		14–17			13–16	
Hip (PB)		16–20				75
Cervical (PB) C1-3		13–17				
Vertebrae (PB) C4-7		10–13				65
(PB) C1-7					10–13	85
Thoracic (PB) Vertebrae		20–23			29–34	85
Lumbar (PB)		17–21				70
Vertebrae					26–30	85
Pelvis (PB)		17–21				70
Skull (PB)		17–21			13–17	
Sinus (PB) frontal		18–21				
(PB) lateral					11–15	85
(PB) maxillary		19–23				
Mandible		21–24				70
		21–24				80
Chest				25–28		85
					29–34	90

kVp should be fixed. Thereafter, all images produced by a given projection will present the same scale of contrast.

(6) Basic mAs. The mAs factor is the one most reliable for regulating the amount of silver (density) in the image. There should be a satisfactory range of densities for interpretations of all portions of the image. The mAs can become a constant within certain limitations for a given projection. A basic mAs value can be established for any average thickness range of a part for a normal person.

(a) Thickness Only a Guide. The thickness of any part serves only as a guide which the specialist can use to expose the normal part and to determine what mAs will compensate for abnormal tissue changes. Knowledge of the structural makeup of the area is necessary when the kVp has been fixed as a constant for the projection. The part should also be judged from a physiologic and pathologic standpoint as to whether it is reasonably normal. If a question arises as to whether the patient is "average" or "in-range", a measurement of the part should be made. The following shows compensations required of the "above-" or "below-range" part.

Below range		In range	Above range	
3-5 cm	1-2 cm	Basic sec	1-2 cm	3-5 cm
1/2X sec	2/3X sec		3/2X sec	2X sec

Since the mA will remain constant, a change in sec will give a corresponding change in mAs. By means of these modifications, the radiographic density obtained will be approximately correct—a "repeat" is seldom required.

(b) Establishing a Basic mAs. First, select the correct quality of radiation for a given projection. Then, determine the quantity of radiation by making three initial radiographs of a part, the thickness of which is approximately at the middle of the average thickness range. In determining exposure factors for a given projection, make the first radiograph with the optimum kVp for the part (table 6-8), and with a mAs value estimated to be correct. For the second radiogram, double the mAs value (2X). Make the

third radiograph with one-half the original mAs value (1/2X). All other factors are constant. The three radiographs are viewed on the illuminator, and the density appropriate for the part is chosen. When using the above method, sometimes none of the densities are exactly correct; however, one of the radiographs perhaps contains a density close to the one desired, so that another radiograph made with an appropriate change in the mAs will provide the required radiographic density and a more nearly correct basic mAs value. The final mAs value is then used on several patients whose measurements fall within the average thickness range. If the density level is satisfactory for measurements at the center and at the extremes of the range, the mAs should be established as basic and used for all patients measuring in the average range. Once the correct mAs is determined, it becomes the basic value to be used for all thicknesses in the average thickness range established for the given projection. Departures from the basic mAs value should be made only when the influence of disease or trauma alters the absorption characteristics of the part or when the speed characteristics of the X-ray film or screens change. The method explained herein for changing density can be used for all projections as long as it is accomplished in a systematic manner. Only one exposure factor should be changed at a time when any exposure technique is to be altered. Changing two factors at a time introduces too many variables that are difficult to control.

(c) Example 1. In PA screen radiography of the adult chest, the average thickness range is 21 to 24 centimeters (approximately 70 percent of patients). A basic mAs may be used when an optimum kVp of 80 is used at a FFD of 72 inches and with average-speed screens. In this projection the basic mAs (X) should be established for a normal healthy adult measuring 22 to 23 centimeters (the middle thickness in the range). Projections that have little variation from the average thickness range, such as a PA of the chest, require refinement in application of the mAs values to those thicknesses slightly in excess of or less than the average. A typical example of a standardized PA chest technique is shown in figure 6-55. The physical characteristics of the patients whose radiographs are shown in figure 6-55 are as follows:

Radio-graph	Thickness (cm)	Sex	Age (yrs)	Height (in)	Weight (lbs)
A	17	F	20	65	105
B	18	F	24	63	110
C	19	F	29	60	101
D	20	F	22	63	107
E	21	M	61	67	135
F	22	F	21	58	132
G	23	F	24	60	123
H	24	M	60	68	165
I	25	M	34	63	130
J	26	M	60	67	173
K	27	M	55	67	199
L	28	M	36	70	206
M	29	M	60	69	193

Radiation that completely penetrates the part and produces a consistently uniform density and contrast is most important in applying a standardized technique as illustrated in figure 6-55. The characteristics of height, weight, or sex cannot per se be used to determine the X-ray absorbing properties of the tissues being exposed.

1. Thickness Greater Than Average. When a chest measurement is slightly greater than average, the only change needed is in the mAs factor. The increased thickness of the 25 and 26 cm chest requires more radiation of the quality as produced with 80 kVp on chests within the average range. The kVp is held constant since it has been predetermined that 80 kVp provides the necessary quality of radiation to penetrate any size adult chest within a reasonable range in the PA direction. When a basic mAs (X) is given to a 25 or 26 cm chest, the radiographic density may be too low. When the mAs is raised to 2X, the density may be too great, largely containing SR fog. Consequently, a value should be used which is one-half the difference between 2X and X, or 1 1/2X the basic mAs. The density produced will then be comparable to that provided by X mAs on a 23 cm chest. The original contrast is maintained because the presence of SR fog is not a problem. Chests with a thickness of 27, 28, 29, and 30 cm can be exposed with 2X mAs because the increase in thickness requires only an increase in mAs and not necessarily in kVp. Chests exceeding 30 cm in thickness require an increase not only in mAs but also in kVp to provide adequate penetration. The higher kVp causes an increase in SR fog which should be eliminated by the use of a stationary parallel-grid. The kVp, therefore, should be raised to 100 to increase penetration and to compensate for the grid. Consequently, a new group of conditions must be set up and a new basic mAs established to assure proper density. The same FFD and screens should be used.

2. Smaller Thicknesses. If the basic mAs is used for a 17 or 18 cm chest, the density will be excessive. A satisfactory result can be obtained, however, by exposing with 1/2X mAs. To balance the densities for the 19- and 20 cm chests, 2/3X mAs may be used and for 13 to 16 cm, 1/3X mAs. For infants (less than 13 cm, 1/4X mAs may be used, but the kVp should be reduced from 80 to 70 to provide increase in contrast.

(d) Example 2. In PA radiography of the hand, over 95 percent of adult hands are in the average thickness range of 2 to 4 cm and the basic mAs value at 50 kVp can be used. When the thickness departs from the average, the mAs may be altered by using the rule of thumb for density.

d. Overexposure:

(1) General:

(a) Modern X-ray film, in combination with intensifying screens, is exceedingly fast and requires only relatively short exposures to produce radiographs of good quality. An overexposed film lacks proper radiographic density and contrast. To the trained eye, the overexposed radiograph is easily identifiable.

(b) One type of overexposure exhibits an overall grayness with low contrast. This appearance is caused by shortened development of the film, a procedure often followed in an attempt to correct the error made in the exposure time or to compensate for excessive kVp. Another type of overexposure produces such a great density of the thinner portions of the part radiographed that they

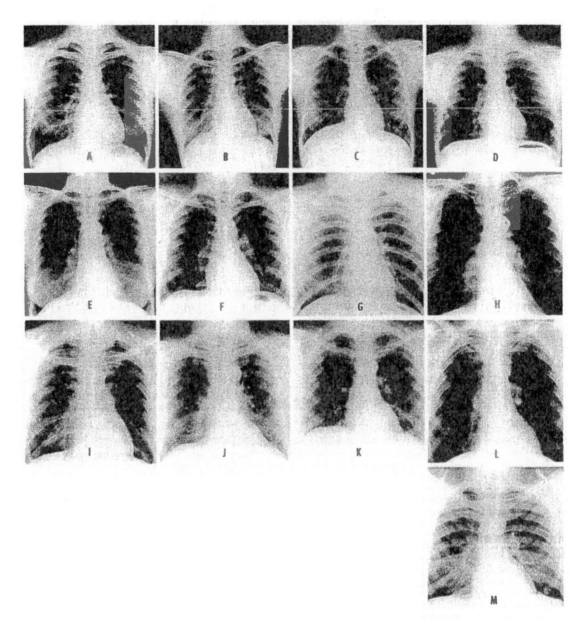

Figure 6-55. Typical Example of Standardized PA Chest Technique.

	Constant Factors		Thickness Ranges	Variable Factors A * Time	B * Time
kVp 80	Cone..............	To cover area	–17 cm	1/40 sec	1/60 sec
mA 100	Film	Screen-type	18–19 cm	1/30 sec	1/40 sec
FFD .... 72"			20–25 cm	1/20 sec	1/30 sec
Screens .... Average speed	Developer	Rapid	26–27 cm	1/15 sec	1/20 sec
Filtration .... Alum., 1 mm	Development	5 min at 68° F	28– cm	1/10 sec	1/15 sec

* To compensate differences in efficiency of X-ray output in various X-ray generators, it is necessary to establish by trial the time category (A or B) that will produce the desired radiographic density. In making the test radiographs, a subject with a 22-23 cm chest should be radiographed, employing an exposure of 1/20 sec (column A). If the density is too great, then 1/30 sec (column B) may be used. The density of this second radiograph will usually be satisfactory; on this basis, the time values for the other thickness groups will be found in column B. The chest radiographs reproduced on this spread were made with the time values listed under column A.

are obliterated. In this case full development is given, and it usually occurs where time-temperature processing is used.

(c) If the kVp is correct, overexposure due to the mAs factor may usually be corrected by making another radiograph with one-half the original mAs (1/2X). Frequently, the density of this second radiograph is satisfactory or is so near in quality that if a third radiograph is made, only a minor adjustment of the mAs is needed to secure the most desirable quality.

(2) Example. To illustrate the procedure in altering density by the rule of thumb method when determining a basic mAs value or correcting a faulty one, a series of AP screen-grid radiographs of the lumbar vertebrae (figure 6-56) was made with 70 kVp and a 36 inch FFD. The first radiograph (A) was made with a trial exposure of 200 mAs. The density was excessive. Applying the rule of thumb for density, the second radiograph (B) was made with 100 mAs. The density was reduced, but it was still somewhat excessive.

mum kVp is used. The experienced X-ray technologist soon recognizes the degree of overexposure and can make short cuts; for instance, the second radiograph (B) can be eliminated by quartering the original mAs and securing a working density that can be easily adjusted, if necessary.

e. Underexposure:

(1) General. A radiograph is underexposed when important details are lacking because of inadequate radiographic density. Details of thin structure may be visible, but those representing the heavier parts are absent. When the kVp is of a value to secure proper penetration of the part yet the mAs is insufficient to secure proper density, the radiograph will reveal very faint detail in image areas corresponding to the greater tissue densities—the kVp is satisfactory for the part, but detail may be better visualized if more silver were deposited on the film. Usually the density will be satisfactory when the mAs is doubled; however, a further

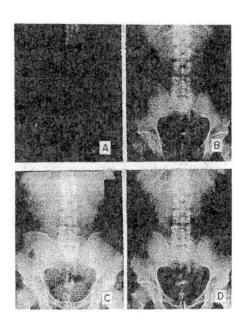

Figure 6-56. AP Screen-Grid Radiographs of the Lumbar Spine.

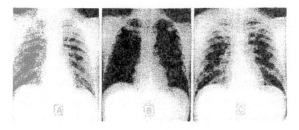

Figure 6-57. PA Screen-Exposure Radiographs of the Chest.

small adjustment may be necessary to provide a satisfactory image.

(2) Example. A series of PA screen-exposure radiographs of the chest (figure 6-57) was made using 80 kVp and 72 inch FFD. The first radiograph (A) was made with 3.3 mAs and resulted in an underexposure. The second radiograph (B) was made with 6.6 mAs and the resulting density was excessive. The third radiograph (C) was made with 5 mAs, approximately midway between the previous mAs values, and a correct exposure was obtained.

f. Phototiming. The use of optimum kVp in radiographic phototiming eliminates many problems in the choice of appropriate factors. Since the FFD is constant for given projections, the burden of regulating the mAs is on the phototimer. When calibrated and operated properly, it will provide the desired radiographic density on the film.

The mAs was halved again for the third radiograph (C), but the density became insufficient. A fourth radiograph (D) was made using 75 mAs, a value midway between 100 and 50 mAs, which yielded a satisfactory image density. Once the basic value is established the need for correcting overexposure or underexposure is seldom required when an opti-

RADIATION PROTECTION

SECTION A—INTERACTION OF PHOTONS WITH MATTER

3-1. Introduction. The definition of the term interaction is quite simple: one force or body having a measurable effect on another force or body. One can see daily evidence of interaction: in a bowling alley, at the lake watching a sailboat, or on the job in the many uses of electrical transformers. The interaction that the radiologic technologist must fully understand is that which takes place when a beam of X-ray photons passes through anything having mass and occupying space, or more simply, matter. An X-ray beam, consisting of photons of pure energy, transfers its energy to the matter through which it is passing, whether it be air, an X-ray film, or the living tissues of the radiologic technologist or the patient. This transfer of energy is not as simple as that seen in bowling, sailing, or electric transformers; it involves the X-ray photons, which cannot be seen, heard, felt, or detected with the normal senses; and, in many cases the interaction itself is not immediately evident without complicated devices to detect these events. Some, if not all, of the X-ray energy seems to disappear in certain materials. The term which best describes this phenomenon is absorption. Absorption is the process by which an X-ray photon transfers its inherent energy to the medium through which it is passing. Some results of this absorption are: (1) chemical changes in film emulsion, (2) electrical changes in a radiation detection instrument, and (3) biological changes in living tissue.

3-2. Ionization. The changes mentioned in the preceding paragraph are all brought about by a process known as ionization. Ionization can be defined as any process which results in the removal or addition of an orbital electron from or to an atom or molecule, thereby leaving the atom or molecule with an overall positive or negative charge. Ionization can occur when an electron is struck by a photon, at which time an energy transfer will take place. Although it is technically possible for this energy transfer to take place in the nucleus, the chances for a photon reaching that vicinity are extremely remote. After an ionizing event occurs, the remaining particles are called a pair of ions (in the case of electron removal). The parent atom (minus

an electron) has an overall positive charge and is known as a positive ion. The ejected electron has a negative charge and is known as a negative ion. This process of ionization is illustrated in figure 3-1. Radiation is measured by the number of ion pairs it causes. The amount of radiation that causes approximately two billion pairs of ions to be formed in one cubic centimeter of air (at normal pressure/temperature) is known as one roentgen (R). The two types of ionization that most generally occur in the diagnostic radiation energy range are the photoelectric effect and the Compton effect.

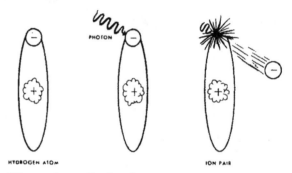

Figure 3-1. Ionization.

a. Photoelectric Effect. The *photoelectric effect*, illustrated in figure 3-2, is an all-or-none energy exchange in that the photon imparts all of its energy to the electron and simply vanishes. The ejected electron, called a photoelectron, departs with all the inherent energy of the photon and can cause secondary ionization due to its increased kinetic energy. In the meantime, as the excited atom returns to the normal state, it quickly attracts another electron to fill the vacant "hole", and radiation is emitted. The energy of the radiation and the sequence of events that causes the radiation is much the same as the replenishment of an electron shell vacancy created by the ejection of an electron by electron collision as explained in chapter 2. The photoelectric effect normally occurs with photon energies up to 100 keV.

b. Compton Effect. The Compton effect also referred to as modified, or incoherent scattering, is the result of a partial transfer of energy from an X-ray photon to an orbital electron as seen in figure 3-3. In this case the

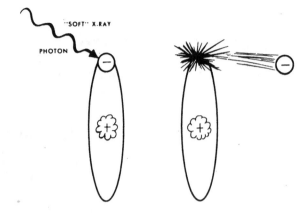

Figure 3-2. Photoelectric Effect.

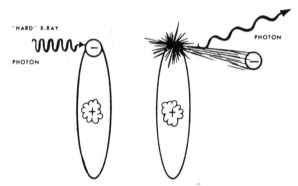

Figure 3-3. Compton Effect.

photon strikes a glancing blow to the electron and ejects it from orbit. Although considerably weakened in energy (longer wavelength), the photon will continue on. While the now "soft" photon will eventually disappear via a final photoelectric effect, the ejected electron can, as in the previous case, continue on to cause another, or secondary, ionization of a nearby atom. In contrast to the photoelectric effect, the Compton effect is predominant with highly energetic X-rays or in the 100 keV to 10 MeV energy range.

3-3. Other Interactions. X-ray photons also undergo other interactions in matter. Two of them are described briefly here although they do not occur with photons in the diagnostic energy range.

a. Thomson Effect. The Thomson effect, also known as unmodified, classical, and coherent scattering, is the result of a photon interacting with a whole atom as shown in figure 3-4. This interaction results in the deflection or scattering of the photon from its original direction without a loss of energy to the atom. The Thomson effect occurs

with photons of only a few kiloelectron volts of energy.

b. Pair Production. For gamma and X-radiation photons of energies greater than 1.02 MeV, pair production occurs. At such energy levels, it is possible that all three interactions can take place in a matter of microseconds. But pair production is predominant among photons with energy in the 5 to 12 MeV range. Only when a high-energy photon passes very close to the nucleus of a heavy atom, can it interact with the electric and magnetic fields in such a way that the photon or part of its energy is converted at the same instant into two particles—an electron and a positron of equal mass and electrical charge (magnitude). Thus, for this conversion into mass, a photon energy of 1.02 MeV is required. The electron, acting like a beta particle can cause ionization in its path, and may end up as a free electron.

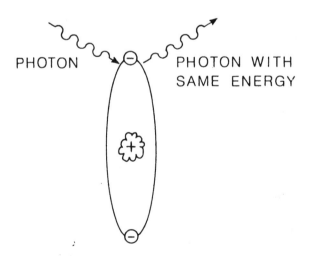

Figure 3-4. Thomson Effect.

The positron, acting as an alpha particle, can also cause ionization in its path. However, the positron, once formed, has a very short life. After losing its speed (energy) by collision and ionizing atoms of matter, the positron undergoes a unique and final interaction with an electron by uniting and annihilating each other to give off two (gamma ray) 0.511 MeV photons. These new photons may produce further ionizations by photoelectric effect or by Compton's effect.

SECTION B—DETECTION AND MEASUREMENT

3-4. Introduction. Since none of the five senses can detect the presence of X-radiation, indirect methods must be employed. Although the ionizing capability is harmful, and in some cases deadly, to living tissue, it is this same ability which is used to provide detection through two means: (1) chemical changes, and (2) electrical changes.

a. Chemical Change. Radiologic technologists are familiar with one of the benefits of chemical change. The ionization of silver bromide crystals in film emulsion causes a chemical change such that those crystals will reduce to black metallic silver when exposed to developing chemicals. The un-ionized crystals remain chemically inert to the developer and are removed during the fixing and clearing process. Thus the degree of darkening on a film badge, when processed under controlled conditions, is used to determine the quantity or total dose of radiation received by the wearer.

b. Electrical Change. The electrical changes brought about by the ionization process are also useful in detecting the presence of X-radiation. It is possible to detect and measure radiation from the number of freed electrons since an X-ray beam will provide a large number of such electrons where there was essentially none before.

3-5. Total Dose and Dose Rate. Total dose, and dose rate, are two terms that must be clearly understood before continuing with the detection and measurement of X-radiation. Total dose is the total amount of radiation received, such as 50 R, with no indication of the time during which it was received. It may have been 1 minute or spread out over 1 year. As the dose gets larger, this time element becomes extremely critical, and in the case of a careless radiologic technologist, perhaps even deadly. Therefore it is necessary to be able to discuss radiation doses in terms of the rate at which they are being received. Dose rate is the amount of radiation received per unit time such as 50 R per hour (50 R/hr). A dose rate of 100 R/min for 4 minutes would result in a total dose of 400 R.

3-6. Ion Chamber. An ion chamber illustrated in figure 3-5 is an example of an instrument that measures radiation dose rate. By applying a difference in potential across the chamber, to cause movement of the free electrons, the rate of current flow would then reflect the amount of radiation striking the chamber. The instrument can be calibrated by using a known quantity of radiation. Figure 3-5A shows no reading on the meter because there is no ionization (no electrons being freed); consequently, there is no electron flow. In figure 3-5B ionization is taking place (electrons are being freed) and the application of a potential difference is causing electron flow which results in a reading on the meter. The meter of course would be cali-

A

ION CHAMBER--AT REST

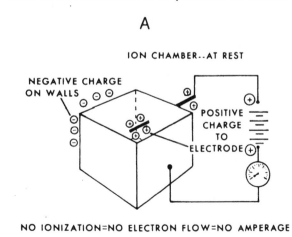

NO IONIZATION=NO ELECTRON FLOW=NO AMPERAGE

B

ION CHAMBER--AT WORK

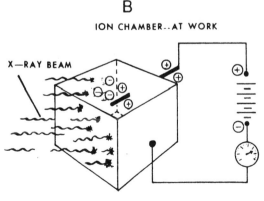

IONIZATION=ELECTRON FLOW=AMPERAGE

Figure 3-5.   Ion Chamber.

brated in roentgens, or some other units. Two examples of instruments used to measure radiation in this manner are the Geiger-Mueller Counter and the Jordan Ion Chamber.

3-7. Film Badge. The *film badge* is an example of a total dose detector. It is the device most commonly used to detect and measure occupational radiation exposures. Precise procedures concerning wearing and maintenance of film badges can be found in the appropriate directives for each service.

a. A film badge consists of a film packet in a film holder usually constructed of plastic or metal. In the film packet are two pieces of photographic film. One has a double emulsion, and one has emulsion on one side only. The single emulsion is of prime importance when loading the film holder. The film may contain only an X-ray sensitive emulsion, or it may be sensitive to X-rays, gamma rays, and beta particles. Special films are available to detect and measure neutrons.

b. The film responds to radiation exactly as does radiographic film; ionization occurs within the emulsion layer, bringing about a chemical sensitivity to developer solution in those silver bromide crystals so ionized. Radiation dosage is then determined by the film density. Processing is carried out under extremely controlled conditions by a central agency to insure accurate and constant results.

c. The film badge should be worn according to the previously mentioned directives, so refer to them for guidance. Generally it is worn on an area of the body expected to receive the highest exposure such as the chest. (Occasionally it may be advisable to wear an additional film badge to determine local exposure. An example would be a wrist badge worn by a radiologist during fluoroscopy to check exposure to that area.) The film badge should not be carried in a pocket, or behind any obstruction such as coins, combs, or cigarette packages as they tend to absorb radiation and reduce the ultimate density reading of the film. Wearing of the film badge in conjunction with a protective apron is described in the appropriate directive. Technologists should avoid receiving a direct exposure of X-rays while wearing the film badge, such as when undergoing diagnostic or therapeutic X-ray exposure themselves. This is because X-ray exposure in those instances is not to be included in the maximum permissible dose. In addition, direct exposures make it difficult to obtain a true density reading. Film badges should also be pro-

tected against direct sunlight to prevent thermal sensitization and possible light leaks in the wrapping paper.

d. When not in use, film badges should be stored in a radiation-free area along with a control film badge. The purpose of the control film badge is to permit the laboratory responsible for processing and evaluating the film badge to take into account such factors as background radiation, temperature variations, et cetera, that would otherwise be recorded as an occupational exposure.

e. When an overexposure is indicated on a film, an investigation is conducted to see if the exposure was indeed accidental or if it was the result of a deliberate act or carelessness. Some of the most common causes of overexposure are:

(1) Deliberate exposure of the film badge.

(2) Improper storage of the film badge.

(3) Failure of the individual to utilize protective shielding.

(4) Improper working techniques.

(5) Inadequate or defective radiation shielding.

(6) Unintentional wear of the film badge while receiving diagnostic or therapeutic X-rays.

(7) Failure on the part of the submitting installation to identify the questionable film packet as having been used for nonroutine recording of radiation exposure.

f. Improper use of film badges results in misleading reports and waste of time and money in unnecessary investigations. Film badge programs are designed to provide radiation workers with a means for detecting accidental exposure to radiation in order that they can be provided with medical treatment if necessary. It behooves technologists to wear the film badge when appropriate to do so and take required measures to insure the success of the film badge dosimetry program.

SECTION C—SHIELDING

3-8. Introduction. Shielding is the intentional use of materials of various densities to limit, control, or modify the electromagnetic energy output of an X-ray tube. To understand the effects of shielding and therefore be able to take advantage of it as a radiation protection tool, it is necessary to review certain facts about X-ray photon interaction with matter. Photon energy is lost by many different methods with photoelectric and Compton effects being the two predominant in the wavelengths associated with medical X-rays.

As X-ray photons travel through an absorber, the amount of reduction, or attenuation is determined by three important factors: (1) the energy of the photons, (2) the atomic mass of the absorbing material, and (3) the thickness of the absorbing material. NOTE: Half-value layer is described in chapter 15.

3-9. Inverse Square Law. Distance from the X-ray source is a highly effective method of reducing the intensity of an X-ray beam. This can be expressed in the *inverse square law* which states that the X- or gamma-radiation intensity from a point source varies inversely with the square of the distance from the source. Expressed mathematically, the inverse square is:

$$\frac{I_1}{I_2} = \frac{(D_2)^2}{(D_1)^2}$$

where

I_1 = intensity at original distance.
I_2 = intensity at new distance.
D_1 = original distance.
D_2 = new distance.

Suppose the intensity of an X-ray beam was 100 R/min at a distance of 2 feet from the X-ray tube; what would the new intensity be at a distance of 4 feet? By substituting the data from the above problem into the formula the new intensity can be found as follows:

$$\frac{100}{I_2} = \frac{(4)^2}{(2)^2}$$

$$\frac{100}{I_2} = \frac{16}{4}$$

$$\frac{100}{I_2} = 4$$

$$I_2 = \frac{100}{4}$$

$$I_2 = 25 \text{ R/min}$$

By doubling the distance from the X-ray tube the intensity of the beam can be reduced to one-fourth its original value—100 R/min to 25 R/min. This is an impressive reduction in intensity, which can be used to advantage by the technologist in keeping his exposure

to radiation to the barest minimum. As stated in the definition of the inverse square law, the formula is applicable only to radiation from a point source such as the target in an X-ray tube.

3-10. Photon Energy Factor. A factor that influences photon absorption or beam attenuation is the energy level of the photons. The higher the photon energy, the more penetrating is the X-ray beam, regardless of the material used for shielding. As kVp is increased, photon energy is increased, thereby causing more penetration. Figure 3-6 shows three blocks of absorbing material. As can be seen, more of the high energy photons penetrate the absorber than do the lower energy photons.

3-11. Absorber Density. A characteristic of an absorber which determines its ability to absorb radiation is atomic density. The more closely packed the atoms, the greater is the probability for photon/electron interaction to take place. Figure 3-7 shows two pieces of absorbing material, wood and lead. Both are of equal thickness but the lead will cause greater attenuation because of its higher density. Due to its density, lead is an excellent shielding material and is widely used in and around radiology departments. The shielding equivalency of some common shielding materials as compared to lead are shown in figure 3-8.

3-12. Absorber Thickness. Another factor which influences attenuation is the thickness of the absorbing material. If photon energy and absorber density remain constant, then further attenuation can be accomplished by simply adding more absorber material. In other words, if 6 inches of concrete is good, then 12 inches is better. Figure 3-9 shows three blocks of concrete of different thickness with each being subjected to X-ray beams having the same photon energy. Attenuation is greatest with the thickest block of concrete.

SECTION D—CELLULAR CONCEPTS

3-13. Introduction. The careless use of X-radiation can incapacitate, disfigure, or even produce death. Since the radiologic technologist plays such a vital role in reducing radiation exposure to himself as well as to his patients, it is necessary for him to be knowledgeable of the concepts involved. This section describes cell structure and activity, how radiation can affect the cell, and the

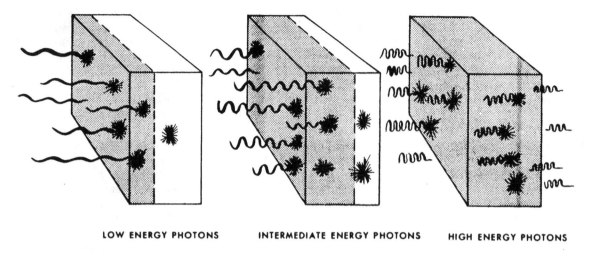

LOW ENERGY PHOTONS   INTERMEDIATE ENERGY PHOTONS   HIGH ENERGY PHOTONS

Figure 3-6.   Effect of Photon Energy on Absorption.

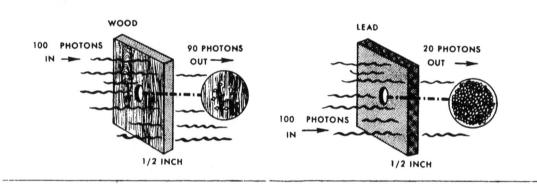

Figure 3-7.   Effect of Absorber Density on Absorption.

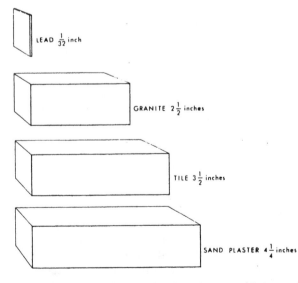

Figure 3-8.   **Shielding Equivalency of Some Common Materials.**

variation in radiosensitivity of different cells.

3-14. Life Cycle of a Cell. Reproduction, maturation, and death are the three phases in the life cycle of a cell. Reproduction is the process of a cell subdividing and producing another cell. As an adult cell subdivides, it gives to its offspring the same operating instructions it had. This second cell then matures and functions in accordance with the operating instructions it received from its parent. Finally, the adult cell wears out and dies; its role is assumed by the offspring. Life span is the total life cycle of a cell and is peculiar to each variety of cell. Some examples of varying life spans are: (1) lymphocytes—8 to 12 hours, (2) intestinal epithelial cells—2 to 4 days, and (3) erythrocytes—120 to 140 days. The recurring life cycle provides constant tissue repair and growth for the

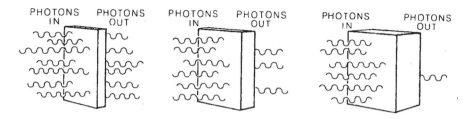

Figure 3-9. Effect of Absorber Thickness on Absorption.

body. However, if radiation alters this life cycle or span, then the cell cannot function correctly.

3-15. Classification of Cells. Cells are classified as somatic or gonadal. Differentiation between these varieties is essential to any discussion of radiation biology since there are distinct effects, depending upon which type of cell is affected.

a. *Somatic Cells.* Somatic cells are those of a specific individual tissue such as heart, lung, or liver. Their functions provide life for an individual. Somatic cells pass on to their offspring operating instructions to act like they themselves acted.

b. *Gonadal Cells.* Gonadal cells insure a species' continuance. When creating a new member of the species, the operating or genetic instructions of two cells interweave, add, subtract, and modify. If either cell has been previously modified, it cannot pass on the genetic instructions it is supposed to.

3-16. Deoxyribonucleic Acid and Ribonucleic Acid. All cells have one common and extremely vital characteristic: they pass on to their daughter cells operating instructions which are extremely detailed, highly complex, and an exact duplicate of the instructions they received from their parent cells. Deoxyribonucleic acid (DNA) and ribonucleic acid (RNA) are the blueprints for cell reproduction.

a. *DNA Molecule.* The DNA molecule is a double helix which has two important functions—replication and controlling cellular activities. The fundamental unit of DNA is the nucleotide, consisting of a phosphate group, a 5-carbon sugar, and a nitrogen base. There are four nitrogen bases found in DNA—guanine, cytosine, adenine, and thymine. They are shown in figure 3-10 with different shapes for illustrative purposes. Note in figure 3-11 that one end of each nitrogen base is identical to the others and that it fits the 5-carbon sugar perfectly but it will not fit the phosphate group. Also note the nitrogen bases fit each other only in specific combinations, guanine with cytosine and adenine with thymine.

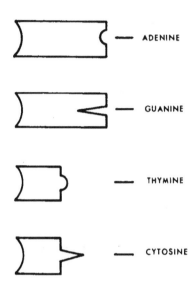

Figure 3-10. 4 Nitrogen Bases Found in DNA.

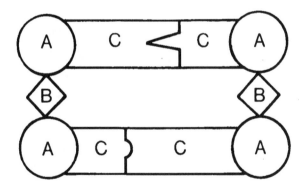

Figure 3-11. Connection of Sugar (A), Phosphate (B), and Nitrogen Bases (C).

(1) The four nitrogen bases constitute the genetic alphabet. They form the blueprints for cell reproduction and are the building blocks of life. Figure 3-12 is an example of an unwound DNA molecule. Notice that the sugar phosphate chain forms the sides of the ladder and various combinations of the nitrogen bases are the rungs. The weakest link in this complex chain is the point where the nitrogen bases join together. This is a hydrogen bond, one of the weakest

chemical bonds known. Also note the sequence of the nitrogen bases in figure 3-12. Each variety of cells will have a certain sequence. This sequence is the critical factor when the DNA molecule performs its two functions—replication and controlling cellular activity.

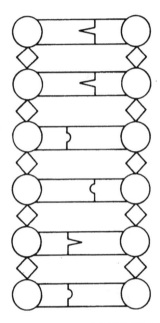

Figure 3-12.   Unwound DNA Molecule.

(2) Replication must not be confused with duplication. In duplication a copy of the original is made and the original remains intact. In replication the original divides and forms two new molecules which resemble the original. Figure 3-13 shows a DNA molecule in the process of mitosis, which means cell division. The weak hydrogen bond between the nirogen bases is released and the DNA molecule starts to split. Each separation leaves an exposed nitrogen base which will recombine with nitrogen bases found in the cytoplasm of the cell. When they recombine, the second molecule will be identical to the original molecule as seen in figure 3-14.

b. RNA Molecule. After replication there are two identical cells. RNA, which is the messenger system for DNA, enables the cells to function as specific cells. RNA is a single-stranded molecule produced by DNA. In the single cell illustrated in figure 3-15 the DNA molecule partially splits and produces an RNA molecule. This molecule is given a set of coded instructions which it takes to the ribosome of the cell. The ribosome of a cell is the protein-producing part of a cell, which manufactures the necessary nutrients for a cell by combining certain amino acids that are

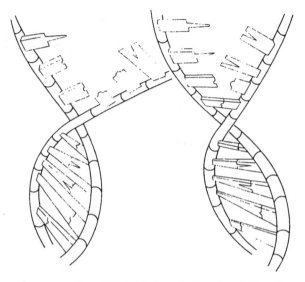

Figure 3-13.   DNA Molecule During Mitosis.

found within the cell. The RNA molecule instructs the ribosome how to combine these amino acids. When this has occurred, then the cell will function as it is supposed to.

c Disturbing the Functions of DNA. The above explanation of DNA and RNA is by no means comprehensive. Cell division is a complex and exacting procedure. Fortunately DNA performs its functions without error as long as its structure is not disturbed. Although other conditions will affect DNA, the one of interest to the radiologic technologist is ionizing radiation.

3-17. How Ionizing Radiation Affects DNA. Ionization, you will recall, is the removal of an orbital electron. If this electron is forming the bond between the nitrogen bases, then the ability to replicate exactly is lost. This means that one of the rungs in a DNA molecule may be incomplete or perhaps incompatible with the free nucleotides present in the liquid cytoplasm.

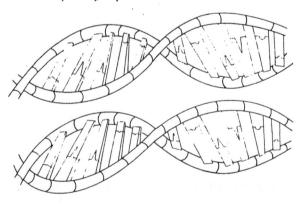

Figure 3-14.   Recombination of Nitrogen Bases.

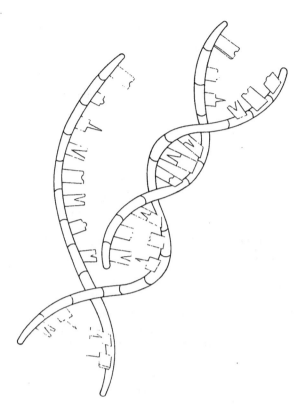

Figure 3-15.   Production of RNA.

a. Any modification in the sequence of nitrogen bases will result in a change of instructions passed from DNA to RNA. When this happens, mutations occur. Mutations are generally considered to be harmful, but, fortunately, they are for the most part recessive and are usually overcome by the dominant characteristics of the normal cells.

b Sickle cell anemia is a mutation not necessarily caused by radiation. It is an inherited defect in man, in which the red blood cells become distorted in the shape of sickles. They tend to form clumps which block the smaller blood vessels, and their tendency to burst brings about anemia, usually resulting in early death. This serious hereditary defect in man is brought about by the substitution of only one nitrogen base in the DNA molecule—a single change in the sequence of the rungs.

3-18. Mechanisms of Radiation Injury. The methods by which ionizing radiation can cause modification of cell structure are known as the target theory and the indirect damage theory.

a. Target Theory. The target theory is also termed direct effects. These effects can be produced at cell level or in the whole animal. In either case they alter cell structure.

(1) At cell level the changes are produced when energy imparted by radiation acts in contact with the biological structure causing genetic effects. In the whole animal direct effects can be produced in a given tissue by virtue of its life span and function. For example, bone marrow continuously produces blood cells. These immature cells are highly susceptible to radiation injury. A high enough dose of radiation received by bone could result in bone marrow depression with a subsequent drop in the blood count of an individual.

(2) One of the possibilities of direct effects is a chromosome break. Such a break would require 20 ion pairs, and could occur as the result of secondary ionization. Gene mutations, on the other hand, can be produced by as little as one ion pair. Chromosome breaks do not necessarily cause immediate cell death. One result of a chromosome break is the possibility of an abnormal recombination. Despite this, the whole cell may still be "operating" normally for the present. There is a definite delay before the injurious effects of radiation are observed. Cell death may occur during attempts at cell division (mitotic-linked death). The sooner the division following radiation, the greater the chances for cell death. Cell death may also occur during subsequent divisions due to loss of chromosome material.

(3) First and second generations may appear perfectly normal and be able to function normally. It should be noted that chromosome damage generally does not bring about cell death unless and until the cell enters division after irradiation.

b. Indirect Damage Theory. The indirect damage theory constitutes all other effects and is produced in the fluid environment and neighboring cells. These effects may be found in one part of the body due to irradiation of the other part. Indirect effects may be the result of circulating toxic substances, histamine imbalance, or auto-intoxication by tissue breakdown products.

(1) Since biological material in general has such a high percentage of water, both inside the cell (cytoplasm) and outside (interstitial fluid), radiochemical effects are usually presented as affecting the water molecule. Under normal conditions water is a stable molecule containing two atoms of hydrogen and one atom of oxygen. When ionization occurs, which results in the removal of an orbital electron, the weak hydrogen bond is broken. The result is the production of free ions and radicals such as H_2,

O$_2$, OH, and so on. To understand the actual chemical breakdown requires an extensive chemistry background. The important fact to remember is that recombination of these free ions and radicals can produce toxic substances.

(2) In the process of recombination these free ions and radicals, which were produced as a result of irradiation of the water molecule, can reform as H$_2$O (water) or 2H$_2$O (heavy water), both of which are harmless. However, another recombination is H$_2$O$_2$ or hydrogen peroxide. The toxicity of hydrogen peroxide is well known and should the quantities of this poison being formed in the cells and interstitial fluid be great enough, cell death will occur.

(3) This mechanical/chemical injury to cells results in cell death. It occurs in both man and animal; however, animals have provided most of the experimental data. Keep in mind a given amount of radiation, say 400 R, will not necessarily produce the same biological effects in man as it does in a rat; in fact, it will not produce the same injury in different cells within a man. It appears likely that both direct and indirect actions contribute to the chemical changes which initiate radiation injury in a biological system.

3-19. Radiosensitivity of Cells. Two important factors influencing the varying responses to radiation or radiosensitivity are cell variety and species variety. These factors are explained by the Law of Berganie and Tribondeau which states "the more undifferentiated physiologically and morphologically, and active mitotically, the longer the cell requires to undergo active mitosis; and the more divisions it has yet to go through, then the more radiosensitive is the cell." Stated generally, this means immature and rapidly dividing cells are more radiosensitive than mature ones and/or those of stable tissues. A cell in mitosis is much more radiosensitive than the same cell at rest. Blood and gonadal cells are most sensitive. Nerve, brain, and muscle cells are least sensitive. The reduced sensitivity of nerve, brain, and muscle is due to the fact that a person is born with all the nerve, brain, and muscle cells he will have. Therefore, according to the Law of Berganie and Tribondeau, since these cells are neither immature nor rapidly dividing, they should have a greater resistance to radiation.

3-20. Radiosensitivity of Species. Species variety shows an even greater variation in radio-

sensitivity, as shown in the following examples. The LD (lethal dose)$_{50/30}$ varies for humans, sheep, poultry and bacteria. LD$_{50/30}$ is the amount of radiation required to produce death in 50 percent of the exposed animals or humans within 30 days.

Species	LD$_{50/30}$
Human	400 R
Sheep	525 R
Poultry	900 R
Bacteria	3,000 to 5,000 R

SECTION E—RADIATION PROTECTION STANDARDS

3-21. Introduction. It is often said that "X-rays accumulate in the body." This statement is about 10 percent correct, but then only if reworded: "Approximately 90 percent of radiation injury is repaired, at the rate of 2.5 percent per day, 50 percent at the end of 30 days, and essentially all repaired by 90 days." The accumulation theory has its roots in the biological fact that 10 percent of the damage caused by any exposure to radiation is permanent and is often referred to as residual dose. It obviously follows that each subsequent dose is less tolerable by the body than the preceding dose.

a. This can be demonstrated by the following hypothetical case. Keep in mind that the figures in this case are intended for comparison only. Assume that a total organ dose of 100 R will kill the pancreas. A patient is exposed to 20 separate doses of 50 R each with 90 days between exposures for biological repair. Remember, that by allowing 90 days between exposures, 90 percent of the radiation damage will be repaired and 10 percent will be permanent. The residual picture would be as follows.

Dose 50 R Each	Repaired Each Time	Residual Dose
1st	90%	5 R
2d	90%	10 R
3d	90%	15 R
10th	90%	50 R
19th	90%	95 R
20th	90%	100 R

After the first exposure the residual dose is 5 R. The second exposure increases the residual to 10 R and the third, to 15 R. Following the tenth exposure, the residual is 50 R and the pancreas is now only 50 percent effective. The nineteenth exposure leaves a residual dose of 95 R, and after the twentieth exposure the pancreas is no longer functional.

b. Note the difference in the ability of the organ to tolerate the first dose of 50 R as compared to the twentieth dose of 50 R. It is for this reason that "safe levels" of radiation exposure have been established. The levels established differentiate between occupational radiation workers and other groups.

c. Although the word "safe" is commonly used in referring to radiation exposure, it should be clearly understood that no amount of radiation regardless of the amount can be considered 100 percent safe. "Biologically acceptable" is more descriptive in that no individual receiving up to that amount would be expected to develop manifestations of radiation injury.

d. There are three organizations involved in establishing the safe limits of radiation dosage. They are:

(1) National Committee on Radiation Protection and Measurement (NCRP).

(2) Federal Radiation Council (FRC).

(3) International Commission of Radiological Protection (ICRP).

Their recommendations cover all types of ionizing radiation and whether it is applied internally or externally. Our major concern is exposure to X-radiation from an external source, the X-ray tube.

e. The safe limits known as Radiation Protection Guides (RPGs) as recommended by the three organizations previously mentioned are divided into two categories: those governing radiation workers and those governing all others, meaning the general population. A further breakdown specifies the limits for whole-body and partial-body radiation exposure.

3-22. Units of Radiation Dosage. Fundamentally, the harmful consequences of ionizing radiation to a living organism are due to the energy absorbed by the cells and tissues that form the organism. This absorbed energy (or dose) produces chemical decomposition of the molecules present in the living cells. The mechanism of the decomposition appears to be related to ionization and excitation interactions between the radiation and atoms within the tissue. The amount of ionization or number of ion pairs produced by ionizing radiations in the cells or tissues provides some measure of the amount of physiological damage that might be expected from a given quantity or dose. The ideal basis for radiation-dose measurement therefore would be the number of ion pairs (or ionizations) taking place within the medium of interest. However, for certain practical reasons, the medium used in establishing a unit of measurement was air.

a. Roentgen. In simple terms, a roentgen (R) is the amount of radiation that will produce one electrostatic unit of charge in 1 cc of air. Since one electrostatic unit of charge is equal to 2.083×10^9 electrons, one R causes 2.083×10^9 (2,083,000,000) ion pairs.

b. Absorbed Dose (rad). The energy absorbed per/R of exposure varies with the type of absorbing material and the quality of radiation. The rad is the unit of absorbed dose and is equal to the absorption of 100 ergs of energy per gram of irradiated material.

c. Rad Equivalent Man (rem). The rem is the absorbed dose in rads multiplied by the relative biological effectiveness of the radiation used on the particular biological system irradiated. Fortunately, in the energy range used for medical radiography, 1 R = 1 rad = 1 rem. In other words for all practical purposes the rad and rem will be the same as the R.

3-23. Radiation Protection Standards. For radiation workers or those individuals whose occupation requires exposure to ionizing radiation on a regular basis, such as the radiologic technologist, radiation protection guides recommend the following maximum accumulated dose. For external exposure, from X- or gamma rays, to the whole body, the maximum average dose rate should not exceed 5 rems per year. The same dose rate applies to the head and trunk, active blood-forming organs, the gonads, and the lens of the eye. When only a single portion of the body is exposed, as compared to the whole body, the maximum permissible dose is generally higher. For example, it is recommended that the average dose rate to the hands and forearms and to the feet and ankles should not exceed 75 rems per year.

a. No occupational dose is allowed persons under 18 years of age. The accumulated dose at any subsequent age, therefore, should not exceed 5(N-18); where 5 is the maximum dose rate per year, N is the age of the worker in years; and 18 is the age prior to which no occupational dose is allowed. Below are two examples of calculating the maximum permissible (accumulated) dose.

Age 20
5(N-18) = 5(20-18) = 5(2) = 10 rems

Age 31
5(N-18) = 5(31-18) = 5(13) = 65 rems

b. Radiation protection guides further state that the maximum exposure for a 3-month period should not exceed 3 rems. This means that a radiation worker could actually be exposed to 12 rems in a single year and still be within permissible limits as long as his accumulated dose does not exceed the maximum established by the formula 5(N-18). For example, we will use the maximum dose for a 31-year-old radiation worker, which is shown above as 65 rems. If his exposure to date was 50 rems, 12 rems in 1 year would be permissible. This is not to say that an exposure of 12 rems during 1 year would be disregarded. An investigation should be undertaken to determine the source of the potential hazard, so the hazard can be eliminated. Obviously repeated exposures of 12 rems per year would eventually lead to overexposure.

c. The maximum permissible dose for the general population group is significantly lower than that of radiation workers. Currently it is recommended that the yearly radiation exposure to individuals in the general population should be held to one-tenth that of the occupational limits. This does not include exposure to natural radiation or medical and dental X-ray. Thus, for whole body exposure the radiation dose should not exceed 0.5 rems per year, and partial-body radiation dose should not exceed 7.5 rems per year. The reason general population rates are less than radiation worker rates is because radiation workers make up only a small percentage of the world population and if long-term effects result, the continuance of the species would not be endangered.

d. Study groups which have spent many years in researching the safe amount of radiation that a radiation worker may receive have taken into account the environmental and other manmade radiation to which he is exposed. This includes everything from cosmic rays to watch dials and TV screen emissions. Man's use of radiation in various forms grows day by day. Consequently, the daily nonprofessional exposure can be expected to rise. Three broad factors contribute to critical decisions of how much radiation we can or should tolerate. They are:

(1) Changing levels of environmental radiation.

(2) Rapid progressions in technology.

(3) Increasing knowledge of the biological effects of radiation, particularly those that may affect or modify the species.

The radiation protection guides discussed here are subject to constant modification and revision. It is the professional responsibility of every radiologic technologist to remain alert to these changing factors.

SECTION F—BIOLOGICAL EFFECTS

3-24. Introduction. Biological effects, also known as radiation injuries, are described as either chronic or acute. Chronic injuries are those that appear a long time after chronic exposure to radiation, in 1, 5, or 30 years or perhaps in succeeding generations. Acute injuries are those appearing relatively soon after acute exposure, within 60 days or so. Acute exposures, if survived, can lead to chronic effects later. The acute effects of whole-body irradiation will probably never be seen in a radiologic technologist, even with the most careless individual imaginable. Therefore, the discussion of these effects will be brief and of academic interest only. Chronic effects are, however, of vital concern to the technologist, not only for his personal interest, but also because of his responsibility to the patient in assuring an absolute minimum of needless exposure. CHRONIC EFFECTS CAN BE BROUGHT ABOUT BY THE CARELESS TECHNOLOGIST.

3-25. Acute Radiation Syndrome. The acute radiation syndrome (ARS), due to whole-body X- or gamma radiation, may reflect a variety of illnesses which are dose-dependent. Three major biological systems emerge as the centers of concern, depending upon the amount of radiation received at the time of exposure. They are the hematopoietic (marrow) system, gastrointestinal (GI) system, and the central nervous (brain) system.

a. The marrow ARS is evident between doses of 200 R and 1,000 R. Extreme depression of the blood cells results in severe anemia and overwhelming infection. Deaths average from 20 percent at the lower end of the range to 100 percent at the upper extreme. Medical treatment is extremely complicated and of long duration, but biological salvage is possible.

b. The GI ARS is evident in dose ranges of 1,000 R to 5,000 R. The classic picture is bloody diarrhea and adynamic ileus, resulting in severe fluid and electrolyte loss.

Deaths are 100 percent as there is no effective medical treatment.

c. The brain ARS, following exposures of over 5,000 R, is also 100 percent fatal. Incapacitation is produced in less than 10 minutes. The classical symptoms are convulsions progressing to coma and death. Cause of death is a sudden and overwhelming cerebral edema. Obviously, there is no effective treatment.

3-26. Chronic Effects. It should be noted that chronic effects are not qualified by the whole or partial-body exposure theories. Chronic effects can and do result from intermediate dose ranges, and even from very low dose ranges if exposure is repeated often enough.

a. Radiation exposures increase the incidence of certain types of cancer in man. While the exact mechanism of this damage is not known, repeated radiation damage and repair seems to account for some cases; whereas in others, the occurrence of somatic cell mutations seems an attractive hypothesis. Earliest evidence was the occurrence of skin cancers at the site of repeated X-ray burns among the early X-ray workers. Bone tumors were markedly increased among the radium watch dial painters.

b. Increases of leukemia incidence have been documented particularly among early radiologists. Since 1911, when four cases were described, the incidence of leukemia among radiologists has increased. The rate in 1952 was some eight times greater than among the general population. This increase does not indicate that radiologists are more careless. It simply reflects the aging of the early radiologists, the time at which the delayed effect becomes more obvious. At present, there has not been a threshold dose established for this phenomenon. In other words, it is not known how much is too much.

c. Extensive animal data has established that radiation exposure produces an acceleration of the aging process. This effect is quite apart from any specific disease manifestation. The animal simply ages faster and dies sooner from causes indistinguishable from those of nonirradiated animals. On the average, the life span is shortened by about 7 percent per 1,000 R of total dose. As with carcinogenesis, no threshold is apparent.

d. As early as 1927 it was reported that radiation increases the rate of mutations in the fruit fly. This work has since been confirmed in other species. As further evidence of the difference in species' resistance to radiation, it has been shown that the mutagenic effect is 10 times greater in the mouse than in the fruit fly for a given radiation dose. Obviously, there is very little human data regarding radiation-induced mutations. However, the following biological facts provide sufficient evidence to warrant concern:

(1) Mutations are transmitted to succeeding generations.

(2) Mutations may be dominant or recessive.

(3) Mutations will eventually result in genetic death.

(4) There is no threshold dose for the genetic effects of radiation.

(5) Any exposure is accompanied by the production of some mutations.

(6) The number of mutations is proportional to the dose.

e. Direct exposure of the gamete or zygote may occur during X-ray examination of the parent. Indeed, any exposure during the first trimester (first 3 months) of pregnancy MAY carry the penalty of an abnormal child. Chromosome activity is at its maximum in early pregnancy. It has been determined on numerous occasions that therapeutic doses of radiation to a pregnant woman can even produce fetal death. The degree of abnormality varies roughly in proportion to dose rates and exposure time, but there is as yet insufficient evidence to establish a minimum threshold dose for humans.

f. Fertility effects are a grossly overrated radiation effect. True, radiation is capable of reducing fertility—the amount of reduction being dependent upon the dose. However, except for direct, repeated exposure to the gonads, no radiation environment in peacetime is expected to be high enough to cause sterility, either temporary or permanent.

g. Irradiation of the eye has been shown to result in cataract formation (lenticular opacity), which appears some time after exposure by X- or gamma rays and corpuscular radiations.

SECTION G—PRACTICING RADIATION PROTECTION

3-27. Introduction. The previous discussion in this chapter shows how adverse biological effects can occur as a result of exposure to ionizing radiation. The discussion also shows that the effects can occur well within the dose levels necessary in medical X-ray diagnosis and treatment. Consequently, radiation protection must be the concern of every radiologic technologist. In addition to having some knowledge of the biological effects of ionizing radiation you must practice positive, protective measures in the exposure room. Furthermore, it is not enough to limit the protection to you, the technologist; the patient deserves, and should be given, equal consideration to keep his exposure also at a minimum. The final responsibility for protecting both yourself and your patient from needless exposure to radiation rests with you. Granted, health physicists, radiologists, supervisors, and other personnel establish and maintain protective programs in the radiology department. But without the constant efforts of the technologist, who makes the radiographs, effective protection against ionizing radiation will not exist. This section will present some procedures to be used by the technologist to reduce exposure to himself, to his patients, and to others who must be present in the exposure room.

3-28. Protection for the Technologist. Good working habits, common sense, and proper respect for ionizing radiation are very important in radiation protection. With present day knowledge and the vast amount of protective resources at your disposal, there is absolutely no reason for you to even closely approach the maximum permissible dose. If proper precautionary measures are practiced daily, the risk involved in being an X-ray technologist is very small, when compared to other risks such as driving a car, crossing the street, et cetera. The steps necessary to keep your exposure at a minimum can be divided into two categories: (1) those that protect you from the primary beam, and (2) those that protect you from secondary and scattered radiation (SR).

a. Protection from the Primary Beam. Protecting yourself from primary radiation is very simple: do not expose any part of your body to the primary beam. This means that during exposure you should never hold a patient or cassette, or in any other way subject yourself to primary radiation. In addition, you should not allow another technologist to perform these tasks. If assistance is needed to obtain a radiograph on uncooperative patients, use someone who is not occupationally exposed to ionizing radiation. Paragraph 3-30 gives further details.

b. Protection from Secondary and Scatter Radiation. Although the intensity of SR is less than primary radiation (for a given technique), the radiation hazard to the technologist is perhaps greater with SR. The reason for this is because SR can reach virtually all parts of the exposure room while the primary beam is restricted to an area which is much smaller by comparison. Therefore, while it is a simple matter to remain clear of the primary beam, it is somewhat more difficult to elude SR. Following are some general rules to adhere to.

(1) Standing Behind a Protective Barrier. Always remain behind a protective barrier when making an exposure. Control booths are designed so that the technologist will not be exposed to any radiation that has scattered only once. In other words, the radiation must scatter at least twice before it reaches you. Use the lead impregnated glass window to observe the patient. Do not defeat the purpose of the control booth by leaning out from behind the barrier to make the exposure.

(2) Using Distance for Protection. Distance is an effective means to reduce exposure. Since radiation intensity decreases as the distance from the source increases, exposure can be reduced by staying as far from the source as possible. This rule is particularly important to remember when taking portable radiographs where protective barriers are usually not available.

(3) Protection During Fluoroscopy. During fluoroscopy be sure to wear a protective apron. When you are not needed to assist the radiologist, remain in the control booth.

3-29. Protection for the Patient. As previously mentioned, any radiation protection program must include patients. There are several ways to reduce radiation exposure to the patient.

a. Repeat Films. A common cause of additional patient exposure is due to repeat films. When a film is repeated because of improper processing, positioning, technique selection, or other technical reasons, the patient (as well as the technologist) is subjected to twice the original exposure. Therefore, getting a diagnostic radiograph on the first attempt helps considerably in protecting the patient.

b. Collimation. A major cause of excessive patient exposure is failure to adequately restrict the primary beam. Always limit the primary beam to the smallest size necessary to include the part or parts being X-rayed. Primary radiation should not cover any areas beyond the borders of the film. In other words if you are using a 14" x 17" film, the beam should never be greater than 14" x 17". There are times when it is advisable to restrict the primary beam to a size smaller than the size of the film. Some examples are sinuses, spot films, and other examinations where a restricted beam will not interfere with the diagnostic information. (An added "bonus" of restricting the primary beam to the smallest practical size is the reduction of SR, and consequently less fogging of the film.)

c. *Filtration.* In most instances, soft or low energy X-rays that exit from the tube serve no useful purpose in diagnostic radiology. They have little or no penetrating power and consequently are absorbed by the patient's skin. To protect the patient from this type of radiation, filters must be added to the useful beam. According to NCRP Report No. 33, total filtration in the useful beam shall not be less than 2.5 mm of aluminum or equivalent for voltages greater than 70 kVp. For voltages between 50 and 70 kVp a minimum of 1.5 mm aluminum or equivalent is required. Below 50 kVp total filtration should be 0.5 mm aluminum or equivalent. This requirement (0.5 mm) may be assumed to have been met if a conventional diagnostic tube is employed since inherent filtration in conventional tubes is at least 0.5 mm aluminum equivalent. If a beryllium window tube is employed, appropriate added filtration will be required.

d. *High-kVp Technique.* The absorbed radiation dose, and therefore, the biologically significant dose, to the patient can be reduced by using high-kVp techniques. Intelligent use of high-kVp techniques produces excellent results, but the technologist must be aware of its limitations. Obviously, when maximum contrast is required, as in mammography, high kVp cannot be used. In terms of radiation protection, high kVp does not necessarily mean 100 to 150 kVp, but it should be interpreted to mean the highest kVp that will produce a good quality radiograph of a particular part.

e. *Films and Screens.* High-speed screens and films are available and their use will certainly reduce the radiation exposure to the patient. Again, they must be intelligently used. Whenever the speed of a screen or film is increased, there is some loss of detail. If the radiologist is willing to sacrifice some radiographic detail in order to reduce exposure to the patient, by all means use high-speed screens and films. He must make the decision since he is the one who interprets the films.

f. *Shielding.* Make it a point to shield the gonadal area of patients whenever possible. Gonadal shields should be used for an examination of the hips on children, but make sure the parts to be examined are not covered. The gonadal dose can be considerably reduced by using lead-rubber shielding on such examinations as femur, hips, and lumbar spines. Lead shielding should be used in addition to collimators and cones since it will protect the patient from SR. The use of lead aprons to cover the part of the abdomen that is not being examined is highly recommended. In the case of children, a special effort should be made to protect the sternum, femurs, and humeri since most of the red blood cells are produced in the marrow of these bones.

g. *Pregnant Patients.* Paragraph 3-26e of this chapter explains the dangers of exposing pregnant women to ionizing radiation, particularly during early pregnancy. The decision as to whether the diagnostic information to be gained outweighs the potential radiation danger rests entirely with the patient's physician. In some cases such as "prenatal" chest films and pelvimetry, diagnostic information may be considered necessary. In other cases it may be appropriate to delay the examination until later in the pregnancy or after delivery. As mentioned before, these decisions rest entirely with the patient's physician because he is more familiar with her particular case than anyone else. The problem arises when the physician does not know that his patient is pregnant. In this case you should inform the patient's physician or the radiologist so a decision can be made regarding her X-rays. How do you know the patient's pregnancy status? Ask her! There are some general rules to observe when asking a patient if she is pregnant. Keep in mind that you should use common sense and good judgment to avoid embarrassing questions.

(1) Do not ask her in the presence of others. Choose a private place such as the exposure room.

(2) Choose words that are in good taste.

(3) Explain why you want to know but do not alarm her with the information that radiation will absolutely result in damage to the fetus.

(4) Ask only those that are procreative. For example, do not ask a 65-year-old patient if she is pregnant.

3-30. Protection for Others. Anyone who is not needed to assist should not be allowed in the exposure room during the examination. At times it will be necessary for others to remain in the room. Some of those needed for assistance and some steps to take to protect them from radiation are discussed below.

a. Parents will sometimes be required to remain in the room with a child. They should not remain in the exposure room during the examination unless they are needed. They may be needed to hold the film, to hold the child, or merely to be present to assist the technologist in getting the child's cooperation. If possible, they should remain in the control booth during exposure. If needed to hold the film or child, be sure to have them wear protective aprons and gloves. (Pregnant women should not be allowed to hold a film or child during exposure.)

b. At times it will be necessary to use other hospital personnel to assist you by holding film, patients, et cetera. Use only personnel not occupationally exposed to ionizing radiation and do not use the same person for extended periods of time. Again, be sure they are properly protected with lead aprons and gloves.

———

GLOSSARY OF RADIOLOGIC TECHNOLOGY

CONTENTS

———

GLOSSARY

1. Abbreviations:

A, amp: ampere

Å: Angstrom unit

AC: alternating current

ADR: air dose rate

AP: anteroposterior

APLO: anteroposterior lateral oblique

APMO: anteroposterior medial oblique

ARS: acute radiation syndrome

ASIS: anterior superior iliac spine

AWG: American Wire Gage

B.E.: barium enema

BSF: backscatter factor

Ci: curie

cm: centimeter(s)

CR: central ray

DC: direct current

DNA: deoxyribonucleic acid

dps: disintegrations per second

DPT: double-part thickness

EAM: external auditory meatus

EFS: effective focal spot

EMF: electromotive force

EOP: external occipital protuberance

eV: electron volts

FFD: focal-film distance, focus-film distance

FRC: Federal Radiation Council

FS: focal spot

FSD: focal spot distance

GB: gallbladder

GCD: greatest common divisor

GI or G.I.: gastrointestinal

G.U.: genitourinary

H.U.: heat units

HVL: half-value layer

Hz: hertz

ICRP: International Commission on Radiation Protection

ICRU: International Commission on Radiation Units and Measurement

I.M.: intramuscular

I.V.: intravenous

IVC: intravenous cholangiogram, inferior vena cavagram

IVP: intravenous pyelogram

IOML: infra-orbitomeatal line

KeV: kilo electron volts (one thousand electron volts)

kHz: kilohertz, 1000 hertz

KUB: kidneys, ureters, and bladder

kV: Kilovolts

kVp: Kilovoltage peak

kW: kilowatt

LAO: left anterior oblique

Lat: lateral

LCD: least common divisor

LCM: least common multiple

LD: lethal dose

LPO: left posterior oblique

mA: milliampere, milliamperage

mAs: milliampere second

MeV: million electron volts

MHz: million hertz

mm: millimeter(s)

MPD: maximum permissible dose

$M\Omega$: megohm, 1000 ohms

μCi: microcurie

μV: microvolt

mV: millivolt

NCRP: National Council on Radiation Protection and Measurements

Obl: oblique

OFD: object-film distance

OML: orbitomeatal line

PA: posteroanterior

PALO: posteroanterior lateral oblique

PAMO: posteroanterior medial oblique

P-B: Potter-Bucky

PE: photographic effect

PF: photofluorography

PFD: part-film distance

PFX: photofluorographic X-ray

PHT: primary circuit of the high-tension circuit

PSIS: posterior superior iliac spine

R: roentgen

rad: radiation absorbed dose

RAO: right anterior oblique

RBE: relative biological effectiveness

rem: roentgen equivalent man

rep: roentgen equivalent physical

r-m-s: root-mean-square value

RNA: ribonucleic acid

rpm: revolutions per minute

RPO: right posterior oblique

RR: remnant radiation

SB: small bowel

SDR: skin dose rate

sec: second(s)

SHT: secondary circuit of the high-tension circuit

SMV: submentovertex, submentovertical

SR: secondary and scattered radiation

TFD: target-film distance

TMJ: temporomandibular joint

TSD: target-skin distance

UGI or U.G.I.: upper gastrointestinal

U.S.P.: United States Pharmacopeia

V: volts

VPT: volts-per-turn ratio

W: watt

2. Prefixes:

a or an	without, not, absence of.
ad	to, toward.
adeno	of or pertaining to a gland.
ambi or amphi	both; pertaining to or affecting both sides.
angio	pertaining to a blood vessel.
ante	before.
antero	in front of, front.
anti	opposite, against, counter.
ap or apo	separation or derivation from.
arterio	pertaining to the arteries.
bi or di	two or twice.
bio	life.
cardio	pertaining to the heart.
cephalo	pertaining to the head or skull.
cerebro	pertaining to the brain.
chiro	hand.
chole	pertaining to bile or to the biliary tract.
co	with, together.
colo	pertaining to the colon.
con	with.
costo	rib.
cysto	cyst, sac, or bladder.
dactylo	finger, toe, digit.
derma or dermato	skin.
dextro	of, pertaining to, or toward the right.
di	twice
dia	through or apart.
dis	reversal or separation.
dys	difficult, painful or bad.
ec, ecto, ex	out or out of; without, on the outer side, external, away from.
en	in, within.
encephalo	pertaining to the brain.
endo or ento	innermost, within.
entero	pertaining to the intestines.
epi	on, upon, above.
extra or extro	on the outside, beyond, in addition.
gastro	pertaining to the stomach.
hema, hemato, hemo	pertaining to the blood.
hemi	one-half; pertaining to or affecting one side of the body.
hetero	different.
homo	the same.
hydro	water.
hyper	above, beyond, or excessive.
hypno	sleep.
hypo	beneath, under, or deficient.
hystero	uterus.
ileo	ileum.
in, il, im, ir	not, in, within, inward, into, toward.
infra	beneath.
inter	between.
intra	within, inside of.
iso	equal, alike, or the same.
kilo	one thousand.
latero	to the side of.
leuko	white or colorless.
levo	of, pertaining to, or toward the left.
litho	stone or rock.
macro	large; abnormal size.
mal	bad, abnormal.
mega	great size, one million times.
melano	black.
meso	middle.
meta	change, after or next.
micro	small, one-millionth of.
mono	one or single.
morpho	form.
multi	many.
myelo	bone marrow or spinal cord.
myo	muscle.
neo	new, recent, young.
nephr, nephro	kidney.
neur, neuro	nerve.
ob	in front of, against.
odonto	tooth.
ophthalmo	eye.
ortho	straight, normal, correct.
osteo	bone.

oto	ear.
pan	all.
para	beside, alongside of, apart from.
peri	around, about.
pneumo	lung, air, or respiration.
pod, podo	foot.
poly	many, much.
post	after.
postero	behind.
prae, pre	before.
pro	before or in front of.
proct, procto	rectum.
pseudo	false.
pyo	pus.
pyr, pyro	fire or heat.
retro	backward, located behind, or against the natural course.
rhin, rhino	nose.
semi	half.
sphygmo	pulse.
sub	under, beneath.
super, supra	excess of, above, upon.
sym, syn	with, together, same.
ter, tri	three, thrice, threefold.
trans	across, through, over.
uni	one.
uro	pertaining to urine or to the urinary tract.

3. Suffixes:

agogue	inducing agent.
agra	seizure of acute pain.
algia	painful condition.
cele	tumor or swelling.
ectomy	excision.
graph	a record.
ia	disease condition.
itis	inflammation.
logy	science of.
mania	excessive preoccupation with something.
meter	instrument for measuring.
oid	like, resembling.
oma	tumor.
opia	eye or vision.
osis	fullness, redundancy, excess.

pathy	a morbid condition or disease.
phobia	morbid or exaggerated fear or dread.
plasty	plastic surgery.
rrhea	flow or discharge.
scope	instrument for making a visual examination.
scopy	visual examination.
stomy	surgical creation of an artificial opening.
tomy	incision.

4. Physical, Radiological, and Medical Terms:

Abduct. To draw away from the midline of the body; opposit of adduct.

Absorption. The attenuation or reduction in intensity of X-rays as they pass through any absorbing material. A condition in which a liquid or gas is taken up by and fills the interstitial spaces of a porous substance.

Acanthiomeatal Line. An imaginary line extending from the acanthion to the external auditory meatus.

Acanthion. A point at the base of the anterior nasal spine.

Acetabulum. The hip socket of the innominate bone.

Acromion. The outward extension of the spine of the scapula, forming the point of the shoulder.

Actual Focal Spot. The area on the X-ray tube target which is bombarded by high speed electrons and from which the X-rays are emitted.

Added Filter. A filter, usually of aluminum, designed to be placed in the portal of the tube housing for additional filtration. It filters out the softer rays and reduces the amount of radiation to the patient's skin.

Adduct. To draw toward the midline of the body; opposite of abduct.

Adipose. Fat; fatty.

Afferent. Leading into or toward an organ, tissue or collection center; opposite of efferent.

Air-Dose. The dose of radiation in roentgens measured in free air.

Alpha Rays. The positively charged particles (helium atom nuclei) which are ejected from the nucleus of certain radioactive atoms.

Alternating Current. A current in which the electrons are periodically reversing direction and speed. Ordinary United States alternating current has 60 cycles per second.

Alternation. One-half cycle of alternating current; one alternation lasts 1/120 second. Also called an impulse or pulsation.

Ambient Temperature. The temperature of the air surrounding the heated parts of an electric circuit.

Ammeter. An electrical instrument which measures current flow in amperes.

Ampere. The practical unit of measurement of electric current, indicating the rate (quantity per second) of electron flow through a conductor. One ampere equals 6.28 x 10^{18} electrons per second.

Angiography. The radiographic examination of the blood vascular system after the injection of an aqueous solution of contrast medium.

Angstrom. The unit of length used for measuring wavelengths of X-rays and other forms of electromagnetic waves. One angstrom equals one one-hundred millionth of a centimeter.

Anode. The positively charged portion of any vacuum tube. In the X-ray tube, the anode contains the target which is bombarded by electrons during X-ray production.

Anode Thermal Capacity. The quantitative ability of the anode portion of the X-ray tube to store and withstand large amounts of heat.

Anterior. Refers to the front portion of the body, or of an organ or part.

Anteroposterior. The positioning of a part so that the CR enters from the anterior aspect and emerges from the posterior aspect.

Antiseptic. A substance that will prohibit the growth of microorganisms without necessarily destroying them.

Antrum. A cavity or chamber, especially one within a bone.

Aorta. The large artery which carries the blood away from the heart.

Apex. The top or pointed end of any conical structure or part, as in the heart or lung.

Apnea. Temporary arrest of respiration.

Arachnoid. Resembling a spider's web.

Armature. The part of a generator or motor that rotates between the field poles and carrying windings in which the electromotive force acts for operating the machine.

Armature Coil. A coil of wire placed on the armature of a generator or motor; part of the armature winding.

Armature Core. The iron cylinder or ring on which, or in which, armature windings are carried.

Arteriography. The radiographic examination of the arteries after the injection of a contrast material.

Arthrography. The radiographic examination of a joint after injection of a contrast material.

Articular. Pertaining to a joint.

Articulation. The place of junction between two or more bones; also called joint.

Artifacts. Foreign or artificial marks on a radiograph which may be caused by static, dirty or damaged screens, loose foreign bodies in the cassette, et cetera.

Aseptic. Free from mircroorganisms which produce putrefaction or rotting.

Aspirate. The act of removing or drawing off by suction, the removal of fluids or gases from a cavity by means of an aspirator.

Atom. The smallest unit of matter which can remain unchanged in chemical reactions.

Atomic Number. The number denoting the total number of protons in the nucleus of an atom; symbol Z.

Atomic Weight. The average relative weight of an atom as compared to the weight of carbon which is represented as 12. It is approximately equal to the sum of all protons and neutrons in the nucleus of the atom; symbol A.

Atrium. A chamber affording entrance to another structure or organ; for example, one of the receiving chambers of the heart.

Attraction. The effect between magnetized bodies, as that between a magnet and iron or steel, by which they are drawn together.

Atypical. Irregular; deviating from the usual or normal.

Auricular Point. The center of the opening of the external auditory meatus.

Autotransformer. A transformer in which part of the winding is in both the primary circuit and the secondary circuit, used to boost or reduce line voltage for voltage corrections, control, et cetera; a transformer in which the primary and secondary are combined.

Axial. Derived from the term *axis* and referring to structures located symmetrically around a straight line or central point.

Axilla. The armpit, or the cavity beneath the junction of the arm and shoulder.

Axis. Any lengthwise central line, real or imaginary, around which parts of a body are symmetrically arranged, as the spinal column in man. Also, the second cervical vertebra.

Backscatter Rays. Secondary rays formed from remnant radiation which has passed through the film holder and is scattered back toward the X-ray film.

Ballistic Milliammeter. A milliammeter having a weighted needle and which measures the product of milliamperes (mA) and time (sec), and is designed to read in milliampere-seconds (mAs). See *mAs meter*.

Barium. A metallic element. The term barium is usually used to refer to barium sulfate, an insoluble compound of barium and sulfuric acid, which is used as a contrast medium in medical radiography because of its high radiopacity.

Basilar. Pertaining to a base or basal part.

Beta Rays. Charged particles (electrons or positrons) which are ejected from the nuclei of certain radioactive atoms.

Bicipital. Having two heads.

Bifurcate. To divide into two branches.

Bilateral. Having two sides; pertaining to both sides; occurring on both sides.

Biliary. Pertaining to the secretion of the liver (bile), the bile ducts, or the gallbladder.

Bregma. A topographical point on the skull at the junction of the coronal and sagittal sutures.

Bremsstrahlung. A German word, meaning "braking radiation," which is used to designate those X-rays which are formed as a result of high speed electrons being braked to a much slower speed. Bremsstrahlung may be of any wavelength up to the maximum energy of the electrons.

Bronchography. The radiographic examination of the bronchial tree using a liquid contrast medium.

Bucky (Potter-Bucky Diaphragm). A device containing a moving grid and which is placed between the patient and the film to reduce the fogging effect of secondary radiation on the radiograph. See *Grid*.

Bursa. A small sack or saclike cavity filled with fluid interposed between parts that move upon one another to prevent friction.

Calcaneus. The heel bone; also called os calcis.

Calculus. Any abnormal concentration of mineral salts within the body. Commonly called "stones."

Calibration. The process of measuring the actual output of a machine as compared to its indicated or metered output.

Canaliculus. An extremely narrow tubular passage or channel (lit. "little canal").

Cannula. A tube for insertion into a body opening.

Canthomeatal Line. See *Orbitomeatal Line*.

Canthus. The angle at either end of the slit between the eyelids; the canthi are distinguished as outer or temporal and inner or nasal.

Capacity. A general term referring to the maximum output of a machine or to the ability that a device possesses to sustain a load.

Capitulum. An eminence on the distal end of the humerus articulating with the radius.

Cardboard Holder (Direct Exposure Holder). A lighttight device for holding film for direct X-ray exposure without the use of intensifying screens.

Cardiac. Pertaining to the heart or to the end of the stomach nearest the heart.

Cardio-angiography. The radiographic examination of the heart and great vessels after intravenous injection of an aqueous solution of contrast medium. Also, referred to as angiography, angiocardiography.

Cassette. A device for holding X-ray film during exposure. It is composed of two fluorescing intensifying screens in a metal and bakelite holder.

Cassette Changer. A piece of radiographic equipment designed for quick changing of cassettes so that successive exposures may be made without changing the position of the patient, as in stereoscopy.

Catheter. A thin tube used for draining fluid from cavities or for distending passages.

Cathode. The negatively charged electrode of any vacuum tube. In the X-ray tube, the cathode contains the filament, which, when heated, produces a cloud of electrons that may be pushed across the tube to produce X-rays.

Cathode Rays. The stream of electrons flowing away from the cathode in a vacuum tube.

Caudad. Toward the tail or the lower portion of the body.

Centigrade. Temperature scale having 100 degrees of graduation, and in which 0° represents the freezing point and 100° the boiling point of water under standard conditions (sea level).

Centimeter. A unit of measurement equal to approximately 0.4 inch.

Central Ray. The theoretical center of the X-ray beam. The central ray leaves the focal spot at 90° from the long axis of the tube housing. Also called principal ray.

Cephalad. Toward the head.

Cephalic. Of or pertaining to the head.

Cephalometry. Measurement of the fetal head in the uterus.

Cerebral Angiography. The radiographic examination of the opacified blood vessels of the brain.

Cervical. Pertaining to the neck or cervical vertebrae; also, to any necklike part.

Cervix. Neck; referring to the neck of the body, or the constricted portion of an organ; for example, the cervix (neck) of the uterus.

Characteristic Radiation. X-rays which are produced by interorbital shifts of electrons within an atom. These rays are characteristic in wavelength of the specific atom which produced them.

Chemical Fog. The overall density of a radiograph produced by contaminated developer or other chemicals not by light or X-rays.

Choke Coil. A device consisting of a coil of wire with an adjustable soft iron core. The choke coil is used as a voltage and current regulator.

Cholangiography. The radiographic examination of the biliary tract following intravenous injection of a suitable contrast medium. It may be performed during or following surgery.

Cholecystography. A radiographic examination of the gallbladder following oral or intravenous administration of a suitable contrast medium.

Cinefluorography. A radiographic procedure wherein motion pictures are taken of images on a fluorescent screen. Also see *Image-Intensifier Cinefluorography.*

Circuit. The complete path through which the current flows; a certain part of the complete part, such as one of its conductors.

Clavicle. The collar bone; a bone curved like the letter s, which articulates with the sternum and the scapula.

Clearing Time. Time required for the fixer to dissolve unexposed salts in X-ray film emulsion.

Closed Circuit. An electric circuit that is complete and through which current may flow when voltage is applied.

Coccyx. The "tail" bone at the caudal end of the spinal column.

Collimator. A diaphragm or other device for confining a beam of radiation within a limited area.

Commutator. A ring of copper segments insulated from each other and connected to the windings of an armature. The alternating impulses from the armature conductors are passed by the commutator into the brushes so that current flowing through any one brush is always in the same direction.

Compression Band. A broad band made of nonopaque material employed for compression and/or immobilization.

Conductance. The conducting power of a body or a circuit for electricity. When expressed in figures, conductance is the reciprocal of resistance. The unit is the mho.

Conductor. Any material which allows easy passage of an electric current through it.

Condyle. A rounded knucklelike articular process of a bone. Applied chiefly to articular prominences occurring in pairs, such as those of the femur, mandible, and the occipital bone.

Cone. A cone-shaped device placed between the X-ray tube and the patient to limit the beam of primary radiation striking the part, thus reducing the amount of secondary radiation that is formed. See *Cylinder.*

Contrast. In general terms, contrast refers to the difference in density between the highlights and shadows seen in a radiograph. Mathematically, contrast may be defined as the ratio of the greatest density to the least density on a radiograph; the larger this ratio is, the greater the contrast is said to be. See *Scale of Contrast.*

Contrast Media. Substances which are introduced into tissues or organs for the purpose of producing radiographic contrast where contrast does not normally exist.

Coracoid Process. The hooklike process which projects anteriorly from the scapula.

Coronal Plane. Any vertical plane separating the body into anterior and posterior portions; also called the frontal plane.

Cornoid Process. A beaklike projection on the upper anterior edge of the mandible; also a process on the proximal end of the ulna.

Corpus. Body.

Cortex. The outer layer of an organ or structure.

Costal. Pertaining to the ribs.

Costophrenic Angle. The angle formed by the ribs and diaphragm; this angle can be clearly seen on a posteroanterior chest radiograph.

Cranial. Pertaining to the head.

Crest. A prominent ridge of the bone.

Cricoid. The ringlike cartilage below the "Adams's apple."

Culdoscopy. Visual examination of the female pelvic organs by means of endoscopy.

Cuneiform. Shaped like a wedge.

Current. The flow of electrons from one place to another.

Cutaneous. Pertaining to the skin.

Cyanosis. Bluish discoloration of the skin resulting from a deficiency in blood oxygen.

Cycle. One complete wave of alternating current or electromagnetic wave curve. A cycle consists of two complete alternations of alternating current.

Cylinder. A cylindrically shaped device which is sometimes used in the place of a cone. A cylinder which may be extended is called an extension cylinder.

Cyst. Any sac, normal or abnormal, especially one which contains a liquid or semisolid material.

Cystitis. Inflammation of the urinary bladder.

Cystography. The radiographic examination of the urinary bladder using an aqueous solution of a contrast medium.

Cystoscope. An instrument used for visual inspection of the interior of the urinary bladder.

Decubitus. A position for radiography in which the patient is lying down and the CR is projected horizontally. The words supine, prone, or lateral are employed in conjunction to describe the particular recumbent position.

Definition. The degree of distinctness with which image details are recorded on the X-ray film. See *Detail.*

Dens. The odontoid or toothlike process on the axis (second cervical vertebra).

Density. The degree of the blackness on a radiograph.

Density Equalization Filter. A radiographic accessory device that is used when it is desirable to cause a variation of X-ray intensity across a part of varying thickness.

Depth Dose. The dose of radiation actually delivered to a point at a specified depth below the surface of the body.

Detail. The relative sharpness of the internal structures of a body as they are demonstrated on a radiograph. This sharpness is affected by geometric factors only, whereas visibility of detail may also be affected by the density, contrast, and fog which are present.

Developer. The chemical solution used to make visible the radiographic image on X-ray film.

Diaphragm. An accessory device which consists of a sheet of lead with a hole in it; as a general rule, a diaphragm is used only when a cone or cylinder is not available. Also, the musculo-membranous partition that separates the abdomen from the thorax.

Diastole. The resting stage of the beating heart.

Dilatation. Natural or artificial enlargment, expansion, or distention of a cavity, canal, or opening.

Direct Current. An electric current in which the current flows in one direction at all times, as opposed to alternating current. A direct current in which the electrons flow smoothly, without change of speed, is called a *uniform direct current;* one in which the electrons are constantly changing speed but not direction is called *pulsating direct current.*

Direct Exposure Film. A type of X-ray film which is made to be especially sensitive in manufacture to the direct action of X-rays. This type of film is designed for use in cardboard holders only.

Distal. Remote, farthest from the center, origin, or head, as, the distal end of a long bone.

Distention. Enlargement or expansion.

Distortion. Difference in size and/or shape of the radiographic image as compared with that of the part examined. When only a change of size is involved it is called *magnified distortion.* When a change of size and shape is involved, it is termed *true distortion.*

Divergent. Radiating outward from a common point; spreading apart.

Dorsal. Pertaining to the back; situated nearer the back than some point of reference. In most cases, same as posterior and opposite of ventral.

Dorsal Spine. See *Thoracic Spine.*

Dose, Absorbed. The amount of radiation measured in rads which is absorbed by the part being exposed.

Dose Exposure. See *Exposure Dose.*

Dose Rate. The dose or amount of radiation delivered per unit of time (for example, roentgens (R) per hour).

Double Focus Tube. An X-ray tube having two focal spots, one of which is smaller than the other. The smaller one is used for maximum detail, the larger one to permit greater energy to be applied to the tube.

Dry Cell. A primary electric cell using carbon and zinc for electrodes with an electrolyte of sal ammoniac and chloride of zinc carried by some absorbent material in the cell. The carbon is the positive electrode and the zinc is the negative.

Duodenal Bulb. The triangular shaped structure forming the first portion of the duodenum and which can be seen on radiographic examination of the upper gastrointestinal tract.

Duodenum. The first or proximal portion of the small intestine, so called because it is about 12 fingerbreadths in length. It extends from the pylorus to the jejunum.

Dyspnea. Difficult breathing.

Effective Focal Spot. The perpendicular projection or effective size of the actual focal spot as it is presented to the film. The x-rays leave the rectangular actual focal spot and appear to be coming from a much smaller square area. In effect, the X-rays are emitted from the square area or the effective focal spot.

Efferent. Leading out of or away from an organ, tissue or collection center; opposite of afferent.

Electromagnet. A soft iron or soft steel core magnetized by the action of current passing through a coil around the magnet. It loses most of its magnetism as soon as the flow of current is stopped.

Electromagnetic Induction. The process by which a current is caused to flow in a circuit due to a magnetic field moving through the wires of a portion of the circuit. There are three types of electromagnetic induction: Relative motion, mutual induction, and self-induction.

Electromagnetism. Magnetism which exists about a wire while it has an electric current flowing through it.

Electromotive Force. The force which drives an electric current through a conductor. It is measured in volts. See *Voltage.*

Electron. The smallest negatively charged particle of matter revolving about the positively charged nucleus of an atom. Electrons moving through a wire constitute an electric current.

Electrostatic Unit. The quantity of electrical charge equal to the charge of 2,080,000,000 electrons.

Emulsion. The X-ray and light sensitive portion of the X-ray film before processing and the portion of the film that contains the image after processing.

Encephalography. The radiographic examination of the brain after the ventricles have been filled with a suitable contrast medium.

Energy. The capacity for performing work (moving a body through a distance).

Ensiform. See *Xiphoid Process.*

Enteric. Pertaining to the intestines.

Epicondyle. A roughened eminence upon a bone above its condyle; especially, the eminences above the condyles of the humerus.

Erythema Dose. The exposure dose which is required to cause a noticeable reddening of the skin within a few days.

Esophagus. The muscular membranous canal extending from the pharynx to the stomach.

Ethmoid. Perforated with small openings like a sieve.

Ethmoid Bone. A thin cancellous bone lying between the sphenoid and frontal bones of the skull.

Eversion. Outward rotation; for example, turning the sole of the foot away from the midline thus raising the lateral border of the foot.

Excrete. To eliminate waste material.

Expiration. The act of breathing out or expelling air from the lungs; exhaling.

Exposure Dose. The amount of radiation, measured in roentgens (R), which is delivered to a specific point.

Exposure, Radiographic. The process of subjecting a sensitive film to the action of X-rays either directly or through an intermediate step using intensifying screens.

Exposure Timer. A timer mechanism on the control panel of an X-ray machine to regulate time of exposure.

Extension. The straightening out of a part.

External. Situated or occurring on the outside.

External Auditory Meatus. The external canal or opening of the ear.

External Canthus of the Eye. See *Canthus*.

External Occipital Protuberance. A prominent eminence on the posterior portion of the occipital bone. Also called the inion.

External Rotation. Rotating a part away from the median plane.

Facial Line. A straight line touching the glabella and a point at the lower border of the face.

Femur. The thigh bone, located between the hip and knee joint.

Fetography. The radiographic examination of the fetus in utero.

Fibula. The smaller of the two leg bones located between the knee and the ankle joint.

Filament. A fine threadlike coil of tungsten which is mounted in the cathode of the X-ray tube. When heated, the filament becomes a source of electrons, the light source in an incandescent lamp and the source of free electrons in an electron tube.

Film, X-ray. The medium on which the radiographic image is recorded. See Screen-type Film.

Filter. See *Added Filter* and *Inherent Filtration*.

Fissure. A cleft, groove or trench.

Fixer. The chemical solution (commonly called "hypo") that clears the X-ray film and hardens the emulsion.

Flexion. The act of bending, or the condition of being bent or brought together.

Fluorescence. The emission of visible light by a crystal when subjected to an activating source.

Fluorescent Screen. A sheet of radiolucent material coated with a crystalline compound which fluoresces when exposed to X-rays.

Fluoroscope. A piece of radiographic equipment including an X-ray tube and a fluorescent screen. X-rays are absorbed by the patient and the resulting shadows are studied from the glow of the fluoroscopic screen.

Fluoroscopy. The process of examining the tissues by means of a fluoroscopic screen. See also *Image Intensification*.

Focal-Film Distance. The distance from the focal spot of the X-ray tube to the film.

Focal-skin Distance. See *Target-skin Distance*.

Focal Spot. See *Actual Focal Spot* and *Effective Focal Spot*.

Fog. A supplemental density (silver deposit) that covers part or all of the film obscuring image visualization. Fog may occur as a result of exposing the film to secondary radiation, light, heat, and chemical fumes; or if outdated film is used.

Foramen. A hole or perforation; especially in a bone.

Foramen Magnum. The large opening in the base of the skull through which the spinal cord passes.

Frequency. Number of cycles per second in an alternating current or electromagnetic wave.

Frilling. Defect in a radiograph associated with separation of the emulsion from the base at the margin of the film.

Gamma Rays. Electromagnetic radiation spontaneously emitted from radioactive deposits or materials, such as radium. Their wavelengths are shorter than those of X-rays used in diagnostic radiography, and they possess great penetrating power.

Gastrointestinal Series. A series of fluoroscopic and radiographic examinations of the gastrointestinal tract, usually using barium sulfate as a contrast medium.

Gastrointestinal Tract. The esophagus, stomach, and the small and large intestines collectively.

Glabella. The anterior protuberance of the frontal bone (between the eyebrows).

Glabella-alveolar Line. An imaginary line extending from the glabella to the upper alveolus; the localization plane of the face.

Gluteal. Pertaining to the buttocks.

Gonion. Anatomical landmark, the most inferior, posterior, and lateral point on the external angle of the mandible.

Grid. A device composed of alternate thin strips of lead and a radiolucent material encased in a suitable binder placed between the patient and the radiographic film to absorb scattered and secondary radiation.

Grid Focus. The point at which all of the radiopaque strips in a grid would meet if they were extended.

Grid Radius. The distance from the grid focus to the center of the grid.

Grid Ratio. The ratio of the height of the lead strips to the distance between them (thickness of radiolucent material).

Ground. An electrical connection to the earth or the metal framework or supports of electrical parts; a wire connecting directly to the earth, usually through a gas, water, or steam line.

Grounded Circuit. A circuit completed through ground, through the earth, or the metal framework of electrical parts.

Half-Value Layer. The thickness of a homogenous filter which will reduce the intensity of the X-ray beam to one-half of its original value.

Heat Unit. An arbitrary unit of measurement of the heat produced in an X-ray tube. Heat units are electrically equivalent to watt-seconds, and are the product of kVp X mA X sec.

Hepatic. Pertaining to the liver.

Horizontal. Parallel to the horizon or ground; at right angles to the vertical.

Hot Cathode Tube. Any X-ray tube utilizing a heated cathode for its source of electrons.

"Hypo". See *Fixer.*

Hysterosalpingography. See *uterosalpingography.*

Ileum. The last portion of the small intestine.

Iliac Crest. Referring to the curving superior border of the ilium.

Iliac Spine. A small but prominent projection on the anterior surface of the ilium; spoken of as the anterior superior iliac spine.

Ilium. The hip bone or winglike portion of the innominate bone.

Image. The deposits of black metallic silver in the emulsion of the film which represent the anatomical structures of the part X-rayed.

Image Intensification. An electronic system of producing flourescent images by amplification of the brightness level so that they may be observed by means of a mirror-optical system or on a television monitor. Viewing may be done in subdued room light and dark adaptation is unnecessary.

Image-intensifier Cinefluorography. A radiographic procedure wherein a motion picture is used with an image intensification system to record a moving study of the amplified images as they occur on the output phosphor or the image-intensifier tube.

Immobilization. The act of rendering a body part immobile during a radiographic exposure.

Impulse. See *Alternation.*

Impulse Timer. An accurate timer for making fractional second exposures.

Inferior. Situated below a particular reference point.

Inferosuperior. Directed or extended from below upward.

Infra-orbital Margin. The inferior rim of a bony orbit.

Infra-orbitomeatal Line. An imaginary line extending from the lower margin of the orbit to the external auditory meatus.

Infusion. The introduction of a fluid, as saline solution, into a vein. An infusion flows in by gravity.

Inherent Filtration. That filtration which is built into the X-ray tube housing. It includes the tube window, a thin layer of oil, and the tube portal; and, usually, is equivalent to apprximately 0.5 mm of aluminum.

Inion. Anatomical landmark, the most prominent point of the external occipital protuberance.

Innominate Bone. One of the major bones of the pelvis; composed of the ilium, the ischium, and the pubis.

Inspiration. The drawing in of breath; the act of inhaling.

Insufflator. An instrument used to introduce a gas (for example, air) into a body cavity.

Intensifying Screen. A screen composed of fluorescent material, usually calcium tungstate, placed in close contact with an X-ray film to intensify the action of X-rays in radiography.

Intensity. Refers to the concentration or quantity of X-rays striking a unit of area per unit of time.

Internal Canthus of the Eye. See *Canthus.*

International Base Line. An imaginary line extending from the external canthus of the eye to the external auditory meatus.

Interpupillary Line. An imaginary line passing through the pupils of both eyes when the eyes are in a neutral position looking straight ahead.

Intravenous Pyelography. See *Pyelography, Excretory.*

Intubation. The process of introducing a tube into a hollow organ to keep a passage open.

Inverse Square Law. The statement of the relationship which exists between the intensity of radiation striking the film and the distance of the tube from the film. The intensity of radiation is inversely proportional to the square of the distance.

Inversion. Inward rotation; for example, turning the sole inward, thus raising the medial border of the foot.

Iodized Oil. A contrast medium in which an oil (poppyseed, olive, or peanut) is combined with iodine. Used as an injection for visualization of the sinuses, bronchi, et cetera.

Ionization. The process of either adding to or subtracting electrons from neutral atoms or molecules.

Ionization Chamber. An instrument for measuring the quantity of radiation in terms of the quantity of ionization produced by the radiation.

Jejunum. The second or center portion of the small intestine.

Kilovolt. A unit of electromotive force equal to 1000 volts.

Kilovolt Peak. The very highest voltage occurring at any time during an electrical cycle; the peak kilovoltage used in making any X-ray exposure.

Kilowatt. A measurement of electrical power equal to 1000 watts.

KUB. An abbreviation indicating a plain radiograph of the abdomen to study the kidneys, ureters, and urinary bladder.

Kymograph. A device for radiographically recording the range of motion of various organs, especially the chambers of the heart throughout the cardiac cycle. The method by which this is done is called kymography.

Latent Image. The invisible image produced on an exposed X-ray film by the action of X-rays or light. It is made visible by the process of development.

Lateral. Pertaining to the side; away from the midline; a positioning of the patient so that the X-ray beam passes from one side to the other.

Latitude. The range of exposure of an X-ray film permissible for a good diagnostic result.

Ligament. A band of tissue that connects bones or supports viscera.

Lithotomy Position. Position of patient on his back, with legs flexed on the thighs, thighs flexed on the belly, and abducted.

Localize. To restrict or limit to one area or part.

Lumbar Spine. The portion of the vertebral column below the thorax; the lower five vertebrae.

Lumen. The cavity or channel within a tube or hollow organ.

Magnet. A body possessing the property of magnetism which causes it to attract materials made of iron.

Magnetic Field. The space about a magnet in which its magnetic properties are present.

Malar. Pertaining to the cheek or cheek bone.

Malar Bone. The cheek bone; same as the zygoma.

Malleolus. A rounded process on either side of the ankle joint. The process at the inner side of the lower end of the tibia is termed the *inner* or medial malleolus. The process at the outer side of the lower end of the fibula is termed the *lateral or external malleolus.*

Mammography. The radiographic examination of the breast.

Mandible. The lower jaw bone.

Manometer. A U-shaped tube used for measuring the pressure of gases.

mAs Meter. See *Ballistic Milliammeter.*

Matrix. Background substance; in bone, intercellular substance containing calcium and phosphate salts; in blood and lymph, the fluid in which cells are suspended.

Maxilla. The upper jaw bone.

Maximum Permissible Dose. The maximum accumulated absorbed dose of radiation to which a person may be occupationally exposed. The maximum permissible dose is calculated by the following formula: MPD = 5(N-18). N = age of individual in years.

Meatus. An opening at the end of a canal; as, the external auditory meatus.

Medial. That portion of a structure or part which is nearer to the midline than some reference point; opposite of lateral.

Median Plane. An anteroposterior plane dividing the body into right and left halves; the mid-sagittal plane.

Mediastinum. The middle compartment of the chest between the lungs. It contains all the thoracic viscera except the lungs.

Meninges. The three membranes (the dura mater, arachnoid, and pia mater) that envelop the brain and spinal cord; the lining of the spinal canal and cranial cavity.

Mental Point. Anatomical landmark, the most anterior medial point of the chin.

Metacarpus. The bones of the hand.

Metatarsus. The bones of the feet.

Meter. An instrument for measurement; a measure of length in the metric system.

Milliammeter. An electrical instrument which measures milliamperes; a milliampere meter.

Milliampere. The unit of measurement of electric current equivalent to 1/1000th of an ampere.

Milliampere-Seconds. The product of time (sec) of an X-ray exposure and the milliamperage (mA) used. The mAs determines the quantity of radiation which is produced by an exposure.

Molecule. The smallest quantity of a material which can exist and retain all its chemical properties. Molecules may be chemically decomposed into atoms.

MOP-Glabella Line. An imaginary line extending from the maximum occipital point (MOP) to the glabella. Considered to be at right angles to the facial line.

Moving Grid. A grid that moves according to a preset time of exposure, or reciprocates continuously.

Mucosa. The membrane lining tubular structures, and containing gland cells that produce a slimy substance (mucus); often called the mucous membrane; for example, the lining of the G. I. tract.

Müller's Maneuver. Making a forced inspiratory effort with the nose and mouth held closed after the patient has emptied his lungs of air. See also *Valsalva's Maneuver.*

Myelin. The fatlike substance forming a sheath around certain nerve fibers.

Myelography. The radiographic examination of the spinal canal following the injection of a suitable contrast medium.

Myocardium. The middle layer of wall of the heart; literally the muscle of the heart.

Nasion. Anatomical landmark where the midsagittal plane intersects with the interpupillary line.

Nasolabial Junction. The point at which the nose and upper lip meet.

Navicular. Shaped like a boat.

Negative Charge. An electrically unbalanced condition which results when electrons are added to a neutral body. A negative charge attracts positive charges and repels other negative charges. See *Positive Charge.*

Nephrography. The radiographic examination of the parenchymal structures of the kidneys during their radiopacification by means of a contrast medium.

Neutron. An electrically neutral or uncharged particle of matter existing along with protons in the nuclei of most atoms.

Node. A small protuberance, knob or swelling.

Nomogram. A graph that enables one by the aid of a straightedge, to read off the value of a dependent variable, when the value of the independent variable is given.

Nonopaque. Radiolucent or penetrable by X-rays.

Nucleus. The heavy centrally located portion of the atom, containing most of the weight of the atom and carrying a positive charge.

Object-Film Distance. See *Part-film Distance.*

Oblique. Refers to a part having been rotated or turned less than 90° with respect to the X-ray film and the tube.

Occipital Bone. The bone that forms the base of the skull, posteriorly.

Occiput. The back of the head.

Odontoid Process. The toothlike process situated on the second cervical vertebra (axis) for articulation with the first cervical vertebra (atlas).

Ohm. The unit for designating electrical resistance.

Ohm's Law. The relationship between voltage (E), current (I), and the resistance (R) in an electrical circuit, and which may be expressed as: $E + I \times R$.

Oil Transformer. A transformer which is insulated by a bath of oil which circulates and cools the heated parts of the transformer while acting as an insulator.

Olecranon. The large bony process at the proximal end of the ulna; commonly called the elbow.

Opaque. Impenetrable by light or X-rays in the diagnostic quality range. Opposite of nonopaque and radiolucent.

Opaque Media. Any contrast media which may be introduced into a body cavity or structure to render it radiopaque to X-rays.

Open Circuit. An incomplete circuit, one broken at any point, so that current does not flow through any part of it.

Optimum kVp. A technique of exposure using a fixed kVp, as opposed to variable kVp.

Orbit. The path in which a body moves as it rotates about another body which attracts it. Also, the bony cavity containing the eye.

Orbitomeatal Line. An imaginary line extending from the external canthus to the external auditory meatus, and used in radiography for localization purposes. It is often called the canthomeatal line. NOT to be confused with the acanthiomeatal line.

Orifice. The entrance or outlet of any body cavity, or tube.

Orthoradiography. An examination minimizing distortion to record a part in its actual size.

Os Calcis. See *Calcaneus.*

Osseous. Of or pertaining to bone.

Ossicle. A small bone.

Overexposure. The result of exposing an X-ray film or person to an excessive amount of X-rays.

Oxidation. The process of changing a compound by removing one or more electrons from an atom, ion, or molecule. Oxidation signifies the loss of an electron.

Palmar. Referring to the palm of the hand.

Parallel. Lying evenly everywhere in the same direction but never meeting, however far extended; running side by side.

Paranasal Sinuses. The accessory sinuses which communicate with the nasal passages: the ethmoid, the frontal, the maxillary, and the sphenoid.

Parietal Bones. The large bones on either side of the top of the cranium. They form the greater part of the top, sides and roof of the skull.

Part-Film Distance. The distance between the X-ray film and the part being examined.

Part-thickness. The measurement, usually in centimeters, of the part being examined.

Pass Box. A two-way, lighttight tunnel for passing exposed and unexposed films in cassettes between the darkroom and exposure rooms. Also called transfer cabinet.

Patella. The knee cap.

Pelvimetry. Measurement of the dimensions and capacity of the female pelvis by radiographic methods.

Pelvis. The bony ring at the posterior extremity of the trunk, supporting the spinal column and resting upon the lower extremities. It is composed of the two innominate bones at the sides and in front, and the sacrum and coccyx behind.

Penetration. Refers to the ability of X-rays to pass through materials.

Percutaneous. Performed through the skin.

Perfusion. A liquid poured over or through something; the introduction of fluids into the tissues by their injection into the arteries.

Pericardium. The membranous sac that contains the heart and first portion of the great vessels.

Periphery. The outer surface or the circumference of a part of the body.

Perirenal Insufflation. Radiographic examination of the kidneys by air insufflation.

Peristalsis. Waves of contractions which pass along tubular organs and move the contents forward. Usually applied to the gastrointestinal tract.

Peritoneum. The serous membrane which lines the abdominal wall and invests the viscera.

Permissible Dose. See *Maximum Permissible Dose.*

Perpendicular. Of or pertaining to any two lines which meet at right angles.

Petrous Bone. The dense pyramidal-shaped portion of the temporal bone which houses the auditory canal.

Phalanges. The fourteen bones of the fingers and the toes.

Phosphorescence. The emission of light by a crystal after the activating source has ceased.

Photofluorography. The radiographic procedure by which a photograph is taken of a fluorescent image on a fluorescent screen. Also called photoroentgenography.

Photon. An individual electromagnetic ray; a "bundle" or "packet" of electromagnetic energy (quantum) that travels at the speed of light. Same as a quantum.

Phrenic. Pertaining to the diaphragm.

Pi Lines. Lines formed on film during automatic processing which were not intended to appear on the finished radiograph.

Placentography. Radiographic examination of the walls of the uterus for localization of the placenta.

Plantar. Pertaining to the sole of the foot.

Pleura. The serous-membrane cover of the lungs which lines the thoracic cavity and encloses the potential space called the pleural cavity.

Pneumoarthrography. Injection of air as a contrast medium into a joint space for the purpose of visualizing cartilaginous structures radiographically.

Pneumoencephalography. The radiographic examination of the ventricles of the brain after removal of varying amounts of cerebrospinal fluid and replacing it with air as a contrast medium.

Pneumoperitoneography. The radiographic examination of the peritoneum and intra-abdominal organs by means of an injection of air as a contrast medium.

Pneumothorax. The presence of air or gas in the pleural cavity may occur spontaneously or be caused by trauma.

Popliteal. Pertaining to the posterior surface of the knee.

Positive Charge. That electric charge which is left when electrons are removed from a neutral body. A positive charge attracts negative charges but repels other positive charges. See *Negative charge.*

Posterior. Toward the back (or dorsal surface) of the body.

Posteroanterior. The positioning of a part so that the CR enters its posterior aspect and exists from its anterior aspect.

Post-evacuation Film. A film of the large bowel made after the patient has evacuated the contrast medium.

Potential Difference. The difference in electrical pressure or voltages between two points in a circuit.

Potter-Bucky Diaphragm. See *Bucky.*

Primary. The part of any electrical device or circuit, attached directly to the source, as distinguished from the secondary which means parts depending directly on the primary in place of the source. Also a source that produces electricity for further action such as mechanical or chemical action.

Primary Factors. The primary radiographic factors to be considered when making an X-ray exposure are (1) kilovolt peak (kVp); (2) milliamperage (mA); (3) exposure time (sec); and (4) focal-film distance (FFD). These four primary factors can be adjusted on an X-ray machine to control the quality and quantity of radiation striking the film.

Primary Radiation. The X-rays which emanate directly from the actual focal spot of the X-ray tube.

Process. A projection, especially on a bone.

Pronation. Turning downward; applied to the hand, turning the palm downward; applied to the foot, lowering the medial margin of the foot.

Prone. A position of the body lying face downward.

Prostatography. The radiographic examination of the prostate gland.

Proton. The subatomic particle found within the nucleus of an atom. The proton is the unit of positive electrical charge.

Proximal. Nearer the point of attachment or origin.

Psoas Muscles. The heavy muscles of the lower spine.

Psoas Shadows. The radiographic appearance of the psoas muscles, which are pyramidal in shape, extending downward on either side of the spinal column from the 12th dorsal vertebra to the level of the iliac crest.

Pulmonary. Pertaining to the lungs.

Pulsating. Occurring in rhythmic beats or surges; for example, the pulsating current in an X-ray tube.

Pulsation. See *Alternation.*

Pyelography, Excretory. The radiographic examination of the kidneys, pelves, and ureters after the intravenous injection of a contrast medium which passes quickly into the urine. Also called intravenous pyelography (IVP).

Pylorus. The orifice between the termination of the stomach and the duodenal bulb.

Quantum. One of the very small increments into which many forms of energy are subdivided.

Radiation. Any kind of particle or wave which leaves a point source and radiates outward in all directions. Light and X-rays are forms of radiation.

Radiation Absorbed Dose. The unit of absorbed radiation dose equal to 100 ergs of energy absorbed per 1 gram of absorbing tissue.

Radioactive. A term referring to atoms which have unstable nuclei. As these atoms change to a more stable form they emit energy from the nucleus as alpha rays, beta rays, or gamma rays.

Radiograph. The record on a film which represents anatomical details of the part examined and which is formed by the differential absorption of X-rays within the part.

Radiography. The use of X-rays in making radiographs for diagnostic interpretation.

Radiologist. A physician who uses all forms of radiation in the diagnosis and treatment of disease.

Radiology. The science which deals with the use of all forms of radiant energy in the diagnosis and treatment of disease.

Radiolucent. That property of a material which allows it to be readily penetrated by X-rays.

Radiopaque. That property of a material which causes it to absorb a relatively large amount of the X-rays passing through it.

Radius. A straight line extending from the center to the periphery of a circle. Also, the bone of the lateral aspect of the forearm.

Ratio of Transformer. The ratio of the number of turns in the primary winding of a transformer to the number of turns in the secondary winding.

Rectification. The process of changing alternating current into pulsating direct current. See *Direct Current.*

Rectifier. A device which is used to rectify alternating current.

Recumbent. Lying down or reclining.

Reduction. The process of changing a compound by adding one or more electrons to an atom, ion, or molecule. Reduction signifies the gain of an electron.

Renal. Pertaining to the kidney.

Resistance. The opposition offered by a substance or body to the passage through it of an electric current, which is measured in ohms.

Respiration. The process of breathing.

Restrainer. In radiography, a chemical employed to check development of the unexposed silver bromide and to control the working speed of the developer with respect to the exposed silver bromide.

Reticular. Having the appearance of a network.

Retrograde. Back or directed against the natural course or flow.

Retrograde Pyelography. The radiographic examination of the urinary tract in which the contrast medium is injected into the pelves of the kidneys through catheters which are inserted into the ureters. Also called retrograde urography.

Roentgen. The unit of radiologic exposure dose designated by the symbol "R". One "R" of exposure will produce in tissues an absorbed dose of approximately one rad. The roentgen, rad and rem may be considered equivalent for purposes of X-ray protection.

Roentgen Rays. X-rays.

Rotating Anode Tube. An X-ray tube in which the target constantly rotates during exposure, thus permitting the heat to be distributed over a much larger area with a corresponding increase in X-ray producing capacity.

Rotation. The movement of a part about its axis.

Ruga. A ridge or fold of the mucous membrane, found in the palate, the stomach and vagina.

Sacrum. A curved triangular bone composed of five united vertebrae, situated between the fifth lumbar vertebra above and the coccyx below and the innominates on each side, and forming the posterior boundary of the pelvis.

Sagittal Plane. A plane which divides the body into right and left portions (not necessarily equal); of, or pertaining to the sagittal suture of the cranium which lies in the median plane of the body.

Salpingography. The radiographic examination of the fallopian tubes following injection of a suitable contrast medium.

Scale of Contrast. The range of densities in a radiographic image; the number of shades of gray demonstrated on the film. In general, a long scale of contrast (many shades of gray) is also a low contrast, while a short scale of contrast (few shades of gray-black against white) is also a high contrast. See Contrast.

Scanography. A method of orthoradiography for measuring the length of long bones.

Scapula. The shoulder blade; a flat, triangular shaped bone forming the posterior aspect of the shoulder girdle.

Scattered Radiation. Those rays that have suffered a change in direction after collision with interposed material.

Scout Film. A preliminary or survey film of a part, usually taken prior to the administration of opaque media; also to check technical factors.

Screen. A device consisting of a rigid backing on which fluorescent crystals are coated. A term applied both to a fluoroscopic screen and an intensifying screen.

Screen-type Film. A film having an emulsion which is designed to be especially sensitive to the bluish light emitted from intensifying screens. It may also be used in cardboard holders but, if so, requires more exposure than *direct exposure film.*

Secondary Factors. The factors which describe the quality of a finished radiograph. These are: density, contrast, detail, and distortion.

Secondary Radiation. X-rays which are produced as the result of the interaction of primary radiation and the absorbing material of the part being examined. Secondary rays go in all directions and may produce an overall density (fog) on the film.

Sella Turcica. A saddle-shaped bone structure at the base of the skull, in the sphenoid bone, which holds the pituitary gland.

Septum. A dividing wall; a partition.

Serial Films. A series of exposures taken to record progressive events; may also refer to films made at specified intervals for small bowel studies.

Serialography. A radiographic technique for making multiple exposures of a part or organ on a single film.

Serrated. Having a sawlike edge.

Short Circuit. An accidental connection of low resistance between the two sides of a circuit so that little or no current flows through the current-consuming device in the circuit.

Sialography. The radiographic examination of the salivary glands and ducts after the injection of a suitable contrast medium.

Sine Wave. A mathematical curve which is used to diagrammatically represent the flow of an alternating current or the change in magnetic and electric fields of electromagnetic radiations.

Sinus. A hollow cavity within a bone; especially those within the face and cranium, for example, the paranasal sinuses.

Skeletal Survey. A series of radiographs taken of the whole skeleton to rule out presence of pathology.

Skeleton. The body framework of the human body consisting of 206 named bones.

Soft Tissue Radiography. A special radiographic technique to demonstrate anatomical details of soft tissue.

Spectrum. A series of electromagnetic radiations arranged in the order of their wavelengths.

Sphenoid Bone. Irregular wedge-shaped bone at the base of the skull.

Sphincter. A ringlike band of muscle fibers which closes a natural orifice.

Sphygmomanometer. A device for measuring blood pressure.

Spinal Fluid. Fluid in the spinal canal surrounding the spinal cord.

Spine. The vertebrae composing the backbone or vertebral (spinal) column. Also, a sharp projection on a bone.

Spinning Top Test. To check an X-ray timer by means of a rotating circular metallic disc with a perforation at its periphery.

Spinous Process. That part of a vertebra which projects backward from the arch, giving attachment to muscles.

Splenoportography. The radiographic examination of the venous circulation in the spleen and related blood channels following introduction of a contrast medium.

Spot Film. A radiograph made of small isolated areas during fluoroscopy.

Stasis. A standing still or stoppage of the normal flow of the contents of the vessels or of any organ of the body.

Static Marks. Artifacts produced on a film due to discharges of static electricity. They may appear as irregularly shaped lines resembling trees, streaks, or smudges.

Stationary Gird. A thin wafer grid placed between the cassette and the part to be examined in order to absorb secondary and scattered radiation.

Stenosis. Narrowing or stricture of a duct or canal.

Step-up or Step-down Transformers. See *Transformer.*

Stereoradiography. The radiographic procedure by which two films are exposed of the same part from slightly different tube positions without moving the patient. The films so produced are then viewed on a stereoscopic viewing box in order to obtain a third dimensional effect not visible on the plain radiograph. Also called stereoscopy.

Sternal Angle. The angle formed by the junction of the manubrium and the gladiolus or body of the sternum. Also called Angle of Louis.

Sternum. The breast bone; it consists of three portions, the manubrium, the gladiolus, and the xiphoid (ensiform) process.

Stop Bath. An acid solution into which film may be immersed before fixing in order to stop the developing action promptly.

Storage Capacity. A term referring to the maximum quantity of heat measured in heat units which may be stored within an X-ray tube without burning out the tube.

Subcutaneous. Beneath the skin, hypodermic.

Submentovertex. The positioning of the head and X-ray tube so that the CR ray enters at a point just below the symphysis mentis and exists from the top or crown (vertex) of the skull.

Superior. Situated above or occurring in a higher position; also referring to the upper surface of an organ or structure.

Superoinferior. Directed from above downward.

Supination. The act of or position of lying on the back. The rotation of the hand so that the palm faces upward.

Supine. Lying face up.

Symphysis. The median point or union of two paired bones; as, the symphysis pubis.

Systole. The period of the heart's contraction; also, the contraction itself.

Target. The portion of the anode of the X-ray tube against which the electron stream is directed.

Target-Skin Distance. The distance from the target of the X-ray tube to the skin; this is a necessary consideration in determining absorbed dose by a patient in radiation therapy.

Teleroentgenogram. A film, usually of the chest, made at a distance of 6 feet.

Temporal Bone. The irregular bone at the side and base of the skull containing the organs of hearing.

Temporomandibular Joint. The joint between the temporal bone and the lower jaw located just anterior to the external auditory meatus.

Therapy. A term used in radiology to indicate treatment with radium, radioactive isotopes, and/or X-rays.

Thoracic. Pertaining to, or situated in the region of the chest.

Thoracic Spine. That portion of the vertebral column to which the ribs are attached. Also called dorsal spine.

Thorax. The part of the body between the neck and diaphragm and encased by the ribs.

Tibia. The longer of the two bones of the leg. The shin bone.

Timer. The device used on an X-ray machine to complete the electrical circuit so that X-rays will be produced for a limited period of time. See *Exposure Timer* and *Impulse Timer.*

Time-temperature Development. A method of film development in which the time or duration of development is dependent upon the temperature of the developer.

Tomography. A special technique in which various selected planes of the body can be clearly demonstrated on a radiograph while structures above or below are blurred in various degrees. Also termed planigraphy, laminagraphy, stratigraphy, and body-section radiography.

Transformer. An electrical device which changes an alternating current of a given voltage and amperage into another alternating current of a different voltage and amperage. A step-down transformer decreases voltage and increases amperage. A step-up transformer increases voltage and decreases amperage.

Transverse. Crosswise; lying perpendicular to the longitudinal axis of the body.

Transverse Plane. Any plane passing through the body perpendicular to the midsagittal and coronal planes.

Transverse Processes of Vertebrae. The bony projections which extend outward on either side of a vertebra to furnish attachments for muscles.

Trendelenburg Position. A supine position in which the pelvis is higher than the head of the patient. For radiographic purposes, the body may be tilted as much as 45°.

Trephining. Removing circular disks of bone from the skull with a crown saw (trephine).

Trochanter. One of two large rounded processes on either side of the femur, just below the femoral neck. The one on the outer side is called the greater trochanter, while the one on the medial side is called the lesser trochanter.

Trochlea. A modified condyle on the distal end of the humerus.

Tubercle. A small rounded projection on a bone.

Tuberosity. A large rounded projection on a bone.

Ulna. The inner and larger bone of the forearm, on the side opposite that of the thumb.

Underexposure. The result of exposing the X-ray film to an insufficient amount of X-rays.

Ureter. A small tube which carries urine from the kidney to the bladder.

Ureterography. The radiographic examination of the ureters after the injection of a contrast medium.

Urethra. The canal through which urine is excreted from the bladder.

Urethrography. The radiographic examination of the urethra after the injection of a contrast medium.

Urography. The radiographic examination of the urinary tract, or any of its parts, after the injection of the contrast medium.

Uterosalpingography. Radiographic examination of the uterus and fallopian tubes after introduction of contrast media. Also called hysterosalpingography.

Uterus. Womb

Vacuum Tube. Any type of sealed tube which has a very low gas pressure and will allow an electric current to flow through it. X-ray tubes and valve tubes are examples of vacuum tubes.

Valsalva's Maneuver. Forced expiration against a closed glottis after the patient has taken in a deep breath.

Variable kVp. Technique of exposure using a changeable kVp, as opposed to optimum kVp.

Vena Cava. One of the great veins the purpose of which is to carry blood back to the heart. It can be visualized on angiocardiograms.

Venography. The radiographic examination of venous structures during the injection of a radiopaque solution.

Venography, Portal. The radiographic examination of the liver following injection of a contrast solution directly into the portal vein.

Ventral. Situated in front of; referring to the anterior surface of the body.

Ventriculography. The radiographic examination of the ventricular system of the brain after removing the cerebrospinal fluid through threphine holes and filling the ventricles with a contrast medium.

Vertex. The crown or top of the skull.

Vertical. Perpendicular to the plane of the horizon; upright. Also, of or pertaining to the vertex of the skull.

Verticosubmental. The positioning of the head and X-ray tube so that the central ray enters the vertex and emerges from just below the chin.

Vesicle. A small bladder or sac containing liquid.

Viscus. Any large interior organ in any one of the three great cavities of the body, especially in the abdomen.

Volt. The unit of electrical pressure or electromotive force. One volt is that amount of electrical pressure (EMF) which is required to force one ampere of current through one ohm of resistance.

Voltage. The electrical pressure which causes electricity to move measured in volts. See also *Electromotive Force* and *Potential Difference.*

Voltmeter. An instrument for measuring electromotive force in units designated as volts.

Vomer. One of the facial bones entering into the formation of the nasal septum.

Watt. The practical unit of electric power. One watt is produced when one volt pushes a current of one ampere.

Wavelength. The distance between consecutively recurring points on a sine wave.

Xiphoid Process. The small triangular bony segment forming the lower end of the sternum. Also called ensiform.

X-rays. A form of electromagnetic radiation possessing very short wavelengths and high penetrating power.

X-ray Tube. A vacuum tube which is designed especially for the purpose of producing X-rays.

Zero Potential. Having neither positive nor negative voltage or pressure.

Zygoma. Same as malar bone.

CPSIA information can be obtained
at www.ICGtesting.com
Printed in the USA
LVHW061315070920
665245LV00016B/1064